The Smithsonian Guides to Natural America

THE PACIFIC

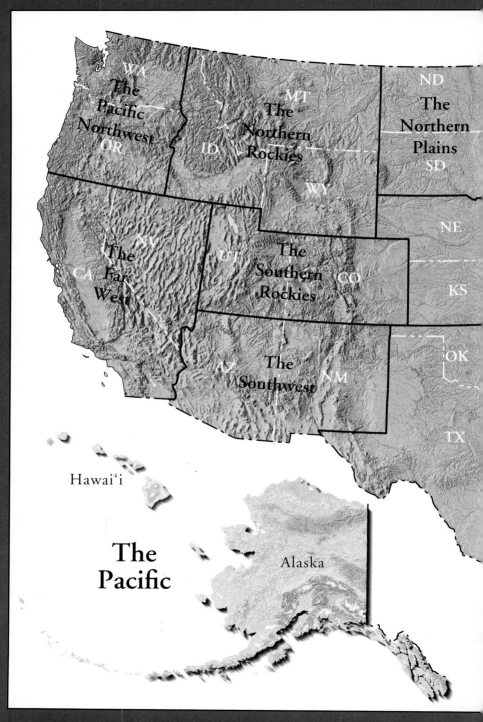

WA

The
Pacific
Northwest
OR

MT

The
Northern
Rockies

ID

WY

ND

The
Northern
Plains

SD

NE

KS

NV

The
Far
West

CA

UT

The
Southern
Rockies

CO

AZ

The
Southwest

NM

OK

TX

Hawai'i

The
Pacific

Alaska

MN

WI

MI

**The
Great
Lakes**

Northern
New
England

ME

VT

NH

NY

**The
Mid–Atlantic
States**

MA
CT RI

Southern
New
England

IA

**The
Heartland**

IL

IN

OH

PA

MD DE

WV

VA

**The
Atlantic
Coast**

MO

KY

**Central
Appalachia**

TN

NC

AR

**The
South
Central
States**

MS

AL

GA

SC

**The
Southeast**

LA

FL

THE SMITHSONIAN GUIDES TO NATURAL AMERICA

THE PACIFIC

HAWAI'I AND ALASKA

HAWAI'I TEXT
Steve Barth

HAWAI'I PHOTOGRAPHY
Richard A. Cooke III

ALASKA TEXT AND PHOTOGRAPHY
Kim Heacox

PREFACE
Thomas E. Lovejoy

SMITHSONIAN BOOKS • WASHINGTON, D.C.
RANDOM HOUSE • NEW YORK, N.Y.

Front cover: Kalalau Valley, Na Pali coast, Kauai, Hawai'i
Half-title page: Onion Portage, Kobuk Valley National Park, Alaska
Frontispiece: Mount Brooks, Denali National Park, Alaska
Back cover: Brown bear, Alaska; lupine and arnica, Alaska; horned puffins, Alaska

THE SMITHSONIAN INSTITUTION
SECRETARY I. Michael Heyman
COUNSELOR TO THE SECRETARY FOR
BIODIVERSITY AND ENVIRONMENTAL AFFAIRS Thomas E. Lovejoy
DIRECTOR, SMITHSONIAN PRESS/SMITHSONIAN PRODUCTIONS Daniel H. Goodwin
EDITOR, SMITHSONIAN BOOKS Alexis Doster III

THE SMITHSONIAN GUIDES TO NATURAL AMERICA
SERIES EDITOR Sandra Wilmot
MANAGING EDITOR Ellen Scordato
PHOTO EDITOR Mary Jenkins
ART DIRECTOR Mervyn Clay
ASSISTANT PHOTO EDITOR Ferris Cook
ASSISTANT PHOTO EDITOR Rebecca Williams
ASSISTANT EDITOR Kerry Acker
EDITORIAL ASSISTANT Seth Ginsberg
COPY EDITORS Karen Hammonds, Amy Hughes
PRODUCTION DIRECTOR Katherine Rosenbloom
DEVELOPMENT EDITOR Mary Luders

Library of Congress Cataloging-in-Publication Data
Barth, Steve
    The Pacific: Hawai'i and Alaska/Hawai'i text by Steve Barth;
 Hawai'i photography by Richard Cooke; Alaska text and photography
 by Kim Heacox.
        p. cm.—(The Smithsonian guides to natural America)
    Includes bibliographical references (p. 258) and index.
    ISBN 0-679-76155-1 (pbk.)
    1. Natural history—Hawaii—Guidebooks. 2. Natural history—
 Alaska—Guidebooks. 3. Hawaii—Guidebooks. 4. Alaska—Guidebooks.
 I. Cooke, Richard Alexander. II. Heacox, Kim. III. Title.
 IV. Series.
 QH198.H3B37 1995
 508.798—dc20   94-29730
                                         CIP

Manufactured in the United States of America
98765432

HOW TO USE THIS BOOK

The SMITHSONIAN GUIDES TO NATURAL AMERICA explore and celebrate the preserved and protected natural areas of this country that are open for the public to use and enjoy. From world-famous national parks to tiny local preserves, the places featured in these guides offer a splendid panoply of this nation's natural wonders.

Divided by state and region, this book offers suggested itineraries for travelers, briefly describing the high points of each preserve, refuge, park, or wilderness area along the way. Each site was chosen for a specific reason: Some are noted for their botanical, zoological, or geological significance, others simply for their exceptional scenic beauty.

Information pertaining to the area as a whole can be found in the introductory sections to the book and to each chapter. In addition, specialized maps at the beginning of each book and chapter highlight an area's geography and geological features as well as pinpoint the specific locales that the author describes.

For quick reference, places of interest are set in **boldface** type; those set in **boldface** followed by the symbol ❖ are listed in the Site Guide at the back of the book. (This feature appears on page 265, just before the index.) Here noteworthy sites are listed alphabetically by state, and each entry provides practical information that visitors need: telephone numbers, mailing addresses, and specific services available.

Addresses and telephone numbers of national, state, and local agencies and organizations are also listed. Also in appendices are a glossary of pertinent scientific terms and designations used to describe natural areas; the author's recommendations for further reading (both nonfiction and fiction); and a list of sources that may be able to help plan a guided visit.

The words and images of these guides are meant to help both the active naturalist and the armchair traveler to appreciate more fully the environmental diversity and natural splendor of this country. To help ensure a successful visit, always contact a site in advance to obtain detailed maps, updated information on hours and fees, and current weather conditions. Many areas maintain a fragile ecological balance. Remember that their continued vitality depends in part on responsible visitors who tread the land lightly.

C O N T E N T S

HOW TO USE THIS BOOK   vii

PREFACE by Thomas E. Lovejoy   xii

PART I HAWAI'I

Introduction   2

ONE The Big Island: Hawai'i   18

TWO Maui   52

THREE Moloka'i and Lana'i   78

FOUR O'ahu   100

FIVE Kaua'i   122

PART II ALASKA

	Introduction	146
SIX	Southeastern Alaska	158
SEVEN	South-Central Alaska and the Aleutian Islands	182
EIGHT	Interior Alaska	218
NINE	Arctic Alaska	240
	FURTHER READING	258
	GLOSSARY	260
	LAND MANAGEMENT RESOURCES	262
	NATURE TRAVEL	264
	SITE GUIDE	265
	INDEX	280

PREFACE

A laska and Hawai'i, which became the last states to join the Union while I was a youth, could not be a greater study in contrasts. Their daylight is distributed so differently throughout the year it is almost hard to believe that all points on the planet—including these two states—have the same total annual amount of daylight. In addition, Hawai'i is an archipelago isolated in the middle of the Pacific whereas Alaska is basically a subcontinent with an appended archipelago.

It is not surprising that their natural history is dramatically different—and their cultural history as well. Alaska's first settlers arrived via the Bering land bridge perhaps as many as 30,000 years ago. The first Hawaiian landfalls by seafarers from the Marquesas probably occurred as recently as A.D. 500.

Yet both states share species such as the lesser golden plover, which nests in Alaska and winters in Hawai'i, and the bristle-thighed curlew, which migrates through Hawai'i on the way to and from its Alaskan breeding grounds. Humpback whales off Maui or Glacier Bay are now considered to be a single population, and we have known for some time that they can communicate across entire ocean basins. Both states share the consequences of the Pacific's ring of fire as the primal energy of the earth bursts forth in volcanic eruption, lava, and gases. They both are vulnerable to consequent tsunamis. In Alaska, one tidal wave climbed 1,700 feet up the side of a mountain.

The United States is fortunate indeed to count both Alaska and Hawai'i as full states with priceless legacies from nature's remaining wild bounty. With this volume, we welcome each reader to these far-flung states through the SMITHSONIAN GUIDES TO NATURAL AMERICA. Over more than a century, Smithsonian explorers have probed these natural wonderlands. In the case of Alaska, the Institution provided the U.S. Congress with the information that convinced lawmakers to authorize

PRECEDING PAGES: *Lush tree ferns called* hapu'u *frame a vista of the Wai-kolu Valley from Moloka'i's Kamakou Preserve, a vital wildlife sanctuary.*

the purchase of this land from Russia. No "Seward's Folly" or "Uncle Sam's Icebox" label could stand up long to the facts, and today some Russians want to regain their former possession.

Hawai'i is another Galápagos where the course of evolution is writ so bold that Darwin could have been inspired as easily by the one as the other. This is a place where early colonizing species radiated into an extraordinary array of life-forms, whether they be the Hawaiian honeycreepers, land snails that seem to have been painted whimsically in a myriad of ways from the evolutionary palette, or even fruit flies with an array of dances that rival those of indigenous Hawaiians.

In this volume, veteran travel writer Steve Barth traces Hawai'i's natural and cultural history, and Ric Cooke's photographs showcase the beauty of his beloved Aloha State. Yankee whalers came to love these ports of paradise, though God-fearing missionaries frowned on the hula and introduced the mu'umu'u, a voluminous Mother Hubbard gown, to cover Polynesian maidens. Remnants of Polynesian culture survive in out-of-the-way settlements. The outsider may be initially shunned, but, Barth says, traditional people will "abandon their reserve and show the true meaning of the aloha spirit. They will take you under their wings, because you are new to old ways."

Kim Heacox, who wrote and photographed the Alaska section of the book, takes similar pains to show tenderfeet the ropes. The icy slopes of Denali, America's highest elevation at more than 20,000 feet, entomb the frozen corpses of half a hundred unfortunate climbers— the ones whose bodies could not be safely removed.

Alaska has been called America's Serengeti. Bears—the Kodiak, the largest brown bear in North America, as well as black bears and polar bears—can be hazardous to the adventurer's health, as can wolves, seals, sea lions, and mosquitoes in the billions with microdraculas' appetites beyond belief.

Kim Heacox does this biological cornucopia justice in language as thrilling and colorful as the mountains, wild rivers, rugged habitats, and molten sunsets of Alaska. With this book people everywhere can cherish the grizzlies, revel in the moose, caribou, and musk ox, and chuckle at sea otters that hold big Dungeness crabs on their tummies, then crack the crabs' shells with rocks to get at their dinner. Bald eagles assemble in squadrons, sea lions and sea elephants round up their harems, and five kinds of delicious salmon run the gauntlet of hungry brown bears.

Yet nature in these states is in peril. The first North American mammal driven to extinction by nonindigenous people was one Rubens might have designed had he applied his art to marine mammals: a gentle creature of the northern seas known as Steller's sea cow. The work of Smithsonian scientist Storrs Olson has revealed that many Hawaiian birds were extinct before the arrival of Captain Cook. Hawai'i is rife with endangered species, many of which are imperiled by exotic, imported species. Smithsonian botanist Warren Wagner's recent flora, a listing of all plants for the state, enumerates more exotic plant species than indigenous ones.

Yet all is not bleak. Parts of the magnificent Tongass forests of peninsular Alaska are now protected in perpetuity. On Hawai'i, S. Dillon Ripley, eighth secretary of the Smithsonian and a renowned ornithologist and conservationist, helped to save the flightless *nene*, descended from Canada geese probably blown far to sea in storms. The Laysan duck was once reduced to a "population" of a single female sitting on destroyed eggs, but who retained enough semen in her oviduct to lay a fresh batch. The species now numbers in the hundreds.

There is still a great deal to enjoy. While glaciers carve fjords in Alaska, torrential rains erode strange headlands on the Hawaiian Islands. Flowers, ferns, and silverswords cling to the lava hills of Maui and elsewhere. In Alaska, forests roll to the horizons until they dwindle to treelessness at the polar circle, where ground-creeping willow, jewellike flowers, crusty rainbows of lichen, and puffs of polar "cotton" spangle the tundra. Here the "barren ground" is never barren, but buzzing with life from bumblebees to butterflies. Ducks, geese, puffins, kittiwakes, snow buntings, and belted kingfishers all have their places in the ecological mosaic.

We are pleased to introduce you to these two states in this volume on the Pacific, part of our SMITHSONIAN GUIDES TO NATURAL AMERICA.

—*Thomas E. Lovejoy*
Counselor to the Secretary for Biodiversity and Environmental Affairs,
SMITHSONIAN INSTITUTION

LEFT: *A humpback whale lifts its tail from the Pacific Ocean. One population of humpbacks shares the waters from Alaska to Hawai'i.*

HAWAI‘I

INTRODUCTION
HAWAI'I

There are cultures that believe that all aspects of the world around them, each rock and snail and flower, are imbued with vitality and power. In Hawai'i, even the most cynical urbanite soon becomes a believer. Every nuance of the Hawaiian landscape reflects the timeless, relentless forces that shape it. From the constant trade winds and pounding surf to the brilliant equatorial sun, the islands seem to vibrate with energy.

Here, in the middle of the Pacific, the air shimmers with scents, the landscape reverberates with color. The terrain—rain-swept valleys, spectacular gorges, cloud-shrouded mountains—might have been invented to showcase every conceivable shade of green. Brilliantly tinted birds and flowers sparkle in their lush tropical settings like exotic jewels. The volcanoes and craters stand stark, gray, and otherworldly, while the beaches are a palette unto themselves, painted dazzling white, jet black, even olive green. And encompassing it all is the sea, turquoise-blue water teeming with rainbow-colored fish and fantastic forms of coral.

Everything on Hawai'i grows at a prodigious rate—jungle vegetation, tropical flowers, commercial crops, even the volcano-created land itself. Everything also changes here faster than anywhere else, as the landscape metamorphoses from rivers of lava to lush jungles to coral atolls to sunken seamounts.

The Hawaiian Islands lend themselves easily to superlatives. The youngest state is also the largest, longest, oldest, and most isolated archipelago on earth. Hawai'i claims the tallest sea cliffs, most beautiful beaches, and the largest and most active volcanoes in the world. It is also home to America's only tropical rain forests. The main islands—Hawai'i, Maui, Moloka'i, Lana'i, O'ahu, and Kaua'i—offer astounding ranges of biodiversity, with delicate ecosystems in underwater coral reefs, high-altitude volcanic moonscapes, and almost every imaginable environment in between. Plants and animals live here that are found nowhere else—among them some of the most endangered species on the planet.

PRECEDING PAGES: *The beauty of the Hawaiian Islands is a result of the combined forces of wind, waves, and volcanoes. Pushed by the trade winds, gilded clouds passing over Goat Island will soon rain on nearby O'ahu.*

Stretching nearly two thousand miles in the middle of the Pacific Ocean, the state of Hawai'i includes some 125 islands. All are the tops of massive underwater mountains created over the last 25 million years by volcanic eruptions. The worn and tiny atolls far to the northwest are the oldest, and the island of Hawai'i (often called the "Big Island" to avoid confusion with the state as a whole), just below the Tropic of Cancer, is the youngest.

The Big Island's highest volcanoes, Mauna Kea and Mauna Loa, rise almost 14,000 feet above sea level, and some 32,000 feet, or 6 miles, from the ocean floor. Following an inevitable process both these mountains will erode from above and below. Once the volcanoes of Kaua'i, O'ahu, and Maui towered over the Pacific as well, but the reign of each in turn lasted less than a million years. Hawai'i's active volcano Kilauea, on the slopes of Mauna Loa, is still growing. And already the next volcano, Loihi, is slowly building up south of the Big Island, only 3,000 feet below the waves. It could become an island in as few as 10,000 years.

The ocean floor beneath the Hawaiian Islands is a slab of the earth's crust called the Pacific Plate. New crust for the Pacific Plate is created by undersea eruptions 5,000 miles south of Hawai'i along the Mid-Pacific Ridge. According to the theory of plate tectonics and continental drift, the crust is then moved to the northwest at a rate of about four inches per year (a human fingernail grows at about the same rate) or 63 miles every million years. When it finally reaches the Aleutian Trench near Alaska it is subducted, or remelted and pulled under.

In the middle of this conveyor belt a hot spot underneath the crust is constantly pushing upward with enough force to punch through the crust with a plume of molten rock, called magma. The magma spreads out on the sea floor around the vent of the plume, gradually building up a sea mound. When the undersea volcano reaches the surface, with great steam explosions, a new island is born. Kilauea, the most active volcano in the world, is now sitting on the hot spot.

In contrast to steep-sided volcanoes found elsewhere in the world, Hawai'i's volcanoes are broad domes, commonly called shield cones because of their resemblance to a warrior's shield. They are built up by one thin layer after another of basaltic lava heavy with iron and magnesium that can flow as far as 30 miles from the vent before it cools and stops. Only the active volcanoes on the Big Island still retain the shield shape. Once the Pacific Plate pushes them away from the hot spot, the volcanoes pass into dormancy and extinction. Erosion seems to acceler-

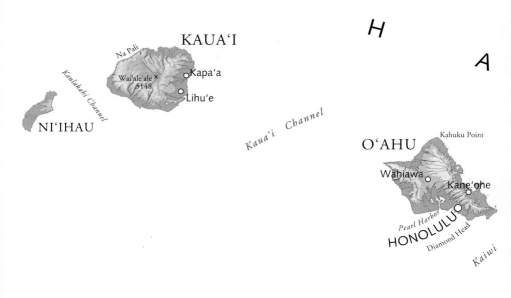

KAUA'I

Na Pali

Wai'ale'ale ✗
5148

○ Kapa'a

○ Lihu'e

NI'IHAU

Kaulakahi Channel

Kaua'i Channel

H

A

O'AHU

Kahuku Point

Wahiawa ○

○ Kane'ohe

Pearl Harbor

HONOLULU ○

Diamond Head

Kaiwi

PACIFIC

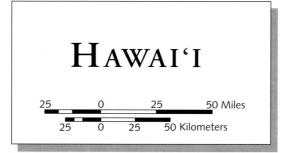

HAWAI'I

25	0	25	50 Miles

25	0	25	50 Kilometers

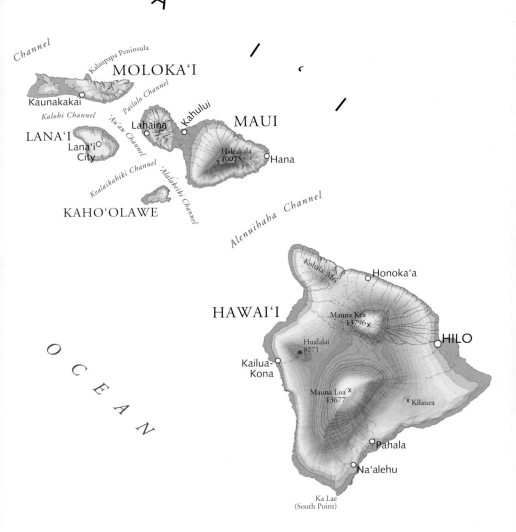

W

A

Channel

Kalaupapa Peninsula

MOLOKA'I

Kaunakakai

Kalohi Channel

Pailolo Channel

Kahului

LANA'I

Lahaina

MAUI

Lana'i
City

'Au'au Channel

Haleakala
×10023

Hana

Kealaikahiki Channel

'Alalakeiki Channel

KAHO'OLAWE

Alenuihaha Channel

I

Kohala Mts

Honoka'a

HAWAI'I

Mauna Kea
13796×

HILO

O

Hualalai
×8271

Kailua-
Kona

C

E

Mauna Loa
13677 ×

× Kilauea

A

N

Pahala

Na'alehu

Ka Lae
(South Point)

ate because it is no longer balanced by the creation of new land.

Clouds cruising the prevailing trade winds from the northeast snag on the peaks of these new mountains. The rain that results—more than 30 feet per year in some areas—promotes heavy vegetation and erosion on what is called the windward coast, usually the northern and eastern sides of each island. Only a few miles away on the opposite, or leeward coast, (generally the southern and western sides) the land is in the mountain's rain shadow, which leaves the land bone dry. As they mature and erode the island's cones, plains, and craters are sculpted by wind, rain, and sea into mountain ranges with valleys, canyons, ridges, and cliffs.

But even as the island is eroding from above, coral polyps and coralline algae drifting through the sea add to the island, enlarging it seaward from the shore. Finding purchase in shallow (less than 200 feet deep) coastal waters, the polyps and algae build their tiny communities into huge reefs, civilizations of uncountable individual organisms. Besides attracting a cornucopia of fish, the reefs also protect the land from eroding waves and provide ground-up coral sand to be deposited by successive tides as beaches.

Endlessly marching toward the Aleutian Trench, continually planed by wind, weather, and waves, all the Hawaiian Islands will eventually become low islets and atolls like Kure, Midway, and the others north-west of Kaua‘i. Over time they will continue to sink into the earth's crust until they are drowned several thousand feet below the waves.

Twenty-five hundred miles from the nearest continental land mass, the Hawaiian Islands began as lifeless, sterile points of bare lava. Over time spores and seedlings floated there on trade winds or equatorial currents, finding a winning combination of sun, rain, and lava rich in chemical nutrients. Animals, too, had to swim, float, or fly here. Only three mammals ever accomplished this feat on their own—Hawaiian hoary bats, the Hawaiian monk seals, and humans. The sea journey was simply too long for any terrestrial reptiles or amphibians to become es-tablished. Seabirds (and any seeds in their digestive tracts) probably ar-rived first, but wayward insects and forest birds came along, too. Given the hospitable island environment and no natural enemies, these early immigrants flourished, eventually evolving into an amazing variety of distinctive native species found nowhere else.

RIGHT: *Kilauea, on the Big Island of Hawai‘i, is the most active volcano in the world. Since 1983, Kilauea has erupted almost continuously from its Pu‘u O‘o vent. Lava flows have covered whole communities.*

Hawaiian native plants are divided into two categories. Those that grow here naturally but also grow elsewhere are called indigenous; those that have adapted completely and become species unique to Hawai'i are known as endemic. Only in Hawai'i do endemics so outnumber indigenous species. Of the almost 1,000 native flowering plant species, for instance, 90 to 95 percent occur nowhere else on earth.

Once a plant or animal species arrives on one of the islands it may go through a process of adaptive radiation, in which a single species diversifies into many different species to fill available niches in the ecosystem. From a lone finch ancestor, for instance, the family of Hawaiian honeycreepers evolved into 45 or 50 different species. Through another trend, commonly known as parallel evolution, plants or animals from different species and different parts of the world come to resemble each other because they occupy the same niche. On Hawai'i some honeycreepers bear more resemblance to parrots or woodpeckers than they do to their finch ancestors.

Compared to the evolutionary lessons the Hawaiian Islands have to offer, the Galápagos are child's play. Among the more innovative survival solutions nature has come up with in the islands are carnivorous inchworms, blind cave-dwelling grasshoppers, and the bizarre but wholly magnificent silverswords, plants of the aster family whose silver hairs collect moisture and reflect sunlight, enabling them to prosper in dry, high-altitude, lava-clad environments.

Because Hawaiian plants were free to adapt and thrive without competition they abandoned or never developed defense mechanisms, becoming tasteless mints, stinkless stinkbugs, and raspberries with thorns that fall off at the touch. Unfortunately, that left Hawaiian native species with little chance for survival when Polynesians and then Europeans began introducing large numbers of animals and plants formerly absent from the native environment. These are called alien or imported.

Within just a few miles on a Hawaiian island there is an amazing cross section of ecosystems. In fact, most of the nearly 150 distinct climatic zones catalogued by biologists around the world are represented in the islands. Unfortunately, few of these zones remain in their original pristine condition—and 80 are generally considered endangered.

Leeward ecosystems have been the most affected. Fragile coastal dunes, once common above many beaches, quickly disappeared after their delicate ground covers were trampled. The savanna grasslands, which covered lowland plains, were regularly burned by Hawaiians in

order to harvest fresh *pili* grass, which they used for thatch. In dryland forests, similiar to mainland chaparral, grazing animals introduced by Europeans decimated trees and shrubs. In their place, aggressive alien species such as *kiawe* (mesquite) and fountain grass thrived in the hot dry climate and fertile soil.

On the windward sides of the islands wet forests (either rain forests at lower elevations or cloud forests higher up) grow from near sea level up to 6,000 feet. These are unlike rain forests elsewhere in the world, where ground debris is quickly broken down by termites and microbes. The process of tree decay in the Hawaiian Islands is extremely slow. There are koa logs on the Big Island's Kilauea, for instance, that are 600 years old. Sometimes three genera-

ABOVE: *In Hawai'i plants and animals evolved in splendid isolation. Species such as the Haleakala silversword brilliantly adapted to extreme environments but were defenseless against aggressive alien species brought from other places.*

tions remain connected, with successive trees growing from the fallen trunks of the ones before. The wet forest was once a diversified ecosystem in which the native *Acacia koa* tree reigned as king. Today the koa, with its fine red wood, has been heavily logged; its decline began, however, nearly a thousand years ago when rats and pigs introduced by the Polynesians developed a taste for its young shoots. Today, especially above 3,000 feet, the *'ohi'a lehua*, a large, wizened-looking tree with brilliant red pompon blossoms, now dominates the rain forest, surrounded by an understory of lush, thickly fronded tree ferns (*hapu'u*).

Higher up, the subalpine cloud belt found on Hawai'i (on Mauna

Avif. of Laysan etc.

J.G.Keulemans del et lith.

MOHO NOBILIS, (MERREM) ♂ & ♀ AD.

Mintern Bros. imp.

Kea, Mauna Loa, and Hualalai) and Maui (on Haleakala) between 6,000 feet and the tree line at 9,000 feet is the realm of the *mamane,* a native tree with distinctive yellow flowers. The sandalwood, once common at this altitude, was almost completely logged in the first century of European contact. Above the tree line only the rarest shrubs thrive, and the highest elevations on Mauna Loa and Mauna Kea, where arctic conditions can prevail during winter storms, are devoid of any vegetation.

Alien species, too, have thrived in Hawai'i's wet and dry forests. The introduction of cattle to the islands in the nineteenth century led to the devastation of vast tracts of forest. Early in this century well-meaning forest managers, frantic to save the watershed and prevent erosion, planted anything they thought would grow: pines, eucalyptus, ironwood. Unfortunately, these new trees did not fill the same biological niches as native species. For every endemic tree that declined, a native bird species that depended on it has been threatened as well.

Archaeological evidence indicates that Polynesians from the Marquesas Islands, approximately 3,000 miles to the south, first colonized the Hawaiian chain in about A.D. 500. In the fifteenth century a new wave of colonists from the Society Islands, about 2,800 miles to the south, conquered or absorbed the earlier group of Marquesan-Hawaiians. They transplanted the Society Islands' rigid customs, social structures, and strict prohibitions (called *kapu*). By the eighteenth century it is estimated that about 250,000 Hawaiians lived in the islands. In January 1778 Captain James Cook, en route to Alaska to look for a northwest passage with his ships the *Resolution* and the *Discovery,* became the first European known to sight the islands and briefly visited Kaua'i. Cook and his crew returned to the islands on their way back from the north the following January to learn more, and although the captain was killed in a dispute on the Big Island, the centuries of protective isolation came rapidly to an end.

The introduction of humans immediately began corrupting the crucible of Hawaiian biology. The Polynesians brought with them animals and plants important to their survival and culture: pigs, chickens, and small dogs (plus stowaway rats); banana, breadfruit, coconut, sugar-

---

LEFT: *The yellow feathers of the 'o'o, seen here in an 1890s lithograph, were once woven into ceremonial cloaks. The species is now extinct.*

OVERLEAF: *Surf crashes against the stark volcanic shoreline of Wai'ana-panapa State Park along Maui's remarkably beautiful Hana Highway.*

With nearly perfect growing conditions, Hawai'i's native species, such as the white hibiscus (upper left), must compete with imported plants such as the plumeria (bottom left), a common garden flower brought from the Caribbean, and the invasive Kahili ginger (right), from northern India.

cane, taro, sweet potato, yam, ginger, and other food staples. They burned forests, cleared valleys, and terraced hillsides for cultivation. Flightless native birds were exploited as a food source, and several species disappeared. Other birds were killed by the tens of thousands to make spectacular, extravagant feather capes for the *ali'i*, or ruling class. Some 80,000 birds each provided their few yellow feathers for just one of the fabled royal cloaks of Kamehameha the Great. Both the black-and-gold Hawaiian *mamo*, first noted by the Cook expedition, and the Hawaiian *'o'o*, a honeyeater and once king of the native plumage birds, were decimated and are now considered extinct.

When other ships followed after Cook's discovery European assaults began on the Hawaiian ecosystem as well. Logging, hunting, cattle grazing, commercial agriculture, pest management, and industrial development accelerated the rate of change to cataclysmic levels. Species of plants and animals were quickly driven to extinction or faced slow death through competition with aggressive alien species.

Introduced to provide meat and sport hunting, pigs, goats, and deer root, trample, or eat entire forests to the brink of extinction. Aggressive alien plants quickly recolonize before native flora has a chance. Delicious guava and colorful lantana are just two of the alien species that have become ubiquitous in the islands.

No ecosystem is truly static. Too many variables intrude for any environment to be completely in balance. Conservation in the islands today, however, has assumed an air of extreme urgency. The numbers are simply overwhelming. With only .2 percent of the U.S. land area, Hawai'i accounts for fully 75 percent of the nation's known plant and bird extinctions. About 1,800 native plant species once flourished in the Hawaiian chain. With the introduction of humans, feral animals, disease, and some 2,000 aggressive alien species, nearly 1,000 endemic Hawaiian plants are gravely endangered—if not already extinct. Of the 110 original species of birds considered endemic to the Hawaiian islands, 40 species were extinct before European contact, another 30 have disappeared since the late eighteenth century, and of the species that remain, 30 are threatened or endangered. Only a few remote and rugged areas remain 100 percent native, with still thriving populations of plant and animal species that predate Polynesian migrations. State and federal agencies and private groups such as the Nature Conservancy are working feverishly to ensure that these areas will be preserved.

Conservationists today understand the importance of restoring integrated ecosystems rather than targeting individual species. Researchers now extend their study of an endangered plant to include the insects and birds that may pollinate it. They have found that endangered birds are more likely to return and prosper when native plants are restored as well.

In addition, simply establishing a refuge does not ensure that its borders will keep alien species out. Preserves have to be aggressively managed, weeded of undesirable plants, and protected from harmful animals. Native species have to be helped along. Botanists have assumed responsibility for pollinating plants whose insect or bird pollinators are extinct. Recently, extinct plant species have even been reintroduced after seedlings were grown from nursery samples or cloned tissue cultures prepared by botanists.

Many people visit the state of Hawai'i because of its reputation for scenic beauty but when they arrive only admire natural Hawai'i from a distance. One benefit that tourism has brought, however, is that at least some sites are now accessible to all varieties of nature lovers. Many driving routes are in themselves nature tours, and Hawai'i offers high-quality helicopter, boat, and horseback tours (see the nature travel listing on page 264). Some parks ('Iao Valley on Maui, for example) have paved trails that entice even the most reluctant pedestrian. There are wheelchair-accessible nature trails and campgrounds designed for the physically challenged. Snuba, a new method for breathing underwater, makes observing reefs up close possible for everyone, including the physically challenged, as it allows the underwater explorer to breathe through a tube connected to a floating tank. Commercial submarines allow visitors to admire marine wonders without even getting their feet wet.

In general Hawai'i's rain forests are undoubtedly the safest in the world, with no malarial mosquitoes or poisonous snakes. But the dangers of flash floods, slippery precipices, and wild pigs all warrant caution. Riptides and unpredictable surf can make swimming dangerous on some of the most beautiful, seductive beaches. Always heed posted warnings. And it should go without saying that the tropical sun can rapidly dehydrate a body already dried out by the conditioned air of planes, hotel rooms, and rental cars. Even a short hike in Hawai'i can feel like an expedition, so be prepared: Get in shape, use proper clothing and equipment, read maps and trail guides, and always carry plenty of water. In some areas it is necessary to register with rangers before going on a hike. And it is always best to tell someone (such as a hotel clerk) of one's destination.

Climates in the Pacific have more to do with geography—which side of the island one is on—than with the calendar. The summer is indeed drier and hotter than the rest of the year, but daily showers are still expected, especially on the windward sides of the islands. Residents use local geography for telling directions, and since every island has two common features—mountains and sea—they use those designations rather than mundane compass directions: *mauka* (toward the mountains) and *makai* (toward the sea).

Some of the most special places in the islands are protected equally by ancient beliefs and by the silence of modern Hawaiians. Please respect their culture by staying on established trails and leaving artifacts

ABOVE: A *hot spot deep below the ocean floor created the volcanoes that formed the islands. Looking west, Moloka'i is in the foreground, Maui's peaks line up behind, and the Big Island rises in the distance.*

and offerings undisturbed. Private property must be respected as such, and visitors should always ask and obtain permission from the owners to travel through. Marijuana growers have also become more militant in defending their secret *paka lolo* patches—take heed.

Finally, the fragility and complexity of the Hawaiian ecosystem cannot be overemphasized. It is vital that visitors—even conservation-minded ones—be aware of the impact they can make and the damage they can do. Boots and clothing, for example, can carry alien seeds into native areas, helping aggressive imports to overrun the endemic species more quickly than they already are. Picking a flower of a plant on the verge of extinction can have devastating consequences. Straying off a path can begin a process of erosion that can destroy a hillside.

Understanding the life-and-death dynamics of the Hawaiian ecosystem, however, can produce strange and marvelous effects for sensitive visitors. To an observer immersed in and alert to the surrounding interplay, flowers become more than just trailside decorations. Tiny tree snails assume a greater importance in the grand scheme of things. Each footfall in the forest is an opportunity for wonder and discovery.

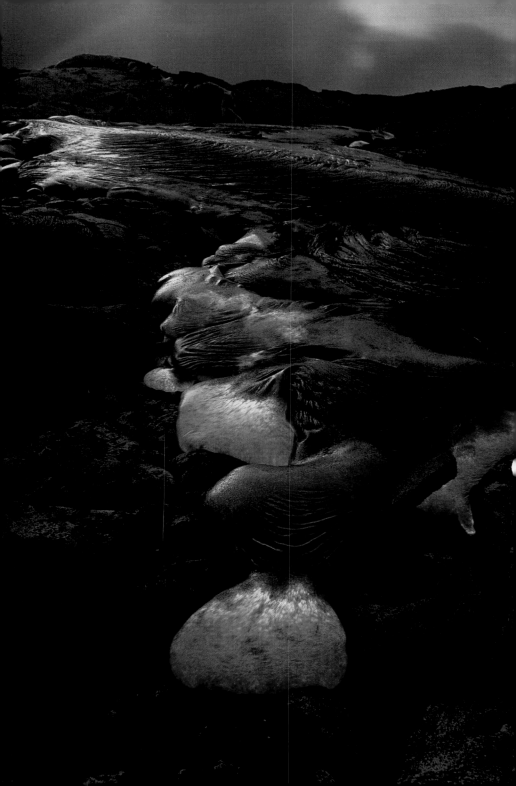

THE BIG ISLAND: HAWAI'I

With twice as much land area as the other islands combined, the Big Island of Hawai'i possesses a landscape of epic proportions, providing a background for virtually any adventure: tropical jungle valleys, Technicolor reefs, rolling ranchlands, stark desert, and the largest and most active volcanoes on earth.

Traditional legends, still chanted to the beat of sharkskin drums, call Hawai'i the first child of Wakea (the sky) and Papa (the earth), references to the ancient gods that early explorers brought from the southern lands known as Kahiki, or Tahiti. It was here on the Big Island that Polynesian seafarers made their initial settlements some 1,400 years ago, and for these first Hawaiians the island offered a remarkable new home.

In geologic terms, the Big Island is actually one of the youngest places on earth, and continuing volcanic activity on Hawai'i adds new acres almost every year. Forming the northern tip of the island, the worn and rounded Kohala, now only about 5,500 feet high, is the oldest (700,000 years) of the island's five volcanoes. Mauna Kea, in the north-central area, stands 13,796 feet above sea level (the highest point in the Hawaiian Islands) and last erupted about 4,000 years ago. On the west, dominating the skyline above Kailua on the Kona Coast, is Hualalai, an 8,271-foot dormant volcano that last erupted about 1800.

LEFT: *Fresh molten lava drips downhill across the landscape from Pu'u O'o, an erupting vent of Kilauea volcano. Cooled by the air, the surface of the flow hardens into a dark, ropy-textured lava called* **pahoehoe**.

The true centerpiece of the island is the still-active Mauna Loa, the world's most massive mountain—more massive than the entire Sierra Nevada combined—with 13,679 feet showing above sea level, some 18,000 feet extending below, and a volume of 10,000 cubic miles. Finally, there's Kilauea, on Mauna Loa's southeastern slope, so far about 4,000 feet tall, whose almost-constant tantrums make it the most active volcano in the world.

Historically, the island has played a key role in the evolving story of the Hawaiian chain. In the late eighteenth century, two men appeared here who would mean the end of the old Hawai'i and the beginning of the modern age. The first was Kamehameha the Great, born around 1758 to an aristocratic family on the northern tip of the island. He became the first *ali'i* (leader or chief) to unite the Hawaiian islands into a single kingdom, which it remained until the monarchy was overthrown in the 1890s by sugar barons, and the nation was annexed by the United States.

The other man who set the islands' destiny in motion was the British explorer Captain James Cook. In 1779, returning from their search for the Northwest Passage, Cook and his men anchored at Kealakekua Bay, on the Big Island's western coast, and went ashore, becoming the first Europeans to visit the Hawaiian Islands (they had anchored off Kaua'i the previous year but had not landed). Cook was killed on his second visit, but other Europeans soon followed, once his men returned home with their stories and navigational charts.

Hawai'i is a three-sided island. The long western or leeward coast is arid. The wet, windward coast faces northeast. And what might be called the "volcanic" coast, dominated by recent lava flows, faces southeast. Frequent commercial flights land both at Hilo, on the eastern side, and at Kailua-Kona, center of the island's western tourist area. It's hard to believe that the two towns, little more than 100 miles apart, belong to the same world: Windward Hilo, the wettest city in the United States, gets ten times the rainfall that sunny, leeward Kona does.

Beginning at Hawai'i Volcanoes National Park in the southeastern part of the island, this chapter follows a generally clockwise route around the 300-mile coastline before turning inland at Hilo and climbing to the summit of Mauna Kea.

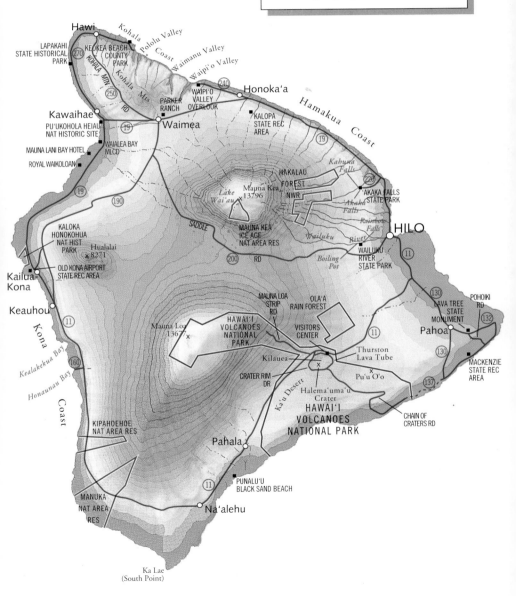

5   0   5   10 Miles

5   0   5   10 Kilometers

Hawi

LAPAKAHI
STATE HISTORICAL
PARK

KEOKEA BEACH
COUNTY
PARK

270

Kohala Coast

Pololu Valley

Waimanu Valley

Waipi'o Valley

240

Honoka'a

KOHALA MTN RD

250

Kohala Mts

RD

PARKER
RANCH

WAIPI'O
VALLEY
OVERLOOK

Kawaihae

Waimea

KALOPA
STATE REC
AREA

19

Hamakua Coast

PU'UKOHOLA HEIAU
NAT HISTORIC SITE

19

WAIALEA BAY
MLCD

MAUNA LANI BAY HOTEL

ROYAL WAIKOLOAN

HAKALAU
FOREST
NWR

Kahuna
Falls

19

190

Lake
Wai'au

Mauna Kea
x 13796

'AKAKA FALLS
STATE PARK

220

Akaka
Falls

Rainbow
Falls

HILO

KALOKA
HONOKOHUA
NAT HIST
PARK

Hualalai
x 8271

SADDLE

MAUNA KEA
ICE AGE
NAT AREA RES

Wailuku

River

OLD KONA AIRPORT
STATE REC AREA

200

RD

Boiling
Pot

WAILUKU
RIVER
STATE PARK

11

Kailua-
Kona

MAUNA LOA
STRIP
RD

OLA'A
RAIN FOREST

130

Keauhou

11

Mauna Loa
13677 x

HAWAI'I
VOLCANOES
NATIONAL
PARK

VISITORS
CENTER

11

LAVA TREE
STATE
MONUMENT

POHOIKI
RD

132

Pahoa

Kona Coast

Kealakekua Bay

160

Kilauea

x

Thurston
Lava Tube

130

Honaunau Bay

CRATER RIM
DR

Ka'u Desert

x
Halema'uma'u
Crater

x
Pu'u O'o

137

MACKENZIE
STATE REC
AREA

Coast

KIPAHOEHOE
NAT AREA RES

Pahala

CHAIN OF
CRATERS RD

HAWAI'I
VOLCANOES
NATIONAL PARK

MANUKA
NAT AREA
RES

11

Na'alehu

PUNALU'U
BLACK SAND BEACH

Ka Lae
(South Point)

ABOVE: *Geological processes of eruption and erosion compete fiercely where new land meets the sea. Even as cliffs in the Kamoamoa area fall under the ocean's wild assault, nearby flows add acreage to the island.*

HAWAI'I VOLCANOES NATIONAL PARK

One of the oldest national parks in the country, **Hawai'i Volcanoes National Park**❖ (authorized in 1916) not only encompasses two of the most active volcanoes in the world, **Kilauea** and **Mauna Loa,** it also protects a great diversity of ecological zones, from jagged coastal cliffs to pristine rain forest to stark desert. The climate—on a single day—can range from tropical sunshine on an idyllic black sand beach to a subarctic blizzard on the windy summit of Mauna Loa, just a few miles away. Because of this unusual variety, in 1980 the United Nations Educational, Scientific, and Cultural Organization (UNESCO) added the park to its Man and the Biosphere Program as an International Biosphere Reserve. The reserves comprise an international collection protecting samples of the world's major ecosystems.

ABOVE: *'Ohi'a trees grow on the rim of the Kilauea caldera, which encloses the Halema'uma'u Crater, or fire pit. Traditional ceremonies and offerings still honor this place as the home of the fire goddess Pele.*

A network (some 150 miles) of backpacking trails and campsites crisscrosses the vast park, but much of it can be seen by road or on short hikes. Given its considerable size and diversity, however, the park still takes several days to explore fully.

Kilauea is a broad shield volcano whose name means, appropriately, "spreading, much spewing." Its almost constant eruptions are an irresistible fascination, all the more so because they are usually safe enough to see up close. Since January 1983 the lava has been pouring out of a Kilauea satellite cone called **Pu'u O'o** on the eastern edge of

OVERLEAF: *Since 1983 Pu'u O'o, a satellite crater along Kilauea's eastern rift zone, has given both geologists and tourists the opportunity to witness volcanic eruptions, which are particularly spectacular at night.*

the park. Here, when the volcano is active, bright magma bubbles up through roiling smoke, only to disappear almost immediately back into the ground; it then reappears downslope from the cinder cone as a lava flow. The surface of the slow-moving lava looks solid enough, its mercury gray only occasionally broken by a glowing orange-red when molten rock flashes through the cracks. At the leading edge of the flow, the molten rock creeps inexorably along the ground, igniting grass and trees, destroying everything in its path—including homes and whole communities—covering highways and beaches, and finally exploding into the sea in colossal clouds of steam.

ABOVE: *The Hawaiian honeycreeper 'apapane (Himatione sanguinea), a common native bird, feeds on the nectar of 'ohi'a lehua blossoms.*

RIGHT: *A mainstay of the Hawaiian environment, the adaptable 'ohi'a lehua (Metrosideros polymorpha), thrives on a dormant volcanic cone in Hawai'i Volcanoes National Park.*

At the summit of Kilauea, about halfway between the coastline and the older Mauna Loa, is the main caldera, encircled by the 11-mile **Crater Rim Drive,** with many turnouts and trailheads. Park headquarters (28 miles southwest of Hilo on Route 11 and 96 miles south, east, then north on Route 11 from Kailua) is perched on the caldera's rim near the park entrance. The visitor center offers current information on conditions and viewing sites within the park as well as a film highlighting recent eruptions. The **Hawaiian Volcano Observatory,** farther along the drive, constantly monitors activity at both Kilauea and Mauna Loa. Sensitive tiltmeters placed in remote locations measure the swelling of the dome beneath the summits, indicating the rise of magma, and are among the tools used to predict eruptions. It is far from an exact science, but in 1982 volcanologists did

26

ABOVE: *A stroll along the park's Devastation Trail underscores the destructive power of Kilauea's eruptions. In 1959 an eruption from Kilauea Iki sent a fountain of lava almost 2,000 feet into the air. The*

manage to post a three-hour warning before an eruption in the caldera. When the U.S. Geological Survey opened a new lab in 1987, the old observatory became the **Thomas Jaggar Museum❖**, with updated exhibits of current eruptions and of the technology used to track them.

Most of the floor of Kilauea's caldera is cool and solid, reminiscent of photographs of the moon's surface, but in some places along the rim the soil only a few feet down is still so hot that trees cannot root in it. Steam wafts in drifting plumes, and acrid sulfur compounds billow invisibly from hidden vents. Brightening the monochromatic landscape, the vivid red *'ohelo* berries growing here are very sweet; they are the favorite food of Pele, the tempestuous volcano goddess, so be sure to offer her a few first. In the caldera floor is the main vent for the magma plume, **Halema'uma'u Crater** ("enduring firehouse"), the traditional home of Pele.

In 1823 when missionary William Ellis paid a visit to Kilauea—he was the first outsider to see it—the boiling floor of Halema'uma'u was almost 1,000 feet deeper than it is today. Subsequent eruptions and

airborne lava cooled too quickly to let gas bubbles escape, forming pumice. Trade winds carried the hot pumice to the southwest, where it rained onto this area, turning lush rain forest into arid desert.

lava flows have raised the floor level of the whole Kilauea Caldera up to about 400 feet below the rim. Until 1924 the crater was a bubbling lake of molten rock, causing much comment from the hardy travelers who struggled their way by foot or horseback to its edge.

Mark Twain chronicled a visit in his 1872 book *Roughing It:* "Occasionally the molten lava flowing under the superincumbent crust broke through, split a dazzling streak, from five hundred to a thousand feet long, like a sudden flash of lightning, and then acre after acre of the cold lava parted into fragments, turned up edgewise like cakes of ice when a great river breaks up, plunged downward and were swallowed in the crimson cauldron."

Beginning at the visitor center, the three-and-one-fifth-mile (about six and a half miles round-trip) self-guided **Halema'uma'u Trail,** which takes about five hours total, descends steeply through forest and rock slides, and then crosses the lunarlike terrain to the Halema'uma'u parking area and lookout on the opposite side of Crater Rim Drive. Along the way subtle color variations in the overlapping black lava

streams are evidence of many different eruptions dating from 1954, 1974, 1975, and 1982 as well as the nineteenth century. Be sure to stay on the trail; solid-looking lava may be only a thin crust over a lava tube or gas bubble. At the Halemaʻumaʻu Crater, where volcanic gases pour out in sufficient quantity to be dangerous over prolonged visits or to anyone with respiratory or heart problems, the trail emerges on Crater Rim Drive. Two rift zones, a series of cracks and fractures that stretch all the way down to the sea, head southwest and southeast from here. Lava tends to erupt along these zones, flowing through the underground fracture systems. Recent eruptions, such as Puʻu Oʻo, have been on the eastern rift.

Nene, Hawai'i's endangered native goose and state bird, can often be seen along Crater Rim Drive. Handsome fowl, they show little gratitude at being rescued from the brink of extinction. Rather, they will beg for food (feeding them is a federal crime) and can get quite nasty when no tasty tidbit is forthcoming. Counterclockwise beyond Halemaʻumaʻu the drive passes through increasingly thick forest punctuated by older craters as it crosses the invisible line between the windward and leeward sides of the island. In such medium-wet forests in Hawai'i the most common combination of native vegetation finds tall *ʻohiʻa* trees sheltering an understory of *hapuʻu,* tree ferns. The ferns are called "mother of *ʻohiʻa*" because the trees' seeds frequently lodge and germinate in the ferns' moist trunks. While the *ʻohiʻa-hapuʻu* symbiosis was probably not always so dominant in the Hawaiian forest (a complete native forest has much more variety), it has proved to be the hardiest native combination in the face of competition from aggressive alien plants.

One of the park's most accessible trails is off this windward stretch of the rim road. Dominated by a looming cinder cone, **Devastation Trail** is a short, paved pathway easily traversed, even by those in wheelchairs, in about half an hour. Skirting an area of dense forest, the trail winds through barren terrain, punctuated by stark silhouettes of dead trees, that was laid waste by pumice ejected by a 1959 eruption.

The nearby **Thurston Lava Tube** was formed when a flow of molten

LEFT: *Reports from early visitors led to the establishment of Hawai'i National Park in 1916. Stylishly overdressed tourists posed amid lush jungle foliage to record their trek to the Thurston Lava Tube in about 1920.*

rock hardened on the top, where it was exposed to the air, while lava underneath continued to flow, like water through a pipe, until the liquid emptied out. Accessible via a 15-minute forested loop trail, the 400-foot part of the Thurston tube open to the public is smooth and flat-floored. Most lava tubes, however, are tortuous mazes of sharp *'a'a* lava.

Crater Rim Drive eventually returns to the park entrance and head-quarters. However, a well-marked turn toward the coast—near Devastation Trail—leads to **Chain of Craters Road,** which descends along Kilauea's eastern rift zone from 4,000-foot-elevation rain forest to sea-level desert in just 20 miles. Like the rim road, Chain of Craters has frequent turnouts at points of interest with educational plaques and side trails. Among the many eruption sites along the way is **Mauna Ulu,** which grew into a new shield cone between two older craters during an almost continuous series of eruptions between 1969 and 1974.

Providing a visual geology primer, after about 10 miles the road overlooks a steep, 1,500-foot escarpment and a broad flat plain of lava at sea level. Here gradual pressure on the flanks of the volcano stressed the outer edges until they broke away along fault lines, creating the escarpment. Long cascades of lava from Kilauea's Mauna Ulu ran down the fault scarp adding more than 200 acres of new land to Hawai'i as it hit the water and cooled.

Toward the end of the road, where it reaches the sea, an easy but hot one-mile walk leads across the lava to **Pu'u Loa** (Hill of Long Life), an area of more than 15,000 petroglyphs of human and animal figures that ancient travelers carved into the soft rock.

Rising up Kilauea's slope from the sea, the two types of lava are quite distinctive: The rough-textured *'a'a* lava absorbs the light, the shiny *pahoehoe* reflects it. *'A'a* is produced by thick, slow-moving streams that solidify into jagged chunks and sharp, stony boulders. *Pahoehoe,* from faster-running flows, stimulates the imagination with its fantastical guises—huge coils of carelessly tossed and twisted rope, whimsical pieces of tortured taffy, endless pillows of frozen stone covered in a coppery glaze. Sometimes the newest lava wears a downy

---

RIGHT: *Volcanic fissures pattern the desolate Ka'u Desert. Precipitation here is mainly acid rain, formed when sulfur dioxide vented from nearby Halema'uma'u Crater combines with air moisture to form sulfuric acid.*

covering of glass strands called Pele's hair. But these fragile fibers, spun when lava is thrown into the air, quickly break down.

As yet, little plant life grows along the eastern rift. Most Hawaiian plants need organic matter and ample rainfall to prosper. They tend to depend on pioneer species—algae, lichens, mosses—to start the regeneration process. Fern spores, blown by the wind into cracks and wrinkles in the flow, are often the first to take root. The *'ohi'a* tree is an early colonizer too.

Chain of Craters Road used to continue northeastward along the coast and on to Hilo, but lava flows from Pu'u O'o in recent years have forged their way to the sea with ruinous regularity, destroying the picture-perfect village of Kalapana, its renowned black-sand beach, the Park Service's million-dollar visitor center, and many miles of highway. One structure was conspicuously spared by the lava: the thirteenth-century **Waha'ula Heiau.** Built during a period of reformation in Hawaiian religion, this temple was the first where human sacrifice was used to give prayers a special emphasis. Access has been blocked by a lava flow. When the volcano is active, it is sometimes possible to hike out to see the actual lava flows as they make their spectacular descent into the sea; a 24-hour volcano-conditions hot line as well as park rangers at the Kilauea visitor center and at checkpoints on Chain of Craters Road provide daily updates on local conditions and the best viewing points.

In a separate section of Hawai'i Volcanoes National Park, just on the other side of Volcano village from Kilauea and the park headquarters, is one of the state's most pristine tracts of native forest, **'Ola'a Forest.** Undeveloped except for a self-guided walk, the area, one of several special ecological zones designated within the park, is so thick with native trees it seems to overflow its boundary fences. Park officials are hopeful that destructive animals such as feral pigs (and eventually even alien plants) can be removed. Feral pigs rooting in the soil to find food uproot and destroy native plant communities. Successful, aggressive alien species are quick to reseed in such an area, squeezing native plants out. Park officials also worry about the effect of commercial helicopter noise (many tour companies operate volcano flyovers) on bird life. The next section of the park to explore is accessed via the Mauna Loa Strip Road. At the bottom of this road **Tree Molds** were made when a Kilauea lava flow washed through a forest. The trees burned, but they left the pattern of their bark in the hardened rock. A similar flow, perhaps 400 years ago, spared the **Kipuka Puaulu** (Bird Park). This oasis of rain forest, rich with native plant and bird life, was preserved by lava flows that isolated it from the surrounding terrain. A one-mile trail loops through a forest grove, where koa, *'ohi'a* and *kolea* trees host such birds as *'elepaio, 'apapane, 'amakihi,* and *i'iwi.*

There is one more section of Hawai'i Volcanoes National Park to explore: Mauna Loa itself. However, the Mauna Loa Strip Road, which leads upward from Route 11, goes only halfway up. The climb up the rest of the way to the summit is serious mountaineering and should not be attempted by anyone unprepared for the dangers of severe weather, high altitude, and challenging hiking. The trail follows Mauna Loa's Northeast Rift Zone, climbing through native forest of koa, *'ohi'a,* and *mamane* trees and rising above the tree line at about 8,500 feet. If the *mamane's* yellow flowers are in bloom, look for native honeycreepers such as the *'amakihi,* which feed on them. Also in evidence are two common native shrubs, *pukiawe,* an abundant narrow-leaved shrub with white or red fruit, and *'ohelo,* a small shrub related to the cranberry with bright red berries. The excursion from the strip road trailhead to the 13,679-foot summit takes about four days round-trip, with nights spent in cabins at 10,035 and 13,250 feet. All climbers who attempt the summit must register at park headquarters.

LEEWARD HAWAI'I: THE KONA COAST

From Hawai'i Volcanoes National Park, Route 11 descends between Kilauea's and Mauna Loa's southwestern rift zones, which run from their respective calderas all the way to sea level, and continues along the island's southwestern coast. Among the glinting lava flows on the south side of the highway just south of Kilauea is the upper limit of the **Ka'u Desert❖**. A short walk (two hours round-trip) through quasi-martian terrain leads to a spot where Hawaiian soldiers were caught by a sudden, unusually violent volcanic eruption in 1790. Their frantic, fleeing footprints became permanent indentations in the ash.

Farther south along Route 11 the desert gives way to macadamia orchards. Several miles past Pahala a road leads down to the black sand beach at **Punalu'u❖**. The black volcanic sand comes as a beautiful surprise to those whose image of a perfect beach includes miles of shining

white sand. Hawksbill turtles nest in the black sand here, so tread carefully. A county campground sits on a grassy bluff above the rocky shoreline.

Just beyond the sleepy town of Wai'onhihu, the narrow, paved
South Point Road leads off the highway through windswept grasslands
12 slow miles down to **Ka Lae❖**, or South Point. Ka Lae is the southernmost point not only of the state of Hawai'i but also of the entire
United States. Ocean currents meet offshore, and the waters below the
cliffs are full of fish, making this spot a favorite of local fishermen for
at least 1,400 years. In prehistoric times they would tie up to mooring
holes in the rock face and let their canoes float out into the current at
the end of long ropes. Modern fishing boats still shelter below these
cliffs, in the lee of prevailing winds.

Green Sand Beach can be reached by parking at the end of Ka
Lae's left fork and following the four-wheel-drive track on foot for
about three miles. (Permission must be obtained from the Department
of Hawaiian Homelands, which manages Ka Lae.) The bright, translu-
cent sand is formed of unusual volcanic olivine crystals.

Past the Ka Lae turnoff, Route 11 turns north, following the rolling
contours of the South Kona Coast about a thousand feet above the
shoreline. The highway crosses alternating strips of arid nineteenth-
and twentieth-century lava flows and lush, healthy forest. **Manuka
Natural Area Reserve❖**, about 12 miles past South Point Road, and
Kipahoehoe Natural Area Reserve❖, 10 miles farther, protect such
areas. Manuka has trails and a small state park along the road.

Perhaps a dozen miles beyond Kipahoehoe Route 160 splits off
Route 11 at Keokea and drops down to Honaunau Bay, a worthwhile
side trip. **Pu'ukohola Heiau National Historic Site❖**, now a serene
seaside oasis on the bay, was once the walled "city of refuge," where
primitive Hawaiians who broke *kapu* (taboos) could seek asylum.
From here a narrow road leads about four miles north to **Kealakekua
Bay State Underwater Park❖**, also a state historical park and the first
of many excellent spots along the Kona Coast for diving and snorkel-

---

LEFT: *The sands and cliffs above Green Sand Beach, near Ka Lae (South
Point), contain volcanic olivine, a distinctive green mineral.*
OVERLEAF: *Coconut palms shade Pu'uhonua o Honaunau, an ancient
refuge where victims of war or breakers of taboos could find safety.*

ing. Many of the best areas, such as this one, are protected as marine life conservation districts, where taking or disturbing sea life is prohibited. At Kealakekua even the shy spinner dolphin can be seen close to shore, and graceful white-tailed tropicbirds, which nest on the nearby sea cliffs, also find rich fishing here. Tour operators from Keauhou and Kailua, both farther up the coast, lead diving excursions and glass-bottom boat cruises here.

Kealakekua is also known for its history. It was long prophesied that the god Lono would return to the land on a floating island streaming with white tapa cloth. Every year a festival in Lono's honor was held here at the Hikiau Heiau. Into this revelry in 1779 tacked the billowing sails of Captain Cook's great ships. For a time, myth and man were one, and Cook received a godly welcome. A broken mast forced the ships to return to Kealakekua shortly after they had left, and an ill-fated series of incidents and misunderstandings led to a skirmish, in which Cook, several of his men, and a number of Hawaiians were killed.

Halfway up the leeward coast, the district of Kona bulges seaward under the least famous of Hawai'i's volcanoes, **Hualalai.** In 1801 Hualalai's last eruption spilled down to the sea, across the area where the airport stands today. Kamehameha, who had established a royal residence in nearby Kailua, paddled out to where the lava flow met the water and politely asked Madame Pele to turn it off. She obliged.

At the bottom of Hualalai's bulge is the town of **Kailua** (also known as Kona, which means "leeward," and as Kailua-Kona). Kailua is the center of the Big Island's tourism industry, with dozens of hotels stretching for miles along the water. Despite the development the waters are full of healthy fish and coral, and the Kona Coast is known for its fishing. The billfishing here—for striped marlin, blue marlin up to half a ton, and black marlin up to 1,800 pounds—is legendary. Snorkel, snuba (an apparatus that allows swimmers to breathe through an air hose attached to a tank that floats on the surface), and scuba-diving trips leave from Kailua's marina and from the tiny beach at the foot of Palani Road.

Largely undeveloped, the **Old Kona Airport State Recreation Area**❖ is about ten miles north of Kailua (two miles north of Keahole Airport), accessible via a road leading down toward the sea from Route 19 (the northern extension of Route 11). Turtles can frequently be seen swimming close to shore here. The Ala Kahakai, or "trail by the sea," once followed the coastline all the way from Kailua north to Kawaihae, some 30 miles. Restoring the trail is a priority of the Na Ala Hele program, affiliated with the Hawai'i Department of Land and Natural Resources. Established in 1988, the group is gradually rebuilding trails of historic importance throughout the islands. On the Big Island, it is beginning here at the state park.

In the nearby **Kaloko-Honokohau National Historical Park❖** lies Aimakapa Fishpond. Once a productive fish farm built by ancient Hawaiians, it is now one of the only wetland habitats on the Big Island. The *ae'o* (black-necked stilt) and *'alae ke'oke'o* (Hawaiian coot), both endangered waterbirds, feed and perhaps nest here.

NORTHWESTERN HAWAI'I: THE KOHALA COAST

It takes a particularly strong spirit not to be put off by the desolate landscape of South Kohala. Endless inhospitable acres of lava extend over the land, baking under the hot tropical sun. The trade winds funnel between Kohala and Mauna Kea, creating powerful gusts called *mumuku,* which blow across the desert and out to sea.

Of course, the land is not as infertile as it looks. Donkeys and goats live off the grass and *kiawe* (mesquite). And even though rainfall averages less than nine inches per year, there is water. Hawaiian divers have long known of the freshwater springs that bubble up offshore under the waves. Every day virtually anywhere around the Big Island (and the others in the chain as well) millions of gallons of fresh groundwater are flushed naturally out to sea along each mile of coastline.

Natural depressions in the land here make for one of the most extensive systems of anchialine pools in the world. Located in porous substrates, these brackish water pools appear to have no link to the sea, yet show tidal fluctuations. Although they are interconnected to the ocean, no evidence is visible. The lack of surface connection allows them to shelter a singular community of flora and fauna.

Such ponds are extremely rare, occurring around the world only in Fiji, the Red Sea, and a few other places in Hawai'i. Everywhere that they occur, in either lava or coralline limestone, they have exactly the same biological makeup: tiny red shrimp (*'opae'ula*) and red coralline algae. The shrimp are the real mystery. No matter how far inland a pool is created, the red shrimp appear within days. The lava on the is-

41

ABOVE: *Nature has largely reclaimed the deep windward valley of Waipi'o.*
Between its high, green, waterfall-laced cliffs, large communities once

land is so porous that anchialine pools two miles inland and 200 feet above sea level rise and fall with the tide.

One of the best places to see anchialine pools is beside the **Hyatt Regency Waikoloa**❖ (about 25 miles north of Kailua on Route 19), where some examples have been preserved. The **Royal Waikoloan**❖ offers tours of the pools on its grounds. Hotels on the Kohala Coast have also been pioneers in finding ways to minimize the impact of development and to maintain the surrounding natural environment. Just up the coast, the **Mauna Lani Bay Hotel and Bungalows**❖ has set aside two archaeological preserves of fishponds, petroglyphs, and lava tubes.

At Kawaihae, the next town, Route 19 turns inland toward the town of Waimea, but the Akoni Pule Highway (Route 270) continues along the arid coast, passing **Lapakahi State Historical Park**❖, a restored fishing village. The waters off the park are also a marine life conservation district. Route 270 continues on to Upolu Point, the northernmost part of the Big Island, and then veers east through the time-lost town of Hawi. The change in vegetation from *kiawe* (mesquite) to pothos (a common houseplant resembling the philodendrons, but which grows

thrived, enjoying the fertile soil and plentiful water. Only a few residents returned, however, after a 1946 tsunami stripped the valley bare.

50 feet high in Hawai'i) indicates the switch to the windward side of the island. The increased rainfall has eroded and sliced the terrain, and the road winds in and out of little valleys.

A few miles farther east Route 270 ends at the **Pololu Valley Lookout,** where a spectacular vista extends 12 miles southeast across the *pali* of the Kohala Mountains' windward coast. One ridge after another arcs into the sea. The deep, overgrown valleys between these cliffs were once populated. Only Waipi'o, at the far southern end, is now accessible by vehicle. From the lookout's northern vantage point a hiking trail leads down into Pololu Valley, a 15-minute trek through a tangle of *hala,* or pandanus, branches and mosquitoes to a black-sand beach.

There is very little in the scenery of the Kohala range to suggest it was the Big Island's first volcano. On the leeward slopes, gently rolling grasslands look like the cattle country of central California. Along Kohala Mountain Road (Route 250), which heads south from Hawi to the town of Waimea, eucalyptus and prickly pear cactus dot the hills, along with plenty of cattle. The **Parker Ranch❖**, which once covered half a million acres, is still the largest individually owned cattle ranch in

43

the United States, currently running 50,000 head on 225,000 acres. In the middle of the ranch, the town of Waimea (also called Kamuela) straddles the wet-dry line between windward and leeward sides of the island.

Following Route 19 east from Waimea, turn left at Honoka'a on Route 240, then go west ten miles to road's end at the **Waipi'o Valley Lookout❖**. Access into the valley is by four-wheel-drive vehicle (tour operators are stationed at the lookout) or by walking down the hill.

The walls of the valley rise more than 2,000 feet on either side, green ramparts that emphasize Waipi'o's isolation in time and space. Long ago thousands of Hawaiians lived here in what was called the Valley of the Kings, working the most productive taro patches in the islands. King Kamehameha spent much of his childhood in this valley, hidden from chiefs afraid of his prophesied power.

But in 1946 a devastating tsunami (often wrongly called a tidal wave) cleaned out the valley, and few families ever moved back. Today the six-mile long valley is a maze of muddy roads, meandering streams, and wild vegetation. At the back of the valley massive twin waterfalls cut into the rock. Smaller waterfalls trickle down the sides of the valley cliffs to fill secluded swimming holes.

Above the beach, on the valley's western wall, a steep trail makes nearly 45-degree switchbacks as it

ABOVE: *Retired San Franciscan Dan Lutkenhouse purchased a 25-acre valley and created the edenic Hawai'i Tropical Botanical Garden, which displays native plants as well as exotic imported flora such as the orchids shown here.*

RIGHT: *Heavy rains on Hawai'i's windward Hamakua Coast create the cascades of 'Akaka Falls State Park and nourish imported gingers, orchids, heliconia, and other flowers as well as tree-sized philodendrons and monstera.*

climbs 1,200 feet. This is the beginning of the seven-mile **Muliwai Trail.** Backpacking this ancient footpath is the only way to get to **Waimanu Valley❖.** Now maintained by the state, the grueling trail crosses 14 *pali* (cliffs) along a coastal plateau, but hikers find refreshment in fern-lined pools and a constant supply of guava and berries within reach of the path. For those who find the whole traverse too arduous to complete in one day, there is an open camping shelter about two-thirds of the way along the trail.

Waimanu was also once a population center, but if Waipi'o is overgrown, Waimanu is positively feral. Since 1976 both the trail and the valley have been protected as a national estuarine research reserve. Inland from the beach a large estuary blends into wetlands fed by five waterfalls on the western wall of the valley. The native bulrush, *‘aka‘akai,* grows in the water here.

In the freshwater streams there are several species of native goby (*‘o‘opu*), two native mollusks, shrimp, and prawns. Native mullets, *moi* and *ahole,* live in the estuary. Two species of waterbirds feed on them, the black-crowned night heron (*‘auku‘u*) and the endangered Hawaiian duck, *koloa.* Hawai‘i’s only native land mammal, the hoary bat, *‘ope‘ape‘a,* also lives in the valley. Small and reddish—with a wingspan of up to 13 inches—it sleeps by day and hunts insects at night. Two other endangered native fliers can be seen: the *‘io* (Hawaiian hawk) and the *pueo* (Hawaiian short-eared owl).

WINDWARD HAWAI‘I: THE HAMAKUA COAST TO PUNA

From Honoka‘a, Route 19 arcs 45 miles southeastward through sugar country to Hilo. The area, the windward slope of Mauna Kea, is known as the **Hamakua Coast.**

Some six miles past Honoka‘a, a well-marked succession of mountain roads winds up to **Kalopa State Recreation Area❖**. A 45-minute self-guided walk down the nature trail here is an ideal introduction to the native flora of Hawaiian forests. The clearly identified and well-described specimens include not just the celebrity natives, such as *‘ohi‘a,* but also the foot soldiers of the ecosystem, such as *kopiko,* a member of the coffee family with black bark, and *kolea,* a tree or shrub with black fruit clustered on its limbs.

Above the highway on Mauna Kea’s windward slopes are endless acres of undisturbed rain forest. A large portion of this forest is currently being organized by the U.S. Fish and Wildlife Service as the **Hakalau Forest National Wildlife Refuge❖**. A more accessible attraction in this region is **‘Akaka Falls State Park❖**. Drive four miles uphill from Route 19 on Route 220, where a half-hour loop hike goes through dense forest decorated with plumeria, ginger, banana, and ti. The real treats here, however, are the waterfalls. **Kahuna Falls** cascades 400 feet down a side canyon, and **‘Akaka Falls** makes a sheer drop of 442 feet into an eroded gorge.

Nearby Hilo is America’s most tropical city, with a lot of rain (some 133 inches per year) as well as plenty of sunshine, so everything natural grows at a prodigious rate. **Wailuku River State Park❖,** which runs parallel to Waianuenue Avenue, affords dramatic vistas into the lovely 80-foot **Rainbow Falls** (a cave beneath them is said to be the home of the goddess Hina, Maui's mother) and **Boiling Pots,** a series of depressions in the Wailuku River that bubble and swirl dramatically, particularly after a heavy rain.

Just north of Hilo, the **Hawaii Tropical Botanical Garden** offers a stunning setting for a large collection of tropical plants from around the world, planted along walkways past waterfalls and the oceanfront. More than 1,000 species are identified in an available guidebook.

In the Puna District south of Hilo there is still more evidence of the island's omnipresent volcanoes. Take Route 130 southeast about 15 miles, then bear left on Route 132 in Pahoa to the eerie forest of **Lava Tree State Monument❖**. In 1790 a 12-foot wave of lava quickly washed through this 'ohi'a grove, cooling where it struck the moist trees. A moment later a fissure quickly opened in the ground, draining away all of the lava except the tree casings, which today are broken columns covered with growth and shrouded in mist.

ABOVE: **Mamane** *trees growing on the volcanic slopes of Mauna Kea provide crucial habitat for the endangered* **palila,** *a native honeycreeper that eats the tree's seedpods and nests in its branches.*

OVERLEAF: *Seen from the Saddle Road, above the timberline dried pasture grasses take on a luminous golden glow. Although not in evidence here, cattle have grazed for decades on parts of Mauna Kea's cinder cones.*

From Lava Tree continue out to the coast on Pohoiki Road, which branches off Route 130, then go left on Route 137 to **MacKenzie State Recreation Area❖**, offering picnicking and camping sites along the dramatic coastline. This shore road used to pass Kaimu (Black Sand)

Beach and Kalapana before rejoining Route 130. But the road, the quaint village of Kalapana, and what many considered the world's most beautiful beach were overrun with lava in the late 1980s and early 1990s. Today the area is largely inaccessible to visitors.

INLAND HAWAI'I: MAUNA KEA

One 14,000-foot volcano is not the same as the next, as a quick comparison of the Big Island's two giants proves. Take the Saddle Road (Route 200) inland from Hilo, climbing upward to the flat 6,000-foot-high plateau between Mauna Kea and Mauna Loa. As a volcano ages, the chemical composition of its exports changes. Early on the magma is rich in iron, and thick, runny lava flows build a broad "shield." Mauna Loa is still in this phase. The magma from eruptions of older volcanoes, such as Mauna Kea, contains more silica-rich minerals. Lava spurts out in violent eruptions that build steep cinder cones and coat the land with cinder and ash. In some places a forested cinder cone may become completely isolated by a lava flow, creating an island of native growth the Hawaiians call a *kipuka.*

The road to Mauna Kea's summit is paved most of the way, but a vehicle with four-wheel drive is recommended. Mauna Kea last erupted along the ridge that the road follows about 4,000 years ago. The slopes are covered with native *mamane* trees, whose flowers bloom bright yellow in summer, attracting the *palila* bird. This yellow and gray honeycreeper is found only on the subalpine slopes of Mauna Kea, where it eats the green seedpods of *mamane.*

Just below the telescopes that dot the mountain's summit a faint trail leads out to **Lake Wai'au.** At 13,020 feet, it is the third highest lake in the United States. More remarkable is the fact that the lake is a remnant of the glaciers that crowned Mauna Kea during the last Ice Age, which ended approximately 10,000 years ago.

Surrounding the lake are numerous quarry sites where Hawaiians came to dig out dense basalt for carving adzes. Strange natural striations along the ground near the lake have never been explained. The area is protected by the state as **Mauna Kea Ice Age Natural Area Reserve❖**. The treeless, barren area receives little more than a foot of rain a year.

Certainly the thinness of the air adds to the surreal impression of the landscape at the top, making it that much harder for the brain to deal

ABOVE: *At almost 14,000 feet, Mauna Kea's summit experiences arctic conditions and despite the tropical sun is often frosted with snow. Its thin atmosphere ensures unparalleled astronomical observations.*

with the tricks of perspective. From December to March, snow caps the peak, delighting hardy downhill and cross-country skiers. The rest of the year the area looks more lunar than terrestrial. Across the ocean channel, Maui's highest volcano, Haleakala, pokes above the clouds. Mauna Kea casts a ghostly shadow of itself against the clouds at sunset.

The unearthly appearance of the terrain is underscored by the spaceshiplike astronomical observatories at Mauna Kea Observatory, where a number of nations have constructed telescopes. Mauna Kea is considered the best place on earth for stargazing. The astronomers who spend their nights here searching the universe are very often oblivious to their otherworldly immediate surroundings (since time on the telescopes costs about $100,000 per night, their narrow focus is understandable).

When measured from their base on the sea floor to their summit, the volcanoes Mauna Loa and Mauna Kea are the tallest mountains on earth. The heights of Everest and K2 will not be threatened for long, though. Hawai'i's volcanic islands wear down so fast that little will be left in a few million years—a blink of an eye in geological time.

MAUI

So much of what you see on Maui seems to belong to another planet: not just the surreal landscape within the vast crater of Haleakala, but the unearthly flora that thrives on the volcano's slopes, from the native silversword to the exotic varieties of imported commercially grown protea. With a semipermanent cloud layer that girdles the mountain about halfway up, the roiling clouds, sunny showers, and rainbows in the moonlight all confound the terrestrial norm. The Big Island inspires awe; Maui inspires a gentler sort of wonder.

The island is named for the demigod Maui, the only member of the Polynesian pantheon to earn such an honor. According to ancient folklore, young Maui, out to impress his scornful brothers, mightily cast his fishing line and, instead of a fish, pulled an entire island up out of the sea, one of the links in what became the Hawaiian chain.

During the last Ice Age, which ended about 10,000 years ago, the level of the Pacific Ocean was some 250 feet lower than it is today. Land bridges connected Maui and the volcanoes that formed the nearby islands of Kaho'olawe, Lana'i, and Moloka'i; the combined land area, an island known as Maui Nui, was about half the size of the present-day Big Island. Over the centuries rainwater dug valleys and

---

LEFT: *A journey through Haleakala Crater's alpine cinder desert is distinctly otherworldly. Color variations in the barren cinder cones at the crater's western end are due to different mineral compositions.*

gorges from above, and melting polar ice raised the level of the ocean, eventually submerging the land bridges and separating Maui from the other islands.

The island gets its asymmetrical figure-eight shape from two volcanoes connected by a narrow isthmus. On the smaller, western side, the worn West Maui Mountains are all that remain of the older volcano, Pu'u Kukui, now eroded to a diminished 5,788 feet. On East Maui towering Haleakala—at 10,023 feet the largest dormant volcano in the world—has only just begun to weather.

The island's regions can be characterized by their cultural geography. Most of the isthmus is planted with sugarcane; in the harvest season cane fires darken the sky with smoke but sweeten the air. Containing the towns of Kahului and Wailuku as well as the main airport, the northern end of the isthmus is as urban as Maui gets. In fact, 75 percent of the island's 728 square miles is wilderness.

The western, leeward shores of both East Maui and West Maui are sunny and dry, rimmed with sandy beaches and resort hotels. Off these western shores, in the tropical waters between Maui and Lana'i, Pacific humpback whales congregate from December through April (they then return to Alaska for the summer and fall). The shallow waters of Ma'alaea Bay, off the southern coast of the isthmus, are a favorite spot for whales to give birth and nurse calves and for whale watchers to enjoy the huge mammals' distinctive spouting and playful breaching.

The windward side of West Maui is rural, remote, and largely inaccessible. The windward side of East Maui, the Hana Coast, is a tropical eden reached via the winding Hana Highway; its spectacular coastline has provided a perfect backdrop for a rich literature of history, mythology, and song.

In the uplands of East Maui, the slopes of Haleakala are girdled with a series of small communities that owe their character to Maui's heyday as cattle country. Much of this open pastureland still belongs to the large Haleakala and 'Ulupalakua ranches, and architecture and fashions here are reminiscent of those of the Old West. At the top, Haleakala National Park offers the wonders of a landscape unlike any other in the world. The park encompasses vast changes in climate and vegetation, ascending precipitously from coastal tropical rain forests to a subalpine desert of gray lava hills strewn with red volcanic cinders.

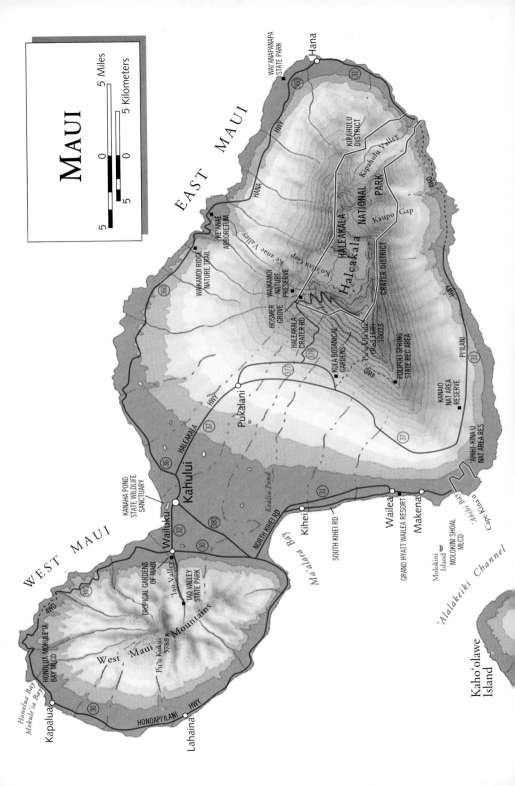

This singular habitat is home to flora and fauna found nowhere else on earth. The mountain, often bathed in clouds and mists, is sacred to Hawaiians. According to legend, when Maui's mother Hina complained that the day was too short to dry her tapa cloth, Maui climbed to the top of the volcano and lassoed the sun. He released it only when it promised to cross the sky more slowly. Thus the mountain, despite its clouds, is known as Haleakala, or House of the Sun.

Much of the island could be seen on one long day's drive—but experiencing and exploring the Valley Isle at its own slow pace is a more rewarding option. This chapter covers West Maui in a clockwise direction from the 'Iao Valley (near Kahului) around to the north shore, then moves on to East Maui, visiting the western shoreline and climbing the slopes of Haleakala Crater through upcountry Maui to Haleakala National Park. The chapter then explores the crater's southern slope and continues along the eastern coast to the Hana area through the vibrant scenery of windward Maui.

WEST MAUI

On the main access road to Kahului Airport, **Kanaha Pond State Wildlife Sanctuary**❖ is one of Hawai'i's prime protected areas for waterfowl. A large population of black-crowned night herons is found here as are Hawaiian coots (*'alae ke'oke'o*), who build large floating nests. Migrating birds from the U.S. Northwest appear periodically. Once a royal fishpond in which fish were raised for food, the sanctuary is home to the endangered Hawaiian stilt (*ae'o*), a graceful wading bird with distinctive orange legs; its estimated statewide population is now only about 1,800. An observation pavilion is near the entrance at the junctions of Routes 36 and 396; to hike the sanctuary's service roads, a permit is required from the Division of Forestry and Wildlife, Department of Land and Natural Resources, in Wailuku.

In Wailuku signs indicate the route west on Ka'ahumanu Avenue (Route 32) toward the West Maui Mountains. Directly ahead the huge, misty **'Iao Valley** gapes above the coastal terrain, reaching back almost to the center of the West Maui Mountains. Follow the signs to 'Iao Valley Road (Route 320), a scenic stretch winding under steep *pali* covered with greenery and extending much of the length of the valley. Early in the route are the **Tropical Gardens of Maui**❖, where de-

ABOVE: *The name of West Maui's 'Iao Valley means "supreme light."*
Amid the lush terrain, the rocky spire called 'Iao Needle (at left) has
outlasted the erosional power of the valley's many streams.

tailed botanical labels describe such island specialties as gigantic
Hawaiian lobelias, with their short succulent stems and long slender
flowers. There are also good displays of unusual gingers and
Polynesian plants. As the road winds higher through Black Gorge a
rock face called **Pali 'Ele'ele** comes into view, said to bear a likeness
to John F. Kennedy.

'Iao Valley State Park❖ is at the end of the road. Short paved
paths cross the stream and wind through the valley. Stairways and
trails provide periodic vistas of the tranquil, lush canyon and rocky
stream below, eventually leading to a lookout pavilion under the **'Iao
Needle,** an unusual rocky monolith covered in verdant vegetation.
This geological curiosity, rising 1,200 feet above the surrounding ter-

ABOVE: *Coral reefs shelter colorful marine life including the whiskered saddle wrasse with its ochre harness, the striped surgeonfish (descriptively called the convict tang), and the bright yellow butterfly fish.*

rain (2,250 feet above sea level), was worshiped in ancient times.

Go back out of the valley and turn south on Route 30 (the Honoapiʻilani Highway), which arcs around West Maui through endless fields of thick green sugarcane. High above the highway as it rounds West Maui's southern tip is the old **Lahaina Pali Trail,** part of the historic route that connected the towns of Wailuku and Lahaina. This stone path has recently been restored by the Na Ala Hele trail rebuilding program and the Hawaiian forestry department. The four-and-a-half mile trail begins from a turnout a quarter mile north of the tunnel off Route 30 and climbs to 1,600 feet. Alongside, endemic dryland plants such as *kuluʻi*, as well as *kiawe* and *pukiawe*, grow. At 1,300 to 1,500 feet, the vegetation changes to the mesic type, with *ʻohiʻa* and koa trees. The sweeping vista takes in the islands of Kahoʻolawe and Lanaʻi and sometimes a pod of wintering whales. The trail comes down near Maʻalaea Harbor, so it's a hike back to the starting point. With almost no shade, the trail gets extremely hot, so start early, wear sunscreen, and be sure to carry plenty of water. The forestry service strongly recommends not straying from the trail.

The coastline from Lahaina all the way to Kapalua is an uninterrupted string of resort communities with luxury hotels and condominiums; all of the beaches have excellent swimming and snorkeling. When Kamehameha succeeded in uniting the islands in 1802, he established his kingdom's capital at **Lahaina.** Soon the seaport was also the capital of a whaling industry that at its height in the 1840s saw hundreds of ships per year. Today the historic town sees mainly tourists, but it is also the site of the largest banyan tree in the country. Planted in 1873, its 16 major trunks, countless intertwined branches, and rooted aerial vines cover nearly an acre.

Past Kapalua, **Mokule'ia Bay** is a popular beach and part of the **Honolua–Mokule'ia Bay Marine Life Conservation District❖**; its protected underwater life provides good snorkeling opportunities. The next left turn off the highway leads down to **Honolua,** another part of the same marine life conservation district. Here the coral is most vibrant on the right side of the bay, and the diving is good. Tour boats from Kapalua come in the morning, but in the afternoon the beautiful cove can be completely deserted. Various surgeonfish, snapper, mullet, wrasses, goldfish, and brighteye damselfish populate the waters, and divers can see rose and lobe corals.

Route 30 swings around the top of the island along a dramatic windswept coastline of bays, sea cliffs, and great red promontories topped by pine that seem to be spilling into the sea. The road, which changes to Route 340, does continue all the way around West Maui back to Wailuku, but beyond a sign that says Area Residents Only, it becomes slow and unreliable, best driven in a four-wheel-drive vehicle. It is easier to return via Lahaina.

Inland, the West Maui Mountains rise to nearly 6,000 feet. Watershed areas in the upper elevations are now almost completely protected by state natural area reserves and Nature Conservancy preserves. Among the important species in these mountains are rare tree snails, the West Maui silversword, bog silversword, Maui bog violet, native lobelias, and three native forest birds: the *'i'iwi, 'apapane,* and *'amakihi.* Although access is severely limited to protect these species, the Nature Conservancy's **Kapunakea Preserve❖** offers guided hikes.

EAST MAUI'S LEEWARD COAST

Much of the leeward coast of East Maui is heavily developed with resort areas. Heading south from Ma'alaea, North Kihei Road passes **Kealia Pond National Wildlife Refuge✧**, a large saltwater marsh and bird sanctuary. Farther south, past the Kihei hotel strip, are Wailea and Makena, two upscale resort areas. Some of the resorts include excellent collections of Hawaiian plants in their landscaping.

Offshore from Makena, **Molokini Island** is a crescent of crater rim sticking up from the channel. The now-eroded volcano, once above sea level, is in a direct line with other eruption sites along a rift zone that points straight to the summit of Haleakala. Above the water the shoal is protected as a seabird sanctuary, and landing is prohibited. The waters sheltered within the crater, **Molokini Shoal Marine Life Conservation District✧**, are the most popular dive site in the state. Giant manta rays (devilfish) cruise the sand channels, undaunted—even intrigued by—divers' air bubbles. The inner edges of the reef are decorated with antler coral and shelter octopus and a great variety of fish, from eels to puffers to butterfly fish. Tour boats from Lahaina, Ma'alaea, and Kihei take advantage of the thriving reef communities with commercial snorkeling and dive tours.

ABOVE: *The native shrub* **pukiawe***, a popular component in colorful leis, grows in dry and wet areas on most islands.*

RIGHT: *In the Waikamoi Preserve, tall* **acacia koa** *trees and shorter* **ohi'a** *provide a vital sanctuary for 14 native Hawaiian birds, including the rare Maui parrotbill and the crested honeycreeper.*

The coast road ends at **'Ahihi-Kina'u Natural Area Reserve✧**. 'Ahihi Bay and Cape Kina'u were formed in 1790 by the lava flowing from Haleakala's last eruption. Today the 2,000-acre reserve is home to a remarkable variety of marine life. Some 100 species of fish and many species of stony coral thrive amid the lava tidal pools, coastal lava tubes, and *kipuka* (oases) in the *'a'a* lava flows that dot the landscape. From here the Hoapili Trail, the old "King's Highway," goes around the is-

land toward Hana. Portions of the foot trail have been restored, but it is still very hard to follow.

UPCOUNTRY AND HALEAKALA NATIONAL PARK

Alongside the Haleakala Highway (Route 37), which starts from the airport at Kahului and proceeds south, miles of sugarcane and pineapple fields lead up the slopes of Haleakala. This region is upcountry Maui, with cattle ranches and a western lifestyle reminiscent of those of rural California. Past the town of Pukalani, about ten miles beyond the airport, take the left fork onto Route 377, then go left again, up Haleakala Crater Road (Route 378) through the vast Haleakala Ranch, where in less than 200 years cactus-strewn grasslands and eucalyptus groves have replaced the dense native forest.

Just inside the entrance to the **Crater District❖** of **Haleakala National Park**, a left turn down a short road leads to the campground of **Hosmer Grove❖** (a self-guided pamphlet is available) and the access point for the Nature Conservancy's **Waikamoi Preserve❖**. One of the largest tracts of native forest in the state, the 5,230-acre preserve borders the park and can be seen only on interpretive hikes led by the Nature Conservancy or by the National Park Service.

The upper part of the reserve was planted by Ralph Hosmer, a turn-of-the-century forestry manager. After the natural watershed on Haleakala had been grazed away, Hosmer experimented by planting a vast array of evergreens, from Mexican weeping pine to Portuguese pine and Japanese sugi pine. The needles proved effective in catching the moisture in the ever-present mist, which then dripped down to soak the forest floor.

Along the ridge native plants grow in isolated communities that emphasize their interdependence. A koa tree might be home to a vase fern, and surrounded by *'ama'u* (*Sadleria* ferns) and *pukiawe* shrubs. Pele's hair, a furry lichen that grows on koa, is home to about 50 different species of insects. The thorns of the raspberries (*'akala*) growing here fall off at the touch, an example of how native Hawaiian plants have adapted to their benign environment and lost their original defense mechanisms. The presence of the berries is also why some local residents can get upset when visitors mispronounce Haleakala. Stressing the third syllable (ha-lay-AH-ka-lah) rather than the fifth (ha-lay-ah-ka-LAH) makes the word mean "House of Berries" instead of "House of the Sun."

Another native berry, in the cranberry and blueberry genus, grows on the *'ohelo* bush. Like those of many other plants, new *'ohelo* leaves have a reddish color to protect them from the harsh tropical sun. The new shoots of the *'ama'u,* the Haleakala *Sadleria* fern, are also red, a color that effectively screens out ultraviolet rays until the fronds toughen up.

At the bottom of **Waikamoi Gulch** is the **Waikamoi Gulch Nature Trail**, where time seems to have stood still. All of the plants in the lava-carpeted gorge are native. Some of the *'ohi'a* are 200 years old. Because the altitude here is too high for the mosquitoes that carry avian malaria, the preserve is especially good for bird-watching. There are a number of rare species found only on the slopes of Haleakala. The Maui parrotbill, an endangered honeycreeper, uses its large, compressed beak like a can opener to split wood and then forage for insects; the crested honey-creeper (*'akohekohe*), a handsome dark bird with a distinctive crest and orange-red nape, feeds on the nectar from the *'ohi'a* flowers. Also found in this valley—and unique to eastern Maui—are Hawaiian mint plants and the world's only known tree geranium, *Geranium arboreum,* which is now on the endangered list.

Haleakala is among the smallest of the national parks. Its plants and animals are also the most threatened. The advent of humans and other alien species has meant hard times for the exceptionally fragile native ecosystem here. Like Hawai'i Volcanoes National Park on the Big Island, Haleakala has been designated an International Biosphere Reserve by the United Nations. Visitors should be prepared for thin air and low temperatures, especially if visiting at sunrise, when tempera-tures can drop below freezing.

A twisting 11-mile drive snakes upward from park headquarters (just beyond the Hosmer Grove turnoff) through subalpine scrubland, bright-ened in spring by the *mamane*'s sprays of yellow flowers. Several over-looks present impressive views of the moonlike landscape. Near the top, at the sheltered visitor center, informative exhibits offer an excellent overview of the park's unusual geology, ecology, and history.

The terrain defies any preconceptions of what a terrestrial landscape should be. The 10,023-foot summit, **Pu'u 'Ula'ula** (or Red Hill), pre-sents an incredible 360-degree vista. As rainwater began carving the outer slopes of the mountain, two huge valleys (Ko'olau and Kaupo)

backed into each other at the summit. The resulting "crater," or bowl, is an enormous erosional depression almost as big as Manhattan Island.

Roads reach only the western rim of the Crater District. The rest of the park can be seen only on foot or horseback along a 30-mile network of spectacular trails. Outings can range from short, self-guided or ranger-led walks near the rim to arduous backpacking hikes of several days. Check with the park service about conditions, equipment, permits, and reservations for overnight stays.

Sliding Sands Trail, recommended for descents but not ascents, enters the crater area near the summit. The higher, drier western half of the crater is an alpine cinder desert. Inside the 3,000-foot-high rim wall the gray and black floor is interrupted frequently by cinder cones, dimpled peaks of red and brown reaching heights of 600 feet. Later lava flows slithered around them, creating ashlike, shiny rivers. For very experienced hikers, the rigorous **Skyline Trail** begins outside the park's boundaries, past the Science City observatories, and descends six and a half miles along the cinder cones of the southwestern rift zone from the

two giant valleys backed into each other at the caldera. Later volcanism brought lava flows and cinder cones. The Koʻolau Gap is seen here.

Air Force tracking station to Polipoli Springs State Recreational Area (covered below in the East Maui: Southern Slopes section).

In the past the flora of Haleakala was devastated both by human souvenir-seekers and by the introduction of wild goats that all but wiped out the tasty silversword and decimated the *mamane* trees. Fortunately, the park service began controlling the millions of two-footed visitors and by 1986 had rounded up the remaining goats and installed 32 miles of fencing around the crater.

The exotic and endangered silversword is related to daisies and sunflowers, so its current appearance shows how extensively it has adapted to fit its environment. A graceful ball of curving silver fingers two feet in diameter, the bush when it finally blooms sends up a two- to four-foot stalk covered with hundreds of purple blossoms. Each silversword flowers only once—often after decades—then withers and dies. The plant's silver hairs not only protect it from ultraviolet rays, increased by latitude and altitude, but also serve to collect moisture from passing mists.

Down on the crater floor, Sliding Sands Trail travels due east through fields of native bracken fern and introduced grasses. Along the base of the southern rim, the *pali* are eroded into parabolas that can echo shouts. Past Kapalaoa, one of three public backpacking cabins in the crater (there are also two campgrounds), the trail turns northeast over rougher terrain. The inhospitable-looking lava on either side of the trail is prime nesting country for the *nene,* the native Hawaiian goose.

Descended from Canada geese probably blown off course to the islands, the *nene* has been terrestrial for so long that its feet have lost 70 percent of their webbing and are now more suited to lava walking than ocean swimming. Most of its natural lowland habitat has been destroyed, and remnant populations now struggle to survive on the volcanic highlands here and on the Big Island. With no natural predators, the original *nene* was as unafraid of humans as the famous dodo—and met nearly the same fate. Popular game birds among Hawaiians and European sailors in the 1800s, *nene* were even exported to feed prospectors during the California gold rush. By the middle of the twentieth century, the birds had practically disappeared on Maui. The *nene* found in the Crater District today are the products of a captive breeding program begun in England in the early 1950s. Since 1962 more than 500 birds have been released into the crater.

The eastern end of Haleakala Crater becomes much wetter. Clouds flow in and out of Kaupo Gap like the tide, wrapping the *pahoehoe* lava and scrubland in thick fog. The *pali* above Paliku Cabin are green and lush. Notches on top of the cliff indicate the beginnings of the Kipahulu Valley, a native rain forest in another section of the park (reached only by leaving the Crater District and proceeding around the island to the Kipahulu District, nine miles south of Hana).

Return westward across the crater via the **Halemau'u Trail** (recommended for ascent), along which cairns of lava called *ahu* mark an old Hawaiian highway. The trail skirts Black Sand Desert, pauses for the **Silversword Loop,** and heads for Holua Cabin. In the distance against the northern crater rim, twisted shapes of lava in narrow volcanic defiles reach up from the burnt earth, and mountains shine palely in the other-

---

RIGHT: *It is fitting that the demigod Maui is said to have captured the sun at Haleakala Crater. Each sunrise seems unearthly as the great bowl fills with light, and color transforms the shadowy landscape.*

ABOVE: *On the brink of extinction only decades ago, the native Hawaiian goose, or* **nene***, was saved through a captive breeding program. Reintroduced at Haleakala, pairs have again nested successfully.*

worldly light. Then the Halemau'u Trail turns north, climbing the *pali* through layer after layer of striated cinder deposits; the trailhead is along the Crater Road at the 8,000-foot level.

EAST MAUI: SOUTHERN SLOPES

The southern slopes of Haleakala can be reached via either the upper or lower Kula roads, Routes 37 or 377, which split off the Haleakala Highway (also Route 37) outside Pukalani. Just north of the point where the two Kula roads come together again (seven or eight miles south of Pukalani), **Kula Botanical Gardens❖** offers the visitor an excellent opportunity to learn more about plant taxonomy. Plantings here give an especially broad glimpse of the enormous range of ferns growing in the islands, from the endangered Haleakala native *Sadleria* to a staghorn fern that grows in a macadamia tree to the pinelike regal fern. Of the 172 fern species native to Hawai'i, 127 are endemic—not found anywhere else on earth.

ABOVE: *The reflective hairs on this young silversword, or ʻahinahina, collect moisture from passing mists and protect the plant from the harsh ultraviolet rays and winter frosts of its high-altitude environment.*

Just as the Upper Kula Road (Route 377) rejoins the Kula Highway (37), Waipoli Road, which is too rough for passenger cars and requires a four-wheel-drive vehicle, splits off and spirals up into the Kula Forest Reserve. **Polipoli Springs State Recreation Area❖** has camping sites and hiking trails that pass through areas of native forest, eucalyptus, Monterey pine, and cypress.

On its way south the Kula Highway (Route 37) offers stunning panoramic views of the slopes below and across the isthmus to West Maui. Past the ʻUlupalakua Ranch, the road becomes the Piʻilani Highway (Route 31), and a sign announces the new **Kanaio Natural Area Reserve❖**, where remaining stands of *hala pepe* (*Dracaena*) and *lama* (native persimmon) trees are typical of the dry-forest species that once covered the southern slope of the mountain. Now the arid lands along the road past the reserve are almost completely barren. The road eventually descends to the rocky shoreline, where streams have cut deep gorges into basalt that seems almost blue. The paved road contin-

ues to the bottom of the **Kaupo Gap,** where all of the alluvium has washed out of Haleakala Crater. The route continues all the way around the southern coast to Hana, but unpaved sections beyond this point can be impassable with a standard passenger car.

THE HANA HIGHWAY: THE WINDWARD COAST

The Hana Highway (Routes 36 and 360) starts in East Maui's northwestern corner, at Kahului, and travels east along the windward coast 51 miles to the town of Hana. The problem with the road to Hana is that it is dangerously beautiful. There's no way to both appreciate the scenery and keep your eyes on the narrow, hilly road as it winds hundreds of feet above the crashing surf and deep gorges. Great batches of yellow ginger bloom along the roadside, and whole mountain slopes are covered with lacy bamboo. Silvery waterfalls cascade down the cliffs—and with 365 inches of rain per year in this area, there are a lot of them.

Fortunately, places to get out and stretch your legs—and your perceptions—abound. The **Waikamoi Ridge Nature Trail❖**, about 20 miles east of the airport, is an easy walk through fragrant eucalyptus groves. A little farther on, at the bottom of Ke'anae Valley, which flows down from Haleakala's Ko'olau Gap, is **Ke'anae Arboretum❖**. Plantings of trees and ornamental and food plants traditionally associated with Hawai'i can be found here. The breadfruit, or *'ulu,* once provided Hawaiians with nourishing fruit, good wood for canoes, and a sticky sap used for glue and chewing gum. Candlenut, or *kukui,* is the state tree, and its nuts produced oil used for candles and laxatives and even exported to Europe to lubricate clocks. The hibiscus

ABOVE: *A tender green fiddlehead of endemic* ama'uma'u *fern unfurls. An early colonizer on new lava flows, it takes root in cracks.*

LEFT: Ama'uma'u, *or* Sadleria, *ferns blanket the rim walls of Maui's Haleakala Crater. The red tint on new fronds provides protection from the ultraviolet rays of the tropical sun.*

71

ABOVE: *The curved beak of the native honeycreeper 'i'iwi is perfectly shaped to sip nectar from flowers. Although extinct or endangered on many islands, some 19,000 'i'iwi thrive in the high forests of East Maui.*

tree, or *hau,* is best known to the outside world for its brilliantly colored blossoms. But its flowers, bark, and wood were important sources of medicine, rope, cloth, and canoe outriggers. Hawaiians used the leaves of the coconut palm (*niu*) as thatch. The trunk could be carved into drums, utensils, even small canoes. The nut has sweet and nutritious milk and vitamin-rich meat; the shell could be crafted into bowls.

Wai'anapanapa State Park❖, off the highway just before Hana, offers cabins, which must be booked in advance, and a campground on a lawn next to an old cemetery, just above the cliffs, under the sea almond trees. A short trail leads to some refreshingly cool lava-tube caves open to exploring. A little black-sand beach directly below the park fronts a bay strewn with lava arches, where the water is green and clear. An ancient foot highway runs in both directions from here. The peninsula on which the park sits is an old hardened lava flow that is still very stark and sharp; it will shear the rubber off sandals, so wear heavy shoes or hiking boots.

In either direction, the trail winds through a huge forest of *hala,* or pandanus trees. With its twisted roots, wandering trunks, and droopy starburst leaves, pandanus figures prominently in Hawaiian culture. The male has flowers; the female has fruit. An extract from the pollen was considered an aphrodisiac. The tough leaves were plaited into mats, pillows, sandals, baskets, and sails. The ends of dried fruits were used as brushes for painting tapa cloth. On the forest floor is a bush called *naupaka,* with white berries and white half-flowers. The story is that when a princess was not permitted to marry her fisherman lover, she asked to be turned into a mountain flower. The fisherman was granted the same wish, but on the beach. So there they are, a beach *naupaka* and a mountain *naupaka,* each flower incomplete, eternally separated. Interestingly, the mountain species is endemic; the beach variety, indigenous.

East from the state park the *hala* forest eventually backs away from the coastline, but the trail stays right along the edge. The only living things to notice are a feisty little grass, some feisty red ants, and a tiny white lichen that looks like a dusting of snow on the black rocks. On this windward coast the seas have carved deep into the lava, leaving some cliffs straight and smooth and others eroded into graceful arches and sea caves.

Beyond Hana (the last chance for food, gas, and water along the road), travelers may see a weasellike animal scurrying across the road, now Route 31, which traverses the pasturelands above the sea. This is the Indian mongoose, introduced in 1883 in an attempt to control the rats, rodent escapees from the many ships that called at the islands. Unfortunately, the rat was nocturnal, the mongoose diurnal, and the problem simply escalated. Today the mongoose is a more voracious predator of native bird eggs than of the rat.

Not far past Hana a side road detours down the hill from Route 31 to Hamoa village, with pretty beaches and lots of introduced tree he-

---

Overleaf: *The rugged margin of Pukiele Point in the remote Kipahulu area is typical of windward Maui, where heavy rains and rolling surf endlessly sculpt the cliffs of soft dark lava flows from Haleakala.*

liotrope, which has silver leaves cupped upward. Along the road, an un-earthly-looking cactus vine that covers walls and climbs utility poles is night-blooming cereus, the squidlike flowers of which begin to bloom in late afternoon and wither by the next noon.

The road continues southwest, threading in and out of small valleys marked by high vistas and waterfalls. Each valley is dominated by different flora. One valley for instance (at mile marker 45) is wooded with breadfruit. The road enters the bottom of the **Kipahulu District❖** of **Haleakala National Park,** an 11,000-acre valley that extends up to the eastern rim of the crater. Neither trails nor roads connect it to the rest of the park; a separate visitor center and campground operate here.

ABOVE: *Imported by sugar growers to control rats, the mongoose quickly developed a taste for native birds instead, joining the rat as a major predator of endangered species.*

RIGHT: *A bamboo forest in 'Ohe'o Gulch is dense enough to block the sun. In contrast to the arid crater, parts of Haleakala National Park's Kipahulu section get 250 inches of rain per year.*

'Ohe'o Gulch, the stream area above and below the road, is terraced with a series of sparkling pools that cascade from one to another. A rare goby spawns in 'Ohe'o, though it spends most of its life in salt water. To breed, it returns to the freshwater pools where it was born. A trail leads up from the parking lot to an overlook above the 185-foot Makahiku Falls. A hidden trail on the left goes to secluded swimming holes above the falls. This area receives nearly 250 inches of rain annually. Torrents from the upper valley can appear quickly, so beware of sudden flash floods, which have washed people away. If the water begins to rise, climb out immediately.

From the overlook the main path climbs up another mile and a half into the forest, past giant banyans, through sweet guava groves, across a side stream, and into bamboo thickets so dense they block the light. At the top of the trail **Waimoku Falls** drapes like lace against a sheer rock

face, dropping some 400 feet down.

Kipahulu's upper valley is pristine rain forest, never disturbed by human settlement; even today it is closed to the public, accessible only to researchers flown in by helicopter. Giant koa trees spread their muscular branches across the valley floors, 'ohi'a launch their red blooms from the steep, overgrown walls, and waterfalls plunge into bottomless pools never enjoyed by even the most intrepid swimmers. Protected by its topography, areas of the upper Kipahulu Valley remain 100 percent native, with such rare birds as the Maui parrotbill and the *nuku pu'u,* Hawai'i's most endangered honeycreeper. Impenetrable hanging valleys (valleys that open or end in a cliff face), steep walls, and now a special fence have prevented wild pigs from tearing up one of the last areas of native Hawaiian vegetation. Even older Hawaiians speak of the upper valley with a special reverence: Its waters were once a source of life for the communities living in the fertile valley below. Today they may be the last refuge for the island's embattled native species.

MOLOKAʻI AND LANAʻI

Located between the islands of Maui and Oʻahu, Molokaʻi and Lanaʻi have shared a reluctance to join the modern age. Both were converted to pineapple production in the nineteenth century; each, in turn, was the largest pineapple plantation in the world. And today both have few tourist resorts. There, however, the similarities end.

Lanaʻi, whose name means hump or swelling, is aptly named because its rounded profile resembles the back of a humpback whale, such as those that winter off its rugged coastline. Traditionally thought to harbor evil spirits, the island has always been sparsely populated. Maui chieftains eventually dominated the island, but the wars in the 1700s severely reduced the population. Today some two thirds of the residents are descendants of twentieth-century immigrant families, mainly from the Philippines and Japan, who worked the pineapple fields.

Very little on arid, tiny Lanaʻi, which was originally prime dryland forest, now resembles its natural state. Nineteenth-century overgrazing and rampant feral animals have caused more ecological loss here—of native forest, plants, and birds—than on any of the other major islands.

Molokaʻi, on the other hand, remains perhaps the most Hawaiian of the major islands. Much of the landscape is untamed, and that's the

LEFT: *Windward Molokaʻi's deep valleys, Wailau and Pelekunu, are separated by high ridges and sea cliffs. The inaccessibility of these valleys has allowed them to remain largely undisturbed in modern times.*

way its 5,000 residents like it. In the 1920s the Hawaiian Homes Act granted 40 acres of land to anyone with a majority of Hawaiian blood— on Moloka'i that was more than half the population. They are *keiki o ka 'aina*, children of the land, who have grown up hunting Moloka'i's valleys and fishing its waters. Long before the great migrations from the Polynesian island of Raiatéa, the earliest Hawaiians lived on Moloka'i, an island where the hula was first danced, the island whose *kahuna* (sorcerers) were feared by the most powerful chiefs. Moloka'i has some of the most sacred sites in Hawaiian history. Moloka'i also harbors some of the most ecologically important places in the islands, from an ancient bog at Pepe'opae to petrified dunes at Mo'omomi.

Formed by three separate volcanoes, Moloka'i is 37 miles long (east to west), but only 10 miles across. The western half is an arid, windswept land with dunes, deserts, and long strips of deserted beach. The eastern half is greener, sloping up from the leeward reefs to rain-soaked ridges, then down steep *pali* striped with waterfalls into four deep canyons. The windward coast's *pali* are famous as the tallest sea cliffs in the world—and infamous for effectively isolating the wretched victims of Hansen's disease, or leprosy, who were exiled to the Kalaupapa Peninsula in the middle of Moloka'i's northern coast.

Lana'i's small size (only 140 square miles) puts all of Hawai'i's land-use issues in a *kukui* shell. The tiny island's dynamics are simplified because 98 percent of the land is owned by a single corporation, and because for the last 70 years or so the island has had a single industry. At one time Dole operated the world's largest pineapple plantation here, producing 240,000 tons per year and employing 6,000 people. But in late 1992 Dole ceased Lana'i's pineapple operations completely to concentrate on real estate and tourism. This pattern is now common on all of the Hawaiian islands, but how it will affect Lana'i's natural environment or its 2,300 residents is a subject of considerable debate.

Sheltered by the rain shadows of Maui (nine miles to the east) and Moloka'i (nine miles to the north), Lana'i is an exception to the weather patterns that normally prevail in the Hawaiian Islands. The reefs face north instead of south and the cliffs face south and east instead of north and west. The windward coast is almost as dry as the leeward, making green vegetation sparse except well up on the island's 3,400-foot-high summit, Lana'ihale. Both cultivation and civilization are con-

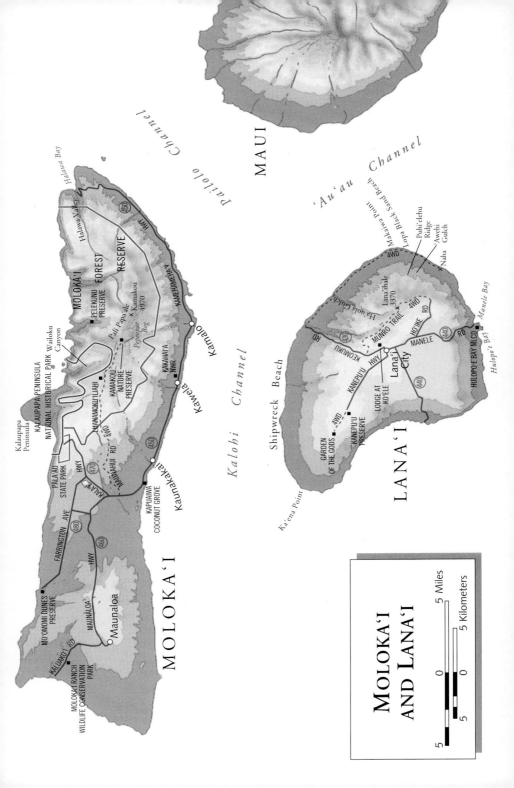

centrated on a high, cool plateau in the middle of the island, thought to be the center of the island's worn extinct volcano, Palawai. Because water was easily trapped on the main, lower part of the plateau, it made ideal plantation land, and row upon row of spiky-leaved pineapples growing in lava-red soil long dominated the landscape.

An imaginary line drawn from Ka'ena Point, on Lana'i's northwestern tip, straight southeast to Naha would bisect the island into its two characters. The northern, windward side has beaches protected by flat, dangerous coastal reefs and steep, eroded valleys leading up the rusty-red mountains. Although the mountains get little rain (only about 35 inches per year), the constant mist of the cloud forest keeps everything green, wet, and muddy. To the south the central ridge looks down on the lee side of the island, where steep sea cliffs tower as high as 2,000 feet over deep ocean water.

Even if very little of Lana'i's flora and fauna is native, most of it is still very wild. The island is so small that conservationists can look at Lana'i as a whole, not as a collection of individual sites, in planning preservation and even restoration of the native ecosystem through replanting.

This chapter will explore Moloka'i first, from its eastern tip across the southern shore, up to the central ridge, down to Kalaupapa, and into the western dunes and beaches. Lana'i follows, starting with the dry western end and then proceeding to the mountain ridge, the lovely leeward shores, and rugged windward side.

ABOVE: *The endangered gardenia Brighamii, or na'u, is still found on Lana'i, but only a few survive. To preserve rare species, conservationists often pollinate by hand.*

LEFT: *Moaula Falls adorns Moloka'i's Halawa Valley, an early site of human habitation in the isles. According to legend, if a ti leaf floats when placed at the base of the waterfall, then it is safe to swim.*

EASTERN MOLOKA'I: FROM HALAWA TO KAUNAKAKAI

Only one road traverses Moloka'i's southeastern coast. This route assumes a drive out to its eastern terminus and a leisurely return. Thirty patient miles east of Kaunakakai, Moloka'i's main town in the middle of the leeward coast, the rural Kamehameha V Highway (Route 450) climbs over the end of the mountain range and suddenly reveals a black-sand beach at the mouth of a deep valley. At the beach the road ends at the beginning of Hawaiian history.

At one time the **Halawa Valley❖** was the most densely populated place in the Hawaiian chain, with about 1,500 families living here. All but a few stragglers moved out after the devastating 1946 tsunami that also wreaked havoc in Hilo on the Big Island. On Moloka'i the wave uncovered an archaeological site at the entrance to Halawa Bay. Relics found here were carbon-dated to about A.D. 650, making Halawa one of only three places in the islands with evidence of aboriginal Hawaiians, the first wave of Polynesian pioneers who are believed to have come from the Marquesas north of Tahiti.

Just inland, a small road heads up the valley from a tiny church (park on the main road). The left fork passes a few homes and quickly tapers off to a foot trail that crosses the full stream and climbs Halawa Valley for about three miles to the first of several waterfalls.

Nowhere else in the islands is there as much intact ancient stonework as along this trail: *he'iau* (shrines or temples), home sites, terraces, and aqueducts called *'auwai*. Hawaiians burned such valleys to clear native vegetation and make room for taro, sugarcane, bananas, and other crops. At one point they tended more than 1,000 individual taro patches here. Like other abandoned valleys, however, Halawa is again overgrown. Most obvious are the many huge mango trees and bushes of *noni* (Indian mulberry), whose ugly fruits were used for an antiseptic. Also in evidence are monkeypod, Java plum, Surinam cherries, and wild taro. In 1939 the largest guava ever picked in Hawai'i—the size of a grapefruit—came from this valley, too. Legend says that the pool below the waterfall is safe to swim in only if a ti leaf floats. If it sinks, the *mo'o*, or mountain spirit, will get you.

The main road (Route 450) climbs steeply out of Halawa on the return to the drier, southern shores of the island. The slopes above the road are covered with sweet strawberry guava, native orchids, and higher up, ironwood and eucalyptus. Along the highest of these ridges, native plants survive in groves or in isolated clumps of great diversity. A simple tree stump may support *'ohi'a,* ferns, mints, and lilies, all wrapped in a furry sweater of liverworts and mosses.

The road dips and winds back around the coast until Kamalo, about 17 miles from Halawa, and then the drive settles down right along the shore. On the *mauka* (mountain) side Java plum and monkeypod give way to *kiawe* as dry slopes climb up to the ridge. *Kiawe,* known as mesquite or algaroba, was introduced to the islands and has quickly naturalized, becoming the predominant tree of dry, leeward slopes. The tall trees have feathery leaves, yellow flowers, and narrow golden seedpods. They also have long thorns tough enough to puncture even rubber soles. On the *makai* (ocean) side fishponds formerly used for trapping and raising fish line the shore inside the state's most extensive fringe reef system. Many of the fishponds are in excellent condition and may soon be used again. The state's first mangroves were planted along this coast around the turn of the century. The trees helped promote aquaculture in the fishponds by providing shade and hiding places, but they also promoted heavy silting of the inner reef area when overgrazed lands upland dumped too much topsoil into the ocean.

Near the town of Kawela some of the wetlands are set aside as the **Kakahai'a National Wildlife Refuge❖**, a haven for Hawaiian stilts, black-crowned night herons, Hawaiian coots, and Hawaiian ducks. The mottled brown native duck, or *koloa,* is probably descended from the mallard. Once common on all the islands except Lana'i, the *koloa* is now endangered. The refuge, not open to the public, is across from the county park of the same name.

Just beyond the tiny metropolis of Kaunakakai the picturesque waterfront **Kapuaiwa Coconut Grove❖,** planted by the fifth and last Kamehameha (who ruled from 1862 to 1872), is still the largest grove remaining in the islands, with about 2,000 trees. Curlews locally known as *kioea* can be seen feeding on mudflats here. The birds breed in the Arctic and winter here and on the island of Ni'ihau.

MOLOKA'I FOREST RESERVE

Just before the eastern road out of Kaunakakai, the Maunaloa Highway (Route 460), meets those going west and north, Maunahui Road, or the Moloka'i Forest Reserve Road, passable only by four-wheel-drive vehicles, leads up into the cloud forest. Four-wheel-drive vehicles can be rented on Moloka'i, but rental companies may impose steep fines if the

ABOVE: *Isolated by high cliffs and the pounding sea, the flat Kalau-papa Peninsula meant cruel exile for victims of Hansen's disease. A*

cars are taken off the pavement. Four-wheel drive is necessary on the forest road, but even with it, the driving is very difficult. The best way to see the reserve is on one of the Nature Conservancy's scheduled trips.

Much of the Moloka'i highlands went through the same cycle of overgrazing and reforestation as other islands. But beyond the pine groves, areas in the upper elevations remain pristine and native. The **Moloka'i Forest Reserve❖** and two Nature Conservancy preserves protect much of the mountain and windward valley areas.

Serving as a reminder of how much sandalwood once thrived here is the Luanamoku'iliahi, a 75-foot pit in the shape of a ship's hold. Beginning in 1791 Kamehameha the Great traded the fragrant wood for foreign goods. When workers had cut enough wood to fill the pit, they would haul it down to the harbor. Only 50 years later hardly a single mature sandalwood tree was left standing in the islands. Young trees, with their leathery leaves and flowers of red, green, or yellow, are still growing in the islands (although scarce), but one of four native species of sandalwood is still endangered.

At 3,600 feet, 10 miles in (just beyond the sandalwood pit), the forest road passes **Waikolu Lookout,** offering a spectacular view down into Waikolu Canyon. The Kalaupapa Peninsula is visible at the bottom. Waterfalls and pools mark the upper gorge. By afternoon, the trade winds push clouds up the valley, and fog envelops the ridge.

few elderly patients still reside here surrounded by stunning views of Moloka'i's deep windward valleys and the highest sea cliffs in the world.

Just past Waikolu the road crosses into the Nature Conservancy's **Kamakou Preserve❖**, named for Kamakou, a 4,970-foot volcanic dome that is the highest spot on Moloka'i. The forest road leads to the beginning of a boardwalk that winds through deep rain forest. At more than 4,000 feet in elevation, the area is usually very wet and quite cold, even in summer. While the leeward shoreline, four miles away, receives only about 15 inches of rain per year, the center of Kamakou Preserve averages almost 15 feet (180 inches) of rain.

In the Hawaiian forest plant life rarely germinates on bare ground. A fallen log or a lichen-covered rock will serve as a platform for dozens of other plant forms, from mosses all the way up to thriving 'ohi'a trees. In Kamakou more than 200 Hawaiian plant species have been catalogued that grow nowhere else except in these islands. Farther into the forest the last known Moloka'i thrush was seen and two honeycreepers, 'amakihi and 'apapane, can still be found. Both birds descend from a single ancestor (as do all Hawaiian honeycreepers) and are among the more common members of the family. The 'amakihi has yellow-green feathers and often feeds on yellow *mamane* blossoms. The 'apapane has bright red feathers that Hawaiians traditionally prized for making royal cloaks. Unfortunately, the small birds rarely survived the plucking.

The walkway quickly reaches **Pepe'opae Bog,** where the forest shrinks to bonsai proportions. Even blooming 'ohi'a trees, which normally reach heights of 20 to 30 feet, are only inches high. Apparently a layer of dense lava beneath the surface retains water with a high level of acidity and a low level of oxygen, stunting plant growth. Soil samples taken here included fern spores about 10,000 years old. Remember to stay on the trail and the boardwalk, which not only makes walking easier but also protects the extremely fragile bog flora.

The trail forks in the bog. To the left is the **Hanalilolilo Trail,** which follows the ridgeline back to the road just above Waikolu Lookout; it can be impossibly muddy and overgrown. The right fork continues on raised boards beyond the bog as the **Pelekunu Trail,** winding another half mile through native forest even more dense and more pristine to the rim of Pelekunu Valley. Another Nature Conservancy preserve, **Pelekunu Preserve❖** is accessible only by boat, and no public use of this fragile area is allowed. On a clear day the overlook has a stunning view 2,500 feet down the Pali Papa'ala, the ridgeline that overshadows the windward Waikolu, Pelekunu, and Wailau valleys. But if the trail ends in clouds, as it occasionally does, then the view from the overlook is completely blank, as if the rest of the world hasn't even been penciled in yet.

MOLOKA'I'S KALAUPAPA PENINSULA

Just north of the start of the forest road, Route 460 reaches a junction with Kala'e Highway (Route 470), which starts a climb past Kualapu'u town to the ridge at the western end of Moloka'i's eastern mountains. It passes by stables, then an unpaved parking area and a chained road, marking the trailhead for **Kalaupapa Peninsula.**

A steep, stairlike footpath descends 1,600 feet to the flat peninsula isolated by the press of cliffs and clouds. The broad, triangular peninsula was formed by the eruption of Pu'u 'Uao, whose crater is now filled with water.

This idyllic setting became a hell on earth in 1866, when victims of Hansen's disease (leprosy) were first quarantined here, condemned by fear and ignorance. Although the disease is now easily controlled by drugs and admittance of new patients ended in the 1960s, a few elderly patients remain, and access to the area is controlled by the Hawai'i State Department of Health, which still cares for these people.

In 1980, the area became **Kalaupapa Peninsula National Historic**

Park❖, and someday the park service hopes to operate a full-fledged national park here. Besides the historic value, the peninsula's assets range from natural rock formations to archaeological sites. Unfortunately, much of the peninsula has become impossibly overgrown with tangled Christmas-berry and other aggressive nonnative plants.

From the top of the Kalaupapa Trail, Highway 470 continues a few miles into **Pala'au State Park❖**. The forested ridge has camping and picnic facilities but is best known for a rock said to be empowered by the god Nanahoa. This phallic stone was a point of pilgrimage for infertile women, who hoped, after spending the night at the site, to return home pregnant.

MO'OMOMI DUNES AND WESTERN MOLOKA'I

Farrington Avenue (Route 480) goes west from Highway 470 at Kualapu'u. This rough, unpaved road continues out to **Mo'omomi Dunes Preserve❖**, also owned by the Nature Conservancy. Again, access is difficult and permission must be obtained from the Nature Conservancy office near the forest road. However, scheduled hikes provide a wealth of information that would otherwise be missed in the subtle landscape.

Mo'omomi is perhaps the most singular environment in the state. The steady trade winds blow sand across the island's western lowlands, building the Mo'omomi Dunes into undulating shapes that mock the ocean swells. Once dunes like these were common on all of the islands; now Mo'omomi is the last intact dune area in the major islands. Sun and salt seem to drift in the wind, and root casings left exposed by loose sand twist up into the glare. Native grasses and shrubs stabilize and cover the dunes.

In stark contrast to the thick jungle of montane rain forests, the floral wonders of this coastal environment seldom rise more than a few inches off the ground. The sweet-smelling heliotrope, or *hinahina,* grows like a mat, with thick leaves covered with silvery gray hairs to protect it from the sun. Besides many other plants seldom seen elsewhere are two of the most common Hawaiian strand plants. Beach *naupaka* has large white berries and curled, waxy leaves. Sharing the characteristic half-flower with its mountain version, the bush has inspired many a legend about separated lovers. Beach morning glory (*pohuehue*) trails vines

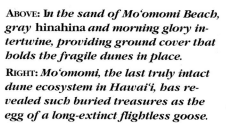

ABOVE: *In the sand of Moʻomomi Beach, gray* **hinahina** *and morning glory intertwine, providing ground cover that holds the fragile dunes in place.*
RIGHT: *Moʻomomi, the last truly intact dune ecosystem in Hawaiʻi, has revealed such buried treasures as the egg of a long-extinct flightless goose.*

covered with heart-shaped leaves and funnellike pink or purple flowers.

There is more to Moʻomomi than rare plants, however. The dunes have become lithified, or hardened, by time and dry weather. Occasionally these petrified dunes have served as time capsules. When they have been opened (perhaps five centuries later) by waves, archaeologists have found sites where houses once stood and where Hawaiians dug fine-grained basalt for adzes. Shells of *ʻopihi* show that the conical mollusk was as much a local delicacy in the past as it is now. The dunes have also revealed secrets to paleontologists, namely, fossilized remains of previously unknown, long-extinct native birds. A giant flightless goose once fed in the low, dry forest above the dunes. Two predatory birds were also discovered, a native eagle and a long-legged owl.

As on a few other places in the islands, the endangered Hawaiian green sea turtle has begun nesting here again. There are hopes that monk seals and Laysan albatross will reestablish colonies along the beach as well. Once common in the islands, the albatross, whose wings,

dark on top and white on the bottom, span as much as seven feet, now nests only in the unpopulated Northwestern Hawaiian Islands.

The rest of western Moloka'i encompasses mountains, dry grasslands, and white-sand beaches. Mountains rise on the south side of Route 460, which goes to the tiny town of Maunaloa, a legacy of Moloka'i's days as a Dole pineapple plantation. The only other road out here is Kaluako'i Road, which goes down to the eponymous resort area. The arid terrain along this latter route is reminiscent of African veld. In fact, the **Moloka'i Ranch Recreation Network❖**, an extensive preserve for African and Asian animals, is just a few miles down the road.

The beaches beside the Kaluako'i Hotel are considered some of the loveliest in the islands. Long stretches of white sand like this are a rare commodity in Hawai'i—and these are all the more precious for being relatively deserted. But beware: Moloka'i residents will tell you never to turn your back on the ocean here. Freak waves on calm days have swept away tourists sitting on the sand.

WESTERN LANA'I

Across the channel from Moloka'i is Lana'i. Despite the island's small size, getting around can be time-consuming because only 30 miles of road are paved; the rest of the island's rough terrain is crisscrossed with dirt tracks and Jeep trails. Inclement weather often makes certain roads impassable. As a result, Lana'i is the only island on which rental companies routinely provide four-wheel-drive vehicles and allow visitors to venture off the main highways. However, it's always advisable to check on conditions and alternate routes before setting out.

The western section of Lana'i is arid and windswept. Before the Polynesians arrived the island was covered with dryland forest, as were the leeward slopes of most of the other islands. The last prime example of this native dryland forest in Hawai'i is on Lana'i at **Kanepu'u Preserve❖,** a Nature Conservancy holding six miles northwest of Lana'i City. From Keomuku Highway (Route 44), west of the resort hotel Lodge at Ko'ele, take the unpaved Kanepu'u Highway, which begins between the stables and tennis courts and heads out through the old pineapple fields; bear left every time the road forks until it crosses a gate and enters an ironwood grove.

In the nineteenth century a Mormon rancher named Walter Gibson gained control of Lana'i and imported thousands of sheep, goats, and cattle to the island, turning them loose to graze. The native vegetation was rapidly destroyed. In 1911 a New Zealand range manager and amateur naturalist, George C. Munro, arrived on the island, and by 1918 he had erected fences and removed stray animals to protect groves of *lama* (native persimmon) and *olopua* (native olive) as well as other plants.

For the next three decades Munro worked to protect the site, and in 1989 Dole, which bought most of the island in the 1920s, donated a conservation easement on 462 acres to the Nature Conservancy. Today the Nature Conservancy holds 590 acres supporting native trees such as *lama, olopua,* and an endangered Lana'i *'iliahi* (sandalwood), which cover the ground with a thick, low canopy. Underneath are many other native species—morning glories, fragrant vines, and *nanu,* a native gardenia.

The wind is strong here above the cliffs. Sisal, resembling a giant century plant, was imported to stabilize the overgrazed dunes before eucalyptus would take root. Alien plants like Christmas-berry and lantana are rampant here, and with no natural predators, animal species once imported in small numbers are thriving. Thousands of feral animals, including axis deer and mouflon sheep, as well as many game birds, such as ring-necked pheasants, chukar partridges, quails, doves, and wild turkeys, still run wild on Lana'i. Restoration plans call for the alien trees and plants to be selectively removed once fences are complete and feral animals are driven out.

Another mile northwest the prevailing trade winds reach Lana'i at **Garden of the Gods❖**, an eerie place suffused with earth tones that are particularly vibrant in early morning and late afternoon. The constant breezes here have eroded the barren landscape, blowing away tons of volcanic dust in long red plumes to expose boulders. Over time the elements have sculpted the lava rocks, peeling away their soft shells to reveal the solid stones inside. Tourists like to stack the rocks, thinking they are imitating some ancient and holy ritual. They aren't, but locals are content to let them believe as they like.

LANA'I'S MUNRO TRAIL

Naturalist George Munro was also concerned about the island's watershed, destroyed by grazing, and spent much of his time replanting the Lana'i highlands with Norfolk Island pines to prevent erosion and catch the mists. The eight-mile **Munro Jeep Trail❖** is a muddy track that now traverses Lana'i's central ridge—and offers an opportunity (to those with a four-wheel-drive vehicle) for some real adventure. It's about an hour and a half by vehicle, or a full day's hike. Follow the Keomuku Highway a mile and a quarter past the Lodge at Ko'ele, then turn right on a paved, tree-lined road to the cemetery. Signs lead to the unpaved Munro Jeep Trail, which can be impassable after rain.

The lower elevations are largely devoid of native plants. An estimated 10,000 axis deer live on Lana'i, trampling the native plants and dropping seeds of exotics. Higher up, however, the practiced eye can view an encyclopedia of ethnobotany. Common in wet forests, 'ie'ie, or climbing pandanus, has fibrous aerial roots that hang from its thick

---

OVERLEAF: *Constant winds at the northwestern tip of Lana'i have exposed these fancifully shaped boulders, called Garden of the Gods, from the surrounding soil; tourists stack them into* ahu, *or cairns.*

ABOVE: *The Munro Trail, a Jeep track across the ridge of Lana'i, offers close-ups of native cloud-forest plants and broad vistas of five islands.*

trunk; they were once woven into helmets for Hawaiian warriors. The mountain shrub *naupaka,* like the beach variety, has only half-flowers. On Lana'i, where wet forest vegetation is less dense, koa trees really branch out, spreading like oaks rather than growing straight and tall the way they do when competing for sunlight under a thick rain-forest canopy. About two and a half miles into the trail, a hiking path leads to an overlook of Ha'uola Gulch—at 2,000 feet, it's the deepest on Lana'i. Axis deer carefully pick their way through the steep gulch.

As the Jeep trail reaches **Ha'alelepa'akai,** the view looks down 'Awehi Gulch, across Puhi'elelu Ridge, and due east across the channel to Maui's west-coast town of Lahaina. The upper elevations of the Jeep road are covered with a variety of Hawai'i's ferns. False staghorn fern, or *uluhe,* common on all the islands, is an important ground cover that fights erosion on steep valley walls because its constantly branching leaves grow on stalks up to 15 feet long and in thickets that can be 4 feet deep. A less common plant is *wawae'iole* (rat foot), so named for its shape. *Pala'a,* lace fern, is used for dyes.

Hawai'i has two types of tree ferns. The *'ama'u (Sadleria)* is not a true tree fern, but is very similar to *hapu'u,* which is. The main difference between the two is in their leaf growth. *'Ama'u's* feathery leaves grow directly off the central stalk, while *hapu'u* has radial stalks, with smaller leaves growing off of those. The *Sadleria* has new fronds shaded in red to protect them from the sun. *Hapu'u* grows in shady, wet

96

areas and can reach up to 20 feet tall.

At the summit, Lana'ihale, the windswept height provides a stunning view of Moloka'i, Maui, O'ahu, and the Big Island—on a clear day. As the trail descends to the east the climate is drier. Many of the dryland plants still found here were extremely useful in Hawaiian culture. *'A'ali'i,* a native hardwood that grows as a stunted shrub on dry, windy Lana'i, grows so strong and straight on other islands that it is used for spears. Its seedpods, with their pink, burgundy, or green sails, are used to adorn *haku* (braided) and *wili* (wound) leis. Also here is *pukiawe,* a bush with tiny, intricate leaves, whose bright red berries are also used in leis. The *pukiawe's* wood smoke was used in embalming. There are tufts of coarse *pili* grass, used for thatch. The meaty root of *'uhaloa,* a ground cover that has mintlike leaves, was chewed as both an antiseptic and an anesthetic for sore throats.

LANA'I'S MANELE BAY

The Munro Trail ends on Hoike Road, less than two miles south of where Manele Road (Route 440) intersects with the Kaumalapau Highway. Manele Road, south of Lana'i City, continues south through the last remaining pineapple fields and winds through virtual desert down to a coastal area where two bays, **Manele Bay❖** and **Hulopo'e Bay Marine Life Conservation District❖**, are separated by a volcanic cone. Manele has a small marina in its crescent-shaped natural harbor. Hulopo'e has tide pools and a beautiful campground that overlooks the long, broad white-sand beach. Trails wind along the leeward cliffs in both directions.

Hulopo'e Bay often hosts visiting spinner dolphins and teems with multihued reef fish and coral, including some rare black coral. The diving in this area is among the most magnificent in the state (some say in the world), especially with the contorted underwater topography—spires and pinnacles rising some 70 feet—caused by volcanism. One of the most popular dive sites is First Cathedral, a vaultlike cavern lit from side openings and with a natural altar in the center.

LANA'I'S WINDWARD SIDE

The paved Keomuku Road (Route 430) winds northeast from the central plateau, over a saddle, descending to Lana'i's unusually dry wind-

97

ward coast. Although the paved road ends when it meets the shoreline, unpaved roads extend in both directions along the coast and are
easily passable by four-wheel-drive vehicles.

The road to the left, toward Shipwreck Beach, goes through a landscape of *kiawe* trees before reaching a dead end in the dunes among
dilapidated hunting shacks. A hot, dry, eight-mile walk along the deserted beach west from here offers perhaps the most rewarding beach-
combing in the world. Bring lots of water and sunblock.

At **Shipwreck Beach❖,** which encompasses the eight miles past the
turnoff from Keomuku Road, the strong winds blow material over the
treacherous coastal reef and onto the beach, leaving the sand covered
with debris ranging from wooden to fiberglass hulls and every sort of
flotsam in between. A World War II liberty ship sits rusting on the reef.
Wild turkeys, which forage in the brush behind the beach, leave fright-
eningly large footprints along the sand. Beach morning glory (*pohuehue*), golden *'ilima,* and *kauna'oa,* a parasitic leafless vine with peach-
colored tendrils that is Lana'i's official flower, flourish along the dunes.

A much longer dirt road goes east from the end of the highway, a
dusty track that stretches a dozen miles to **Naha.** The road follows the
water very closely, and in some places waves even wash over it slight-
ly. The drive can take two hours, one-way, if the road is bad.
Homesteads sprout palms, bananas, and derelict vehicles. Game birds
gather in the road in daylight. In the dark axis deer cross the road to
lick salt off the sand. Native to India, these small, white-spotted animals
are extremely shy. Halepalaoa Landing, about seven and a half miles
from the end of Route 430, has been closed as a boat landing site for
several years but still has one of the better beaches on eastern Lana'i.
Past Makaiwa Point is **Lopa❖,** a beautiful black-sand beach with sheltered picnic tables and a view of Maui.

The road continues to Naha, but the scenery changes little from
what preceded Lopa. It's a spot, perhaps, to pause before turning
around, and consider the contrast between this island and lush Maui,
visible across the waves, practically bustling compared to quiet Lana'i.

RIGHT: *A liberty ship was left to rust on the reef off Lana'i's Shipwreck
Beach, where great swaths of indigenous beach morning glories and
miles of pristine sand greet the flotsam blown in by prevailing winds.*

CHAPTER FOUR

O'AHU

Because O'ahu is home to 80 percent of Hawai'i's population, a visitor might expect that the island would have little left that's natural. But as urbanized as this tropical isle has become, O'ahu still holds plenty of natural areas that are accessible to visitors, even by the island's bus system, which provides round-the-island as well as urban transportation.

The third largest of the Hawaiian Islands at 617 square miles, O'ahu is roughly diamond-shaped. Its geographic character is defined by two parallel mountain ranges with broad plains in between, ending in the south at Pearl Harbor. The easternmost range, Ko'olau, continues on to the southeast, and on its southern side slopes down to metropolitan Honolulu and the beaches of Diamond Head and Koko Head. O'ahu's two parallel mountain ranges are remnants of a pair of volcanoes that created the island. Running the length of the leeward, or western, side of the island, Wai'anae, the older of the two, breached the ocean's surface four to five million years ago. When the volcano's summit collapsed, Wai'anae's caldera was on the eastern slope, and lava continued to flow on that side. Streams flowing down the western, leeward slopes dug three huge amphitheaters, forming the Makua, Makaha, and Lualualei valleys.

LEFT: *With the conical shape of a cinder cone, Mokolii Island, or "Chinaman's Hat," seen here from Kualoa Regional Park, is actually a sea stack, part of Ko'olau Volcano, one of two O'ahu volcanoes.*

Because the eastern side of the volcano was still active, however, new flows prevented the normal process of erosion from cutting the deep valleys usually found on windward slopes. In addition, the lava was so porous that rainwater simply seeped through the ground instead of forming erosive streams.

The second volcano, Ko'olau, arrived a few million years later, popping up to the east and putting the older mountain in its rain shadow. Eventually lava from both volcanoes filled in the space between them to create a single island. Wai'anae became extinct first, and lava flows down Ko'olau's western slope continued to wash up against the flanks of its older sibling.

Erosion had free reign on Ko'olau for three million years. On the windward side water cut valleys, then amphitheaters, then steep cliffs (*pali*). About 250,000 years ago a new period of secondary volcanism filled in some of the valleys (such as Nu'uanu and Manoa above Honolulu) and formed the tuff cones at the island's southeastern tip.

After human settlement the island was divided into *ahupua'a*, traditional designations still used today to describe the land districts that extend from upland areas to the sea. Traditionally every valley and ridge had a trail, and many were heavily traveled in the days before European contact. Although there are far fewer trails today, organizations such as the Hawaiian Trail and Mountain Club and the Sierra Club lead hikes most weekends.

O'ahu's geography can make linear exploring difficult, even with a map. As on the other islands, mountains make certain areas inaccessible, and it is sometimes necessary to trace the perimeter of an area to get access to it. The chapter begins in the Honolulu District, which includes all of metropolitan Honolulu and its valleys. Moving up the center of the island we visit the 'Ewa District, which encompasses the lower region between the two mountain ranges as well as Pearl Harbor, the military bases, and the communities that support them. We then proceed northward through the Wahiawa District in the central valley, called the Leilehua Plateau, now largely agricultural, to the spectacular North Shore Waialua District, and then down the lush windward coast, encompassing the Ko'olau Loa and Ko'olau Poko districts. The chapter concludes its exploration of O'ahu on the leeward coast, in the Wai'anae District.

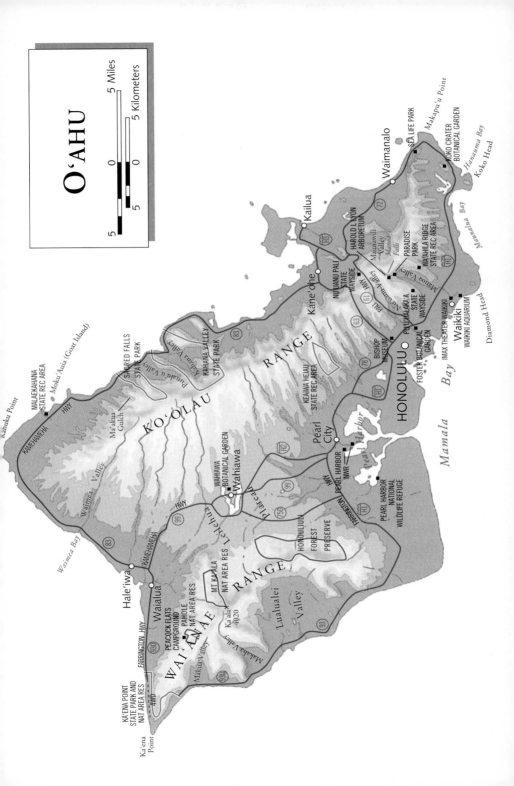

ABOVE: *Nu'uanu Pali, on the east side of the Ko'olau Range, towers 3,000 feet. Windward rains over millions of years shaped the high, in-*

SOUTHEASTERN O'AHU: HONOLULU, WAIKIKI, KOKO HEAD

For anyone interested in Hawaiian natural history, Honolulu is a good place to start. Exhibits at the **Bishop Museum❖** (in the Kalihi neighborhood, northwest of Waikiki and downtown) illustrate the important connections among the geology, biology, and history of the Hawaiian Islands. The museum's ongoing research in Hawai'i and throughout Oceania has added much to current understanding of ancient Pacific peoples.

An obligatory stop right in downtown Honolulu is the **Foster Botanical Garden❖**, flagship of the island-wide Honolulu Botanical Gardens system. Each garden is designed to provide the optimum climate for a different group of tropical plants. Foster is ideal for those requiring both high temperature and humidity, such as orchids, plumerias, and palms.

The Pali Highway (Route 61), which is the main artery connecting

land cliffs, cutting deep valleys and eroding all traces of ridges between cascading streams until only steep head walls, or pali, remained.

Honolulu to O'ahu's windward cities, Kane'ohe and Kailua, climbs up the next major valley. Signs point to **Nu'uanu Pali State Wayside❖**, which commemorates an ancient battle and commands a fabulous view down the sheer cliffs to the windward side of the island.

Behind Honolulu the valleys and ridges of the southern Ko'olau range offer hikes and vistas within easy reach of the city. **Manoa Valley,** directly above Waikiki, is home to the University of Hawai'i. At the head of the valley is **Paradise Park❖**, a botanical theme park. A three-quarter-mile trail leads to 100-foot **Manoa Falls,** a jaunt amid eucalyptus and African tulip trees and colorful flora such as wild purple orchids and red ginger. Drawing large crowds on weekends, the trail is frequently very muddy—and insect repellent is essential.

At the very top of Manoa Valley the university's **Harold L. Lyon Arboretum❖** grows about 6,000 species of plants on 195 acres and has one of the most extensive collections of palm trees in the world. The botanical garden has become involved in the fight to save native

105

plant species from extinction, making important scientific contributions in the field of tissue cultivation. Scientists there now have more plants of some almost-extinct endemic species in their nursery than exist in the wild. An *Isodendrion* species thought to be extinct was revived from only twigs.

The Lyon's ethnobotanical garden features many plants important in Hawaiian culture. Tree fern stalks are rootlike structures with *pulu* fibers among them, which Hawaiians used for embalming and to stuff pillows and mattresses. The roots of *'awa* (kava) were chewed to numb the mouth and relax muscles. The juice of *'awapuhi* (wild ginger) flowers was used as a shampoo and contained chemical compounds that acted as mild disinfectants.

Above Manoa Valley on the eastern side, **Wa'ahila Ridge State Recreation Area❖** is a small ridgetop park at the top of Saint Louis Drive, where trade winds cool conifer-lined forest trails, and hikers are treated to panoramic views of the city below. On the opposite, northwestern side of Manoa, the **Pu'u'ualaka'a State Wayside❖**, accessible via winding Round Top and Tantalus drives, has miles of tended trails that wind through lush forests.

Before European sails ever darkened the horizon the rich and famous of old Hawai'i were surfing off the beaches of Waikiki. Today some of these waters are a marine life conservation district, a designation that protects the numerous varieties of fish that congregate around the natural and artificial reefs, and even sunken planes and ships. Yellow-margin moray and other eels, eagle rays, and schools of bluestripe snapper pull duty around a U.S. Navy oiler sunk in 1989 as an artificial reef. Tour operators lead trips below using snorkel, scuba, or snuba equipment. (Snuba allows divers to breathe underwater through hoses attached to floating air tanks.) Those who don't want to get wet can opt for an excursion by submarine.

The **Waikiki Aquarium❖** in Kapi'olani Park (on the Diamond Head end of Waikiki Beach), affiliated with the University of Hawai'i, offers another chance to see the diversity of Hawai'i's underwater environments. The complex dynamics of reef systems are detailed in a series of spectacular exhibits of living corals, jellyfish, giant clams, and exquisite reef fishes, including the reef triggerfish. Also on display is the latter's flamboyant cousin, the lagoon triggerfish, whose wild and

ABOVE: *In an 1857 engraving British artist George Henry Burgess depicted a small fishing village called Honolulu. It was already the kingdom's capital—even before Europeans discovered its fine anchorage.*

colorful patterns have earned it the nickname Picasso fish. Both triggerfish varieties have the same Hawaiian name, *humuhumunukunuku apuaʻa*, which describes their piglike snouts. The aquarium has also pioneered methods of culturing large quantities of *mahimahi* for consumption. This delicious tropical gamefish can measure nearly three feet long only 12 months after hatching.

Waikiki's **Imax Theater**❖ features a large-screen film, *Hawaiʻi: Born in Paradise,* a spectacular natural-history documentary of the past, present, and future of the Hawaiian ecosystem.

Dominating the skyline at the eastern end of Waikiki is **Diamond Head,** a tuff cone that blew up some 100,000 years ago. The crater rim averages 400 feet high. The distinctive landmark was named for its glinting rock face by British sailors in 1825. Although the sparkle turned out to be calcite crystals, the name has endured. At **Diamond Head State Monument**❖, a trail leads from the picnic area into the cone itself,

107

emerging at Leʻahi ("the brow"), a 763-foot-high peak on the crater's rim, affording spectacular views of the city and coastline.

East of Diamond Head, beyond Maunalua Bay, H1 turns into Route 72 and proceeds through the Koko Head area. About 30,000 years ago a volcanic vent emerged here right at water's edge. When it exploded the outer rim formed a seawall. Several thousand years ago the sea broke through the outer wall of the crater and created Hanauma Bay. Today **Hanauma Bay State Underwater Park**❖ is a beach park and a marine life conservation district. Although reef-building creatures quickly colonized the bay when it formed, almost all of the coral has been killed by overuse of this extremely popular beach. Even so, the bay is a good place to get an introduction to snorkeling and snuba, although in 1993, restrictions were placed on use its use. The view from the cliffs above is one of the most spectacular sights in the islands.

Just before **Sandy Beach** the cinder cone that rises off the land is the site of the **Koko Crater Botanical Garden**❖, part of the Honolulu Botanical Gardens system. Planted on the inner slopes and floor of the crater are a large grove of shrubs, herbs, and grasses native to Hawaiʻi's dryland forests, including the *wiliwili,* a tree with red seed-pods and hooked flowers. The collection

---

LEFT: *Hanauma Bay was originally the crater of a tuff cone created about 30,000 years ago. The sea eroded the outer wall and flooded the basin in the last few thousand years, creating a perfectly shaped bay.*

also includes a large number of dryland species from around the world, some quite rare.

Southeast of Waimanalo Beach the easternmost cliffs of the Ko'olau Range press down on the shoreline, with Route 72 squeezed in the middle. Many seabirds nest here: great frigatebirds, red-footed boobies, and albatross. Just after **Makapu'u Point,** at the southeastern tip of O'ahu, is **Sea Life Park Hawai'i❖**. Along with amusements like dolphin and sea-lion shows, the marine park has a 300,000-gallon tank displaying thousands of creatures native to local waters—hammerhead sharks, eagle rays, eels, and many other reef species. The park plays an important part in educational and conservation activities in the state. For instance, injured Hawaiian monk seals are brought here to be nursed back to health, and breeding colony areas have been set aside for Hawaiian green sea turtles and endangered Humboldt penguins.

THE CENTRAL 'EWA PLAIN

Take the main urban artery, H1, through Honolulu and continue north and west around Pearl Harbor, skirting a series of secondary craters. Although given over to the modern naval base and historic monument, **Pearl Harbor** is also an important natural-history site. Its three sections (bearing the un-Hawaiian names of West, Middle, and East lochs) are actually a trio of river valleys dating back to a time when sea levels were lower than they are today. Parts of the harbor are still natural habitats for migratory birds, and certain areas, restricted to the public, have been designated as parts of the **Pearl Harbor National Wildlife Refuge❖**.

While little evidence is visible to the untrained eye, **Barber's Point,** just beyond Pearl Harbor to the west, is an important area to archaeologists and geologists. Ancient campsites have been found as well as evidence of native flightless birds—a goose, a rail, and an ibis—that became extinct early in the Polynesian occupation. The area is reserved for the use of military personnel, their family, and guests only.

Northeast of Pearl Harbor many of the trails climbing into the central section of the Ko'olau Range are long and difficult, requiring much effort

---

RIGHT: *An ancient volcanic tuff cone, Manana—or Rabbit—Island (seen here from Makapu'u Point) is now a bird sanctuary and important breeding ground for sooty terns and wedge-tailed shearwaters.*

ABOVE: *A common seabird in the islands, the frigatebird , or 'iwa, (meaning "thief") has earned its nickname for stealing the catches of other birds. Males puff out their red pouches enticingly during mating rituals.*

over unpaved roads and through private lands just to access the trailheads. Much effort is also required to gain permission for access over private and government lands. The short **'Aiea Loop Trail** in **Keaiwa Heiau State Recreation Area❖**, however, is easy to get to, just a few miles off H1 southwest of the 'Aiea golf course. The park has an ancient temple dedicated to the healing arts and a garden of plants once used as medicines, including *noni* (Indian mulberry), whose pale-yellow fruits eased heart problems; *kukui* (candlenut), whose nuts were chewed as laxatives; and *'ulu* (breadfruit) whose sap soothed chapped skin.

WAHIAWA AND WAIALUA
Routes 99 and H2 head northwest from Pearl Harbor right through O'ahu's central Leilehua Plateau. The two routes rejoin in the plateau's center, in the town of Wahiawa. **Wahiawa Botanical Garden❖**, a gully that has been landscaped with tropical plants needing a moist climate—cooler than that of Honolulu—was originally an experimental nursery sponsored by the Hawaiian Sugar Planters Association. A self-guided tour details the names and uses of such plants as Australian

ABOVE: *Red-footed boobies are frequently seen at Ka'ena Point. Too tame for their own good, they were dubbed boobies (*bobo *is Spanish for stupid) by European sailors who found them easy to catch.*

tree ferns, Chinese and true cinnamon, Indian mahogany, Mindanao gum, and *loulu* palms, native to Hawai'i.

O'ahu's broad central plain is planted with pineapple on the upper elevations and sugarcane lower down, and the sweet smell of burnt sugar often hangs in the air. To the west is 4,020-foot Ka'ala, the peak of the Wai'anae Range and the highest point on the island. At the **Mount Ka'ala Natural Area Reserve**❖ an elevated boardwalk protects a fragile bog area. Bogs form where there is more rain than the land can absorb or drain. The standing water becomes acidic, forming peat and dwarfing trees and shrubs to natural imitations of bonsai. The reserve can be reached only by roads and foot trails that cross private or military lands (requiring permission to access).

Kamehameha Highway (Route 99) proceeds to the North Shore's main towns, Waialua and Hale'iwa. Farrington Highway (Route 930)

OVERLEAF: *Driven against the shore by the trade winds, the legendary waves of O'ahu's North Shore can reach as high as 30 feet in winter, earning the area a reputation for the best surfing in the world.*

113

travels west from Waialua, paralleling the Wai'anae mountains as they curve out toward Ka'ena Point at the western tip of O'ahu. Off Route 930 just before Mokule'ia a road provides hiking and bicycling access to a high campground at **Peacock Flats❖** and to the **Pahole Natural Area Reserve❖**. Trails through the *'ohi'a* and fern forest lead up to the ridge, where it is possible to look down the western side of the Wai'anae Range into the Makua Valley. Once considered one of the healthiest *'ohi'a* forests, in recent decades the region has been hard hit by a natural dieback cycle, which has left it especially vulnerable to introduced plants. Watch for the conical shells of the rare and endangered tree snails on leaves along the trail.

Back on Route 930, a few miles west of Dillingham Airfield, now used to lift sailplanes, the pavement ends. An easy three-mile walk down the unpaved road leads to **Ka'ena Point Natural Area Reserve❖**. Here strong winds and surf have ground sea coral and ancient lava into sand, which has then blown into dunes. In the 1980s human use of the point, especially by off-road vehicles, severely damaged the delicate dune environment. With access now restricted to hikers, the ecosystem is beginning to recover. Common seabirds, wedge-tailed shearwaters, and boobies frequent the area. Laysan albatross breed here, and monk seals bask on the shore. Rare green sea turtles occasionally swim by.

Ka'ena Point's lava boulders are sea-polished to the shine of eight balls. In early morning dolphins can sometimes be spotted beyond the breakers. Around the point are excellent views to the south of the Wai'anae coast and its cavernous valleys. The trail on the southern side of the point presents a few tricky sections where the old dirt highway, which once made a circuit of the coastline, has crumbled away. Ka'ena Point can also be reached by proceeding north along the leeward, Wai'anae coast, up Route 93.

From the North Shore town of Hale'iwa the Kamehameha Highway (now Route 83) continues northeast along the coast. Inland from picture-perfect Waimea Bay, whose shimmering turquoise waters were sacred to early Hawaiians, lies **Waimea Valley❖**, containing **Waimea Falls Park,** a commercial operation. Easy trails wander through extensive botanical gardens and a bird sanctuary, with trams available for anyone not able to walk. The Waimea Arboretum contains rare plant specimens and has been instrumental in returning some to the wild.

The *Kokia cookei,* or *koki'o,* here, for instance, was the last of its kind until cuttings took root. It remains among the rarest plants in the islands. Once a month the park remains open after dark and visitors can walk up the valley by the light of the full moon, when all the colors of a tropical paradise are reduced to subtle shades of silver.

THE WINDWARD COAST AND KO'OLAU RANGE

Past **Sunset Beach,** an international winter surfing mecca, Route 83 swings around Kahuku Point to the long sweep of the eastern, windward coast. South of the town of Kahuku on the island's northern tip, the **Malaekahana Bay State Recreation Area❖** is a two-part park. The northern section is a privately run campground specializing in access for the physically challenged. The southern part has beautiful sandy beaches. Just offshore is **Moku 'Auia❖** (Goat Island), a seabird sanctuary that can be reached on foot at low tide.

Ko'olau Loa, the top half of the windward coast, is characterized by deep valleys. The highway traces the beautiful shoreline, as waves break on reefs off palm-shaded beaches. Many of the valley areas have excellent hiking trails. In the forest reserve above **Hau'ula** three trails branch off the end of Hau'ula Homestead Road (across from Hau'ula Beach Park). The middle trail climbs up **Ma'akua Gulch❖**, a gorge that towers a hundred feet high and narrows in places to only a dozen feet across (a unique sight in the islands). The valley is full of trees bearing delicious mountain apples at lower levels and refreshing swimming holes higher up. But be warned: The narrowness of the gorge makes flash floods a deadly danger.

Sacred Falls State Park❖, a few miles farther south, has an often-muddy but popular trail that leads up a narrow gorge from a roadside parking lot to Kaliuwa'a waterfall, with a 1,520-foot drop. Again, flash floods can be perilous here.

The next section of the coast just north of **Ko'olau Poko** finds huge consolidated valleys backed by steep *pali.* Consolidated valleys form where several very eroded valleys run into each other. The first to the south is Punalu'u Valley. The next, on a small bay, encompasses **Kahana Valley State Park❖**. Kahana is one of the wettest valleys on O'ahu, receiving about 300 inches of rain per year at the upper elevations (about 2,700 feet) and 75 inches along the coast. Before the polit-

117

ABOVE: *At Sacred Falls State Park, Kaluanui Stream has cut through dense rock to flow at the bottom of a shady, narrow canyon with walls towering some 1,600 feet.*

---

ical changes of the late eighteenth century and the introduction of European culture, Kahana was an efficient, self-contained *ahupua'a,* providing itself with all the crops and seafood its residents needed. Archaeologists have found terraces and canals in the valley and a fishpond at the bottom of the stream. Cattle egrets, small white herons with a slow, graceful flight, and water-loving black-crowned night herons, called *'auku'u,* roost in the lowlands. A loop trail just over a mile long circles part of the valley through dense vegetation.

Serrated silhouettes cutting into cottony clouds, the *pali* of the windward coast are transformed by the sun into ribs, flutes, and buttresses— jagged outlines in tones of jade, making hiking among them a spectacular visual treat. The **Maunawili Trail❖**, cut by the Sierra Club, is a beautiful trail running along the windward side of the Ko'olau between the Pali Highway and the town of Waimanalo and can be reached from the town of Waimanalo on Waikupanaha Street. The sky can be particularly dramatic here as the wind pushes clouds over the razor's edge of the mountain spine. Around the promontories, huge koas come into

ABOVE: *Windward O'ahu is a garden of tropical vegetation, such as this stand of red ginger, growing in the shadow of the Ko'olau Range. All of Hawai'i's gingers were introduced by either Polynesians or Europeans.*

view, spreading their branches over the terrain, shading tree ferns and palms. Mountain apples, guava, avocado, and *kukui* grow abundantly.

LEEWARD O'AHU: THE WAI'ANAE COAST

The dry, western side of the Wai'anae Range, northwest of Pearl Harbor (take H1 to Route 93), until recently was considered a "locals-only" area. Much of the region still is used by the military and closed to the public. Many camping facilities are restricted to local residents only.

North of the town of Wai'anae the **Makaha Valley** opens its giant mouth into the mountains. According to local lore, the name Makaha (meaning "fierce" or "savage") derives from the violent robbers who lived in these valleys and preyed on passing travelers. (Although the robbers may prey no more, it is always wise never to leave anything of value in a car while hiking.) A large cave opens into the mountain beside Route 93, but it has unfortunately been littered with graffiti and beer bottles.

The valley's boundary ridges run up to Ka'ala, the highest point in the Wai'anae Range. On weekends the Board of Water Supply leaves a gate

119

open on the upper portion of the Wai'anae Valley Road for hikers. Through here is the base of the **Wai'anae-Ka'ala Trail,** which climbs to the Mount Ka'ala Natural Area Reserve. This hike (six and a half miles round-trip) is one of O'ahu's most spectacular outings. With 11 ropes on the steep upper head wall, going all the way to the summit is rugged, however, and should be attempted only by experienced, well-conditioned hikers or climbers.

Makua Valley, the next one north, is a military firing range. Soon after that the road ends at **Makua-Ka'ena State Park**❖ and a truly beautiful white-sand beach. From here a trail winds along the coastline up to Ka'ena Point.

The point is a perfect place to watch the sunset. Here at the northernmost reaches of the Wai'anae Range, especially at dusk, the once-great volcano, now reduced to eroded bluffs, looks for all the world like a row of old men sitting on a porch. And out to sea bumper-to-bumper cumulus clouds commute home after a long day of watering the gardens of paradise.

RIGHT: *Ka'ena Point, now a natural reserve at the westernmost tip of O'ahu, looks back southeast to the dry, gaping valleys of the starkly beautiful Wai'anae coast.*

120

KAUA'I

Compared to other land on the planet, Kaua'i's terrain is in its infancy. In the life cycle of a Hawaiian island, however, the "Garden Isle" is the grand old man, the oldest of the major islands. A single volcano created Kaua'i some six million years ago, giving erosion plenty of time to work its inimitable ways on the surface. Today the island has alluvial plains, river systems, and great canyons carved by millions of years of runoff from the almost constant rains at its summit.

Kaua'i is the smallest of the four major islands and the most remote, at the northwestern end of the chain. It doesn't attract the huge numbers of tourists that O'ahu and Maui pull in, but its stunning scenery has provided the backdrop for films from *South Pacific* to *Jurassic Park*—and more than a few honeymoons. Waimea Canyon, the Alaka'i Swamp, the sea cliffs of the Na Pali Coast, and the Hanalei Valley are among the masterpieces of Hawaiian geologic evolution. Each of these in their way is a product of the heavy rains at the island's center, where Wai'ale'ale, Kaua'i's second highest peak, receives more rain than anyplace else on earth. Nearly round, Kaua'i measures 33 miles east to west and about 25 miles north to south—with some of the most dramatic landscapes on earth concentrated in the northwest quadrant.

LEFT: *Sliced by streams from above and pounded by surf from below, the buttresses and sea cliffs of Kaua'i's Na Pali Coast hide deep valleys and lonely beaches as they stand silent vigil facing the open ocean.*

All the Hawaiian Islands are at the mercy of the elements through the process of erosion, but the elements can be particularly violent on Kaua'i. The island seems to catch more than its share of tropical storms. In September 1992 it took the full force of Hurricane 'Iniki, the strongest storm to hit in nearly a century. With winds of 175 to 200 miles per hour, it tossed even huge banyan trees aside, their trunks snapped in half, branches crumpled and left dangling like broken arms.

Although many trees were completely defoliated, amazingly 'Iniki did not do as much damage to the island's inland *mauka* forests as Hurricane 'Iwa had ten years earlier. Still, hundreds of thousands of the island's trees and shrubs were killed. For some endangered native species—so threatened that their last individual members were personally watched over by conservationists—the price was high. When field researchers hurried to check on them after the storm several were reduced to a dozen specimens or even fewer. The last remaining *Caesalpina kauaiense,* a rare tree with delicate purplish flowers, was blown over, and no living specimens remain.

Occasional catastrophes—fires, floods, hurricanes—occur in all ecosystems, and nature has adapted to meet these periodic disasters. In fact, Kaua'i probably represents a textbook case of nature's power to destroy and then regenerate. Native trees seemed to withstand 'Iniki's winds better than alien imports such as guava and mango. Even though some endemics, such as koa, do not grow deep roots and are easily blown over, they are able to reorient themselves and continue to grow after they are downed. Stripped of their leaves and branches by 'Iniki, trees quickly recovered with the strong sun, fertile soil, and frequent rains. Whole forests of koa, their bare, limbless trunks bleached by the sun, eventually showed new leaves growing directly on the trunk—an odd sight. Some plants, such as cycads, produced an abundance of seeds. The imported African tulip trees, with their orange-red flowers, received an ideal pruning and were soon blooming exuberantly all over the island.

A belt road circles three quarters of Kaua'i. So rugged is the terrain

OVERLEAF: *The most prodigious rainfall in the world, hundreds of inches per year, has sculpted the Waimea Canyon into a vast pinnacled tableau that inevitably invites comparison to the Grand Canyon.*

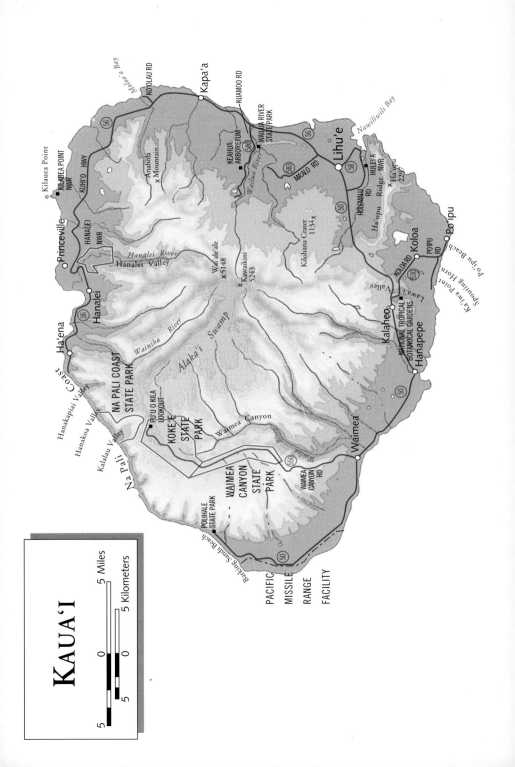

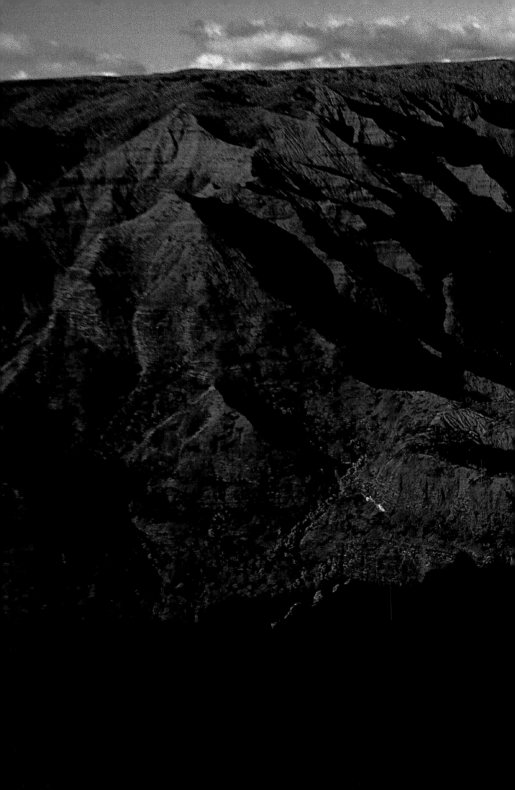

ABOVE: *Easily spotted along Waimea Canyon, the native Kauai* iliau *is a relative of the Maui silversword, but keeps leaves and flowers at the top of its stalk.*
RIGHT: *The steep sides of Waimea Canyon, seen here from the Po'omau Canyon Overlook, funnel moisture up to the mountains, where it falls as rain.*

in the unpaved part that although it measures only a few miles in length, it is necessary to drive almost 360 degrees around the island to see either side of it. The chapter begins in the island's western interior highlands, an area covered by two state parks and several wilderness and forest preserves, followed by the southern coast, from the sands of Polihale in the west to the valleys and dramatic coastline south of Lihu'e, in the east. The route continues up the east coast, where the Wailua River is found, and along the beautiful North Shore. The last—and most spectacular—section of the island, the Na Pali Coast, is a series of sheer cliffs extending along the coast in the island's northwestern corner. No roads traverse this incredibly beautiful but rugged area, which can be seen only by air, by boat, or from an ancient footpath that snakes its way precariously along about half its length.

INTERIOR HIGHLANDS:
WAIMEA CANYON AND KOKE'E STATE PARKS

Kaua'i's highest peak is 5,243-foot Kawaikini. But the second tallest, nearby **Wai'ale'ale,** is more famous. Humid northeasterly trade winds are funneled from the coast up the island's wide stream-fed valleys, and the air rises rapidly as the valleys narrow. The moisture quickly cools and then precipitates, falling as rain—lots and lots of rain. A

ABOVE: *The fluted walls of the Kalalau Valley offer a magnificent vista from Kokeʻe State Park on a clear evening. Inaccessible by roads, the fertile, isolated valley was once home to thousands of Hawaiians.*

record came in 1982 when the rainfall on Waiʻaleʻale was measured at 681 inches. The average annual rainfall is a staggering 451 inches, making the 5,148-foot mountain at the center of the island the wettest place on earth. Scientists even suspect these measured totals are often low because strong winds blow much of the rain past the gauge. Surprisingly, the abundant moisture ensures that Waiʻaleʻale is barren. The almost-constant rains so saturate the ground that the soil is leached of nutrients and almost nothing will grow.

Wet, desolate Waiʻaleʻale is inaccessible, but the waters running off its summit bring lush greenness—and a deeply carved landscape—to other parts of the island. To the summit's west Waimea Canyon Road (Route 550, a right turn off Route 50, the belt road, in the island's southwestern corner) climbs 4,000 feet in about 20 miles from the coastal town of Waimea to Waimea Canyon State Park and adjacent Kokeʻe State Park. Summer temperatures in the highlands are about ten degrees cooler than those at the beach. The differences are even more pronounced in the winter, when night temperatures can drop to 30 degrees Fahrenheit in the highlands. Because clouds often cover the area at midday, views are generally clearest before 10 A.M. and after 4 P.M.

As the road ascends, the scenery gets better and better, especially on clear, sunny days. Frequent turnouts overlook **Waimea Canyon**, a vast gorge painted in desert shades of red and orange that seem strangely out of place in the green tropical Hawaiian landscape. Although the nickname "the Grand Canyon of the Pacific" may be an exaggeration, the chasm is indeed a singular geological feat and a spectacular sight after a rain, when cascading waterfalls plunge over its red walls. One mile wide and 14 miles long, in places it plummets 3,600 feet, exposing rusty layers of volcanic time. It was created by a sliver of a stream, barely discernible at the bottom, and it graphically demonstrates how the erosion process accelerates: As watery runoff carves ever deeper valleys, more moisture is funneled up to become rain in the highlands, eroding the land at a faster and faster rate as the rainwater rushes back down to the sea.

One of the most unusual plants in **Waimea Canyon State Park❖** is the *iliau,* a native woody species found only in the western mountains of Kaua'i. A cousin of Haleakala's endangered silversword, this dry-forest plant has a starburst cluster of green leaves at the top of a slender stalk rather than at the bottom as the Maui species does. Conical clusters of flowers bloom on ten-foot stems. The rare endemic plant is showcased along the **Iliau Trail,** a short roadside loop, walked in about ten minutes and well marked to point out important flora. Halfway around the loop is the head of the **Kukui Trail,** which snakes down the western side of Waimea Canyon, a steep—but stunning—2,000-foot descent.

Route 550 continues up into **Koke'e State Park❖**, which encompasses some 4,400 acres of rain forest and is a prime breeding ground for the only native Hawaiian land mammal, the hoary bat (*'ope'ape'a*), whose ancestors migrated here thousands of years ago. The tiny **Koke'e Natural History Museum** at park headquarters has a surprising number and diversity of exhibits on the area's natural history. The wild chickens often seen in the vicinity are called *moa,* or jungle fowl. Once prevalent on all the islands, the *moa* today lives only on Kaua'i because the mongoose, an imported species that eats bird eggs, is not

131

found here. The nearby campground makes a good base for exploration of the Alaka'i Swamp, Waimea Canyon, and the forested ridgetops overlooking the Na Pali Coast. In addition, the **Koke'e Lodge** has rustic cabins available. At the museum, hikers can get information on the 45 miles of trails in the vicinity.

Trails leading west from Route 550 descend through dry forest to the top of the Na Pali Coast, with dizzying views down the valleys to the crashing surf thousands of feet below. The **Awa'awapuhi Trail**, just past the Koke'e headquarters and museum, has labeled plants; an accompanying botanical guide is available free at the museum.

All the way at the top of the ridge—about 20 miles in from the town of Waimea—is the **Kalalau Lookout**. With the sea glinting in the distance, the vista down the sheer but thickly forested cliffs is magnificent, a bird's-eye view into one of the largest valleys of the Na Pali Coast, where thousands of Hawaiians made their homes before the social changes brought by European contact. (Unreachable from here, the bottom of the Kalalau Valley will be visited later in this chapter, from the northern end of the belt road.) The 4,000-foot cliffs are frequently painted with rainbows when afternoon showers end.

Taking the road's eastern fork, continue past Kalalau Lookout to **Pu'u o Kila Lookout,** at the very end of Route 550, with more views of the Kalalau Valley. This is also the start of the **Pihea Trail**, the easiest way to hike into the **Alaka'i Swamp❖**. The state publishes a free plant guide to the Pihea Trail, with illustrations identifying many of the area's native ferns and flowering plants.

When Kaua'i's shield cone collapsed to form the largest caldera in the islands, *pahoehoe* lava, less porous than *'a'a* lava, filled the depression. The muddy bogs and forests of the 16-square-mile Alaka'i Swamp formed on top of this smooth, unbroken ground. Today this high, nearly inaccessible swamp-forest has some of the wettest land on earth and is home to the state's greatest concentration of native birds. Many are endangered, such as the extremely rare *kama'o,* which was the island's most common forest bird in 1891 and whose population may be down to less than two dozen birds, as is that of its cousin the *puaiohi*. Since Hurricane 'Iniki struck Kaua'i only one *puaiohi* has been observed. Several bird species now believed extinct, including the Kaua'i *'o'o 'a'a,* a black honeyeater (*Moho braccatus*), were last sighted here.

132

LEFT: *Kaua'i's vast Alaka'i Swamp is home to some of Hawai'i's rarest birds. Increasingly, alien species are threatening native birds and their habitats; only two* nuku-pu'u *(shown above in a nineteenth-century print) have been spotted in recent decades.*

Many endangered species survive here because introduced birds and invasive plants—as well as insects carrying destructive avian diseases—generally find the wet, chilly habitat so inhospitable. The conditions also dwarf the vegetation. 'Ohi'a treees, normally 20 to 30 feet tall, grow to only a tenth that size. One of the more intriguing bog plants is the tiny *mikinalo (Drosera anglica)*, which attracts and traps insects with a shiny gel that sparkles in the sun and then dissolves and digests the bugs.

The swamp's confusing topography, often submerged trails, and sudden fogs made for treacherous going until recent years, when wooden boardwalks were installed on the worst parts of the trails, turning one of the islands' toughest treks into one of the easiest. (Still, hikers must register at the Koke'e Natural History Museum.) The trail first follows the Kalalau Valley ridge, turning south after about a mile into the swamp; it then descends along a wide boardwalk through well-preserved native wet forest to the drier mesic forest along the beautiful Kawaikoi Stream. At about a half mile in, the Pihea boardwalk crosses the **Alaka'i Swamp Trail** boardwalk, whose trailhead is otherwise reachable only with four-

133

wheel-drive vehicle. The boardwalk does not yet extend along a third trail, to the east, which reaches into the wettest part of the swamp.

THE SOUTHERN COAST: POLIHALE TO LIHU'E

While the interior of Kaua'i may get up to 56 *feet* of rain in a year, parts of the coastal desert only a dozen miles away average a mere five *inches* of annual precipitation. At the leeward end of Highway 50, the western tip of Kaua'i is occupied by the Pacific Missile Range Facility. However, from Mana, about ten miles past Waimea town, a well-marked dirt cane road leads five miles out to the shore at **Polihale State Park❖**, a vast stretch of sand under the first looming walls of the Na Pali coastline. Along the beach black, rounded hills of striated lava chronicle eons of eruptions. At ground level are common strand flora such as *naupaka* and beach morning glory as well as a rare variety of the *'ohai* bush, a low native shrub with pale hairy leaves and reddish yellow flowers.

To the north the *pali* (cliffs) line up in receding silhouettes facing the open ocean. Three miles south is **Barking Sands Beach❖**, so named for an auditory illusion that some claim sounds like a dog barking. (Visitors can walk to the beach from Polihale or gain access through the military base.) Across 20 miles of open sea, the island of **Ni'ihau** is visible. At the very northwestern end of the chain of main islands, it is privately owned and was closed to outsiders for more than a century. A helicopter tour that makes two brief stops and a hunting safari are now offered on the island, but access is very restricted.

Heading eastward through sugar country, Route 50 crosses many of the island's "rivers"—a designation given to ten of Kaua'i's longer streams draining the rainfall from the interior—and turns inland after Hanapepe (some six miles past Waimea). East of the town of Kalaheo, Papalina Road leads downhill to the **National Tropical Botanical Garden❖** (NTBG). Chartered by Congress in 1964 as a research center for tropical botany and horticulture, NTBG has the largest collection of Hawaiian native plants in the world as well as an extensive collection of flora from equatorial forests. Special collections of plants include species of nutritional, medicinal, ethnobotanical, or economic value.

The deep Lawa'i Valley is an ideal location for this collection of some 7,000 species. The NTBG's 300 acres, a sampling of which can be seen on three-hour guided tours, include many different microclimates, each with the appropriate volume of rainfall to accommodate its own particular tropical plants. The garden's careful landscaping and the valley's natural features combine for a truly stunning setting. In addition to property in the Lawa'i Valley, NTBG also maintains satellite gardens on Kaua'i's north shore, on Maui's Hana coast, and in Florida, and staff members care for endangered plant species in preserves throughout the islands. Hundreds of new acquisitions arrive every month to be grown from seeds. After Hurricane 'Iniki the NTBG was frantic to save what it could of its valuable collection, approaching the task as if it were battlefield triage. Damaged trees and plants that could not be righted and repaired were gleaned for cuttings and seeds. Garden scientists surveyed and tended the rare plants they had been keeping an eye on in the wild.

The stretch of coastline east of the Lawa'i Valley and below the town of Koloa boasts a dramatic landscape. Take Route 530 south to Koloa and continue all the way south, turning west on Lawa'i Road. The road ends at Ka'iwa Point, where an exposed lava flow meets the sea in a unique natural feature called the **Spouting Horn❖**. When conditions are right, waves reach into a lava tube and send a column of water straight up through the rock into a blowhole. The resulting spray looks and sounds just like the spouting of a breaching whale.

Travel east along the same coastline on Po'ipu Road, past the expensive resorts, to reach the dunes at **Po'ipu Beach❖**. Besides lovely scenery Po'ipu offers ancient petroglyphs and some of the best snorkeling and diving on Kaua'i. Turtles, eels, and lobsters can be found here, and fish species include the Hawaiian lionfish and the long-nosed butterfly fish (*Forcipiger longirostris*), known in Hawaiian as *lauwiliwili nukunuku 'oi 'oi.*

Northeast of Lawa'i Route 50 passes around the isolated spine of Ha'upu (Hoary Head) Ridge, in which some may recognize the commanding profile of Queen Victoria. The last side trip before the island's main town of Lihu'e is **Hule'ia National Wildlife Refuge❖**, 238 acres along an estuary that is home to some 30 bird species, including 4 endangered waterbirds—the Hawaiian stilt, Hawaiian duck, Hawaiian gallinule, and Hawaiian coot. Viewing is difficult as access is restricted, and many of these species can be more easily seen at **Hanalei National Wildlife Refuge❖** in the north of Kaua'i. Hulemalu Road swings off the highway through cane fields, overlooking the reserve, the

135

ABOVE: *A fluffy Laysan albatross chick nests on the ground at Kilauea Point National Wildlife Refuge.*

BELOW: *The once common Hawaiian monk seal was hunted to the brink of extinction and is now rarely seen.*

RIGHT: *The long legs of the endangered Hawaiian stilt are perfect for wading through a wet taro patch at the Hanalei National Wildlife Refuge.*

Alakoko Fishpond (also called Menehune Fishpond), and the Hule'ia Stream as it empties into Nawiliwili Bay.

EAST COAST: WAILUA RIVER AREA

North of Lihu'e the main road around the island becomes Route 56, Kuhio Highway. Route 583 (Ma'alo Road), which splits off from the main road just north of Lihu'e, at Kapaia, climbs three miles to overlook the 80-foot **Wailua Falls.** Hiking to the falls is prohibited, but the Wailua River below is one of the state's few navigable waterways, and kayaks and commercial barges can travel about three miles inland. The most popular feature along the river is the **Fern Grotto,** a natural amphitheater in the rock wall dripping with water and ferns (generally accessible only to barges run by tour companies). **Wailua River State Park** protects the lower banks, where the river has cut a deep valley into the surrounding alluvial plain. The most spectacular views of this uniquely un-Hawaiian river valley are from the knife-sharp ridge just to the east of the falls lookout. From the falls return to

Route 56 and drive north to Wailua, taking a left on Route 580 (Kuamoo Road), which climbs a narrow ridge north of the river, while the river winds 250 feet below. On the opposite side of the road the Opaeka'a Stream plummets over wide, 40-foot-high falls into its own deep gorge.

Surrounded by a forest reserve is **Nounou Ridge,** said to resemble a sleeping giant (its nickname) when seen from the coastal town of Kapa'a. Three short trails, from 580, from Wailua, and from 581, converge into one well-marked trail to the peak, which rewards hikers with a 360-degree panorama, including views across the plain to the main mountain range. Visible to the south, inland of Lihu'e, is 1,133-foot-high Kilohana Crater, the only volcanic feature on the island that retains its crater shape. At the end of Route 580 is the **Keahua Arboretum❖,** which has been undergoing renovation, and several excellent hiking trails.

NORTH SHORE: KILAUEA TO HA'ENA

Agriculture has altered the roadside landscape along Route 56 as it continues up toward Kaua'i's fabled North Shore. *Mauka* views become more dramatic as the main range reaches the coastline about ten

ABOVE: *Although ravaged by Hurricane 'Iniki in 1992, Kaua'i's North Shore is still considered an idyllic paradise. After rains, waterfalls lace the sur-*

miles north of Wailua and the needlelike rocky aiguilles of Anahola Mountain come into view. The highway crosses valleys bisected by streams and waterfalls. African tulip trees offer their brilliant orange-red blooms to the sky. Below the main road side tracks lead down to numerous secluded beaches. **Moloa'a Bay,** in Kaua'i's northeastern corner, has one such beach, reached off Ko'olau Road a few miles past Anahola. Sea-polished lava boulders ring the bay, and cattle trails lead up and over a hill on the northern side. There are more stunning beaches to come on the North Shore, often with crevices and lava tubes that shelter a vast array of marine life. Among the best are 'Anini, Lumaha'i, and Ke'e.

As long as a year after Hurricane 'Iniki the North Shore from Kilauea to Ha'ena had the look of a forest recovering from a fire. The eye of the storm passed directly over this shore not once but twice, scouring it from one direction then another, devastating the towns of Kilauea, Hanalei, and Ha'ena. Forests were damaged, and unprotected coastal areas were stripped of every plant, including large ironwood and Java plum trees. Whole groves of pandanus were knocked over. While residents struggled to rebuild, nature quickly accomplished a remarkable regeneration.

Kilauea Point National Wildlife Refuge❖, two miles north of the town of the same name (the first North Shore town the highway reaches), occupies 160 acres at the northernmost tip of the inhabited Hawaiian

*rounding cliffs draining into the Hanalei Valley. Although much of it is
cultivated, the valley protects bird life as a national wildlife refuge.*

Islands. On the end of the point a picturesque lighthouse sits on a sheer
palisade 200 feet above the sea. Below, humpback whales ply the waters
between December and April, rare (and endangered) Hawaiian monk
seals sunbathe on secluded rocks, and sea turtles and porpoises glide
about in the cove. Public use of the refuge is restricted.

But it is the birds that truly star here. At sunset red-footed boobies return home from the sea, their feathers lit by the setting sun as they turn
and hover on the updrafts along the cliffs. Great frigatebirds, with their
seven-foot wingspans and forked black tails, lurk above, swooping in to
steal the boobies' catches. Wedge-tailed shearwater chicks nest in holes
dug into the point along the park's path, and Laysan albatross travel
down from the atolls in the north to gather in grassy areas near the point.
Red-tailed and white-tailed tropicbirds perform overhead, creating an aerial ballet as pairs poise on the wind, long tails streaming behind, and then
swoop into elaborate courtship spirals.

More seabird species can be seen at Kilauea Point than almost anywhere else in the islands. The large avian population is a fairly recent feature of the point, perhaps due to World War II shelling of offshore islets
or to simple overflow from growing bird populations in the
Northwestern Hawaiian Islands; restoration of native plants has also
helped. Three new species have nested here in the last decade alone.
Volunteer naturalists lead one-mile hikes, lasting a couple of hours, in

139

ABOVE: *At the end of a precipitous but stunning 11-mile trail along the cliffs of the Na Pali Coast, Kalalau Beach offers rest and relaxation for the weary hiker. The beach can sometimes also be reached by boat.*

the refuge and the adjacent Crater Hill preserve.

Passing the resort town of Princeville the highway suddenly overlooks, then drops into, the verdant Hanalei Valley, a patchwork of dark green taro fields, rippling grasslands, and sparkling water. Especially prominent after rain, numerous waterfalls shimmer as white lines on the high walls that enclose the area. Much of the valley—some 900 acres—has been set aside as the **Hanalei National Wildlife Refuge❖**, where wetlands protect native and migratory species of waterfowl including the Hawaiian coot (*'alae ke'oke'o*), the Hawaiian black-necked stilt (*ae'o*) and the Hawaiian duck (*koloa*)—all considered endangered. The rare Hawaiian gallinule (*'alae'ula*) also nests among the broad taro leaves. According to legend this dark gray bird, with its brilliant red brow and bill, brought fire from the gods to the Hawaiian people. Bird-watching boat trips into the refuge leave from Hanalei town. Kayaks can be rented for a peaceful tree-shaded outing; a nine-mile round-trip through the refuge takes three to four hours.

The narrow one-lane bridge over the Hanalei River protects the rest of the North Shore from large buses or heavy trucks. Even so, the region was the fastest growing area in the state during the 1980s. Past Hanalei town, which fronts a scenic, crescent-shaped bay, the road crosses two more rivers, and after the Wainiha River several wet and dry caves open into the rock on the *mauka* side of the road.

THE NA PALI COAST

Undeniably one of the most exceptionally scenic places in the world, **Na Pali Coast State Park❖** encompasses 20 miles of sheer volcanic buttresses pounded by the Pacific Ocean, hanging valleys that open up high above the shore in the cliff wall, clogged with waterfalls and jungle, and windy promontories with vast views of successive *pali*. (Na Pali literally means "the cliffs.") But this beauty has a price of admission: exertion. Helicopters and Zodiac rafts view it from air and sea, but the only way to truly see Na Pali is along a difficult, strenuous 11-mile trail following an ancient footpath used by early residents. Beginning as early as A.D. 1200, some 6,000 Hawaiians are believed to have lived in some of the valleys of the Na Pali Coast.

The **Kalalau Trail** begins at Ke'e Beach on cobblestones left over from the original Hawaiian trail. Even a half-hour walk along this trail provides a breathtaking view of the remote windswept coastline with its precipitous emerald cliffs and deep fertile river valleys spilling down to turquoise-blue seas. On this rain-forest side of the coast pandanus (*hala*) trees cover the slopes, with an understory of purple orchids, wildflowers, and pothos (an *Araceae*), growing far larger in the wild than it does as a popular houseplant. Soon the trail is hundreds of feet above the shore, descending a mile later into **Hanakapi'ai Beach,** whose name means "Valley of the Weavers," for the master artisans who used to make sails, baskets, mats, and other products from the leaves of the pandanus that grow so well here. Off the beach the water may look inviting, but deadly riptides are common here. A clearing above the beach marks the first

OVERLEAF: *Na Pali means "the cliffs," and the Na Pali Coast, with its high buttresses facing the ocean is spectacular even by Hawaiian standards. Here the remote Kalalau Valley breaks through to the sea.*

of three campgrounds along the trail.

A side trail, which occasionally gets washed out, goes up the lush and peaceful valley. Coffee, guava, and mango growing along the way are left over from a 1920s mill. At the top of the valley **Hanakapi'ai Falls** tumbles lacily down a 400-foot cliff into a blue-green pool in the middle of a huge amphitheater.

After Hanakapi'ai the main trail switchbacks up to its highest point, about 900 feet. (The repeated ascents and descents of the trail, however, as it weaves in and out of the remote valleys make it the equivalent of a 3,000-foot climb.) White-tailed tropicbirds soar on updrafts off the cliffs. One alien species that is definitely thriving along this stretch is the century plant. After the hurricane fallen stalks sprouted hundreds of bulblike offspring, ready to grow when they hit the ground.

The campground in the **Hanakoa Valley** marks the trail's halfway point. It is a hanging valley; it ends in a cleft high in a cliff overlooking the ocean. The rushing stream plunges into the ocean downhill from the trail, and no beach graces the shore below.

Beyond Hanakoa, in an immediate transition, the trail rounds to the dry, leeward side of the island. Instead of thick forest the valleys are carpeted with lush grasses that can prove razor sharp to bare legs. Quiet hikers are likely to come upon the many wild goats living in the park. At about ten miles into the hike, about one mile from its end, the trail descends through a desert-dry slope of dusty red soil into **Kalalau Valley**, where hikers must ford a heavy stream. A trail climbs the valley, an all-day hike, but the main path continues out to the third campground, on Kalalau Beach. Impassable sea cliffs make the valleys beyond this point accessible only by boat (commercial outfitters run wilderness trips). But the campsites here, on a low rise above the beach, with a shower-perfect waterfall plunging down from overhead, make this one of the best places in the world to pitch a tent.

While summit rains continually erode this island from above, the constant sea undercuts these cliffs, which recede about two inches per year. In only a few million years, the forces of nature that have created the masterpiece that is Kaua'i will erase it from the face of the earth.

Beyond Kaua'i there are—and were—other Hawaiian islands. They have been weathered down to atolls. Now the **Hawaiian Islands National Wildlife Refuge,** the ten groups of tiny, barren islets of the

ABOVE: *Due to erosion, all of Hawai'i will one day resemble French Frigate Shoals to the northwest of Kaua'i. Such tiny, low islands are ideal habitats for seals, native birds, and the rare sea turtles seen here.*

Northwestern Hawaiian Islands provide important habitats for endangered Pacific seabirds, land birds, and mammals. Among the approximately 15 million seabirds on these islands are boobies, albatross, noddies, shearwaters, petrels, and millions of sooty terns. Laysan and Nihoa islands are each home to two endangered or threatened endemic species: the Laysan duck and finch and the Nihoa finch and miller bird. Endangered Hawaiian monk seals breed only in the refuge.

As the Pacific Plate continues to move to the northwest, these tiny map dots, and even older, sunken seamounts farther north, will make a long retreat toward the Aleutian Trench, where they will slide downward, reclaimed by the earth's deep inner layers.

The impermanence of these islands, even on a time scale beyond our human comprehension, gives added weight to their beauty. Each mountain and valley, each beach and coral reef is here for only the blink of an eye in the life of the planet. The delicate flowers and shy birds of Hawai'i, as fragile as they are, seem to convey this sense of time. A visit to the islands can capture only a slice of this time, but in that snapshot the whole of creation seems to come into focus.

INTRODUCTION
ALASKA

Somewhere inside each of us lives an image of Alaska. It is the call of the wild, the land of extremes, the American Serengeti. It sweeps us down the wildest rivers and up the highest mountains, revealing its breathtaking vision—intimidating at times, inspiring at others, yet always as big as our dreams. Often bigger.

The Aleut people called it Alyeshka, or Alakshak—the great land— from which we carved the word Alaska. More a subcontinent than a state, it is roughly one fifth the size of the entire contiguous United States. "Scale and diversity foil all who try to simplify Alaska," wrote National Park Service historian William E. Brown in *This Last Treasure*. "Its immense and ceaseless grandeur numbs the mind, glazes the eye, and plagues the writer who would describe it. The intellect cannot close the suitcase on the subcontinent. Always a spare peninsula or archipelago or coastal plain dangles out after the sweaty struggle to buckle the straps."

The southeastern panhandle runs more than 500 miles from Misty Fjords to Yakutat Bay, and the Aleutian Islands stretch more than 1,000 miles from the Alaska Peninsula across the Bering Sea toward the Russian Far East. Point Barrow, the northernmost point in Alaska and the United States, lies above 71 degrees north latitude, more than three times closer to the North Pole than to the equator. Here, the sun does not set from mid-May to early August, nor rise from mid-November to late January.

This is Alaska, much of it blessed with light in summer, condemned to darkness in winter. A temperature of minus 40 degrees Fahrenheit is not uncommon in interior Alaska in January and February, nor is a temperature of 80 degrees in June, July, and August. It is a land of contrasts and extremes, showcasing some of nature's most spectacular sights: the midnight sun, rippling northern lights, rain-forest cathedrals,

---

PRECEDING PAGES: *Dwarfed by peaks of the towering Fairweather Range that rise more than 10,000 feet above sea level, a cruise ship navigates the upper West Arm of Glacier Bay in Glacier Bay National Park.*

Introduction

blue tidewater glaciers, steaming volcanoes, sockeye salmon, brown bears, clouds of seabirds, and rivers of caribou. Alaska is the last, best hope for a wilderness ecosystem in America, perhaps in the world.

In July 1741, Vitus Bering and Alexei Chirikof arrived in small wooden packet boats and dropped anchor to claim this land for Mother Russia. Although theirs became the first recorded occupation of Alaska, 60,000 to 80,000 native people were already living there and had been for thousands of years. Their ancestors had crossed over from Siberia during the end of the Ice Age, when sea levels were lower and a land bridge connected the two continents where the Bering Strait separates them today. It was not a finger of land that joined Siberia and Alaska then, but a broad causeway hundreds of miles wide—cold, treeless, windswept—across which moved the people who would become the first North Americans. They followed the earlier migrations of plants and animals, moving incrementally, mile by mile, year by year, generation after generation, not in a conscious effort to populate a new continent, but in simple pursuit of food and shelter. While some traveled by foot, others came by boat, following southern, fish-rich coasts. And although glaciers were extensive then, this central part of Alaska was relatively ice-free.

These people settled in every corner of Alaska: the Yupik and Inupiat Eskimo in the far west and north, the Aleut on the Alaska Peninsula and the Aleutian Islands, the Athabascan in the interior, and the Tlingit and Haida (and later the Tsimshian) along the southeastern coast. Their descendants still live in Alaska today, and although most have been integrated by varying degrees into white culture and a cash economy, others have done their best to retain their subsistence culture, hunting, fishing, trapping, even gathering berries every summer and fall.

The Russians occupied the southern coasts of Alaska for 126 years, from 1741 to 1867, plundering the sea otters to near-extinction before putting the land up for sale. The British were interested in the purchase, but they had recently battled the Russians in the Crimean War. So the czar took the American deal, as offered by secretary of state William Seward: $7.2 million, roughly two cents per acre. American newspapers called it "Seward's Folly," maintaining that Alaska was nothing more than an "icebox."

Three decades later the Klondike gold rush sent a tide of humanity flooding into Alaska in pursuit of gold and Lady Luck, and historians

commented that the same avarice and adventure that had pulled people across the American West was bringing them to the last frontier.
How long, they asked, would the last frontier last?

The answers to this objective question always have been and probably always will be as colorfully subjective and diverse as the people
giving them, especially Alaskans. Oil field or national park, clear-cut
wood or ancient forest, fish farm or wilderness, what exactly is Alaska?
The litmus test that best defined natural Alaska, and foretold its future, occurred while Klondike miners were grubbing their way through
the mud of the Yukon—a little-known and largely forgotten event

Russian artist Mikhail Tikanov did rare portraits of native Alaskans during an 1817 trip. Above: *Nangquk, a Kodiak Island toyon, or chief, poses in ceremonial dress.* Left: *A seafaring Aleut hunter in a bidarka, or seal-skinned boat, stalks a whale off the Aleutian Islands.*

called the Harriman Alaska Expedition. It was financed by the railroad magnate Edward H. Harriman, who in the summer of 1899 filled a steamship with distinguished American scientists, naturalists, writers, artists, and photographers, and headed north from Seattle. For three months they traveled the coast of Alaska from the bottom of the southeastern panhandle to the end of the Seward Peninsula, near Siberia, marveling at every nautical mile up and back.

Their collective assessment developed a rift, for they saw not one Alaska, but two. The first was for the taking: fish, minerals, and timber (and later oil) to sustain a young, growing nation. The second was for the saving: bears, caribou, tundra, wolves, fjords, and forests, all beating

153

to a cadence undisturbed by man, the North American wilderness on a grand scale.

Six years earlier, in 1893, historian Frederick Jackson Turner had pronounced the American frontier dead. Now America had a second chance to save a part of herself—wild Alaska—and with the Harriman Alaska Expedition completed, passenger Henry Gannett, chief geographer of the U.S. Geological Survey, made a prophetic entry in his journal. "The Alaska coast is to become the show-place of the earth," he wrote, "and pilgrims, not only from the United States, but from far beyond the seas, will throng in endless procession to see it. Its grandeur is more valuable than the gold or the fish or the timber, for it will never be exhausted. . . . If you are old, go by all means; but if you are young, wait. The scenery of Alaska is much grander than anything else of the kind in the world, and it is not well to dull one's capacity for enjoyment by seeing the finest first."

Tidewater glaciers tower out of the sea and calve massive shards of ice into the fjords. Grizzly bears patrol over open, roadless tundra and ridges, leaving their tracks along sandy river shores and atop 8,000-foot summits. Lynx bound through winter's whiteness after snowshoe hares. The midnight sun arcs across the northern Arctic sky, dipping rather than setting as it paints the land in shades of sienna, ocher, and orange. A single sandpiper nests on the ground, motionless, soundless, wary of the nearby fox trying to find it. Winter locks the sea in ice that groans with the movement of the tides, restless and creaturelike as great slabs splinter into ridges 20 feet high. Mountains rise like fangs from the earth, snowy year-round, creating their own weather as if it were January in July.

Everything seems taller, bigger, and longer in Alaska. Consider that it contains 33,000 miles of coastline (more than the entire contiguous United States), an estimated 100,000 glaciers (the largest of which is bigger than Rhode Island), 3 million lakes, and 17 of the 20 highest mountains in the United States. Before the Alaska Statehood Act of 1959, the territory was 100 percent federally owned. Today it is roughly 60 percent federal land, 28 percent state land, 11.8 percent native land, and 0.2 percent private land. Within this vast area of 560,000 square miles live only 550,000 people, nearly half of them in the state's largest city, Anchorage. The result, as poet Robert Service described long ago, is "a land where the mountains are nameless, and the rivers all run God knows where," and with "hardships that nobody reckons, and valleys unpeopled and still."

The Alaska National Interest Lands Conservation Act of 1980 created 105 million acres of new national parks, monuments, preserves, wildlife refuges, and wild and scenic rivers in Alaska. Most of these differ from parks and preserves elsewhere in three ways: they have few or no visitor facilities, they allow varying degrees of sport and subsistence hunting, and they are reachable only by boat or plane in summer and snowmobile and plane in winter. These conditions also apply for 70 percent of the villages in the state. As bush pilots like to say, "Where the road ends, the real Alaska begins."

A laska contains 63 percent of the acreage in the U.S. National Park Service system, and 88 percent of the acreage in the U.S. National Wildlife Refuge system. Wrangell–Saint Elias National Park and Preserve, for example, covers 13.2 million acres, an area greater than the combined sizes of Massachusetts, Connecticut, and Rhode Island. Yukon Delta National Wildlife Refuge, at 19.6 million acres, is 50 percent larger than Wrangell–Saint Elias.

For all their size, ruggedness, and remoteness, however, the natural areas of Alaska are not out of reach. You can drive to some, including Denali and Wrangell–Saint Elias national parks, take a boat to many, and fly to the rest. Getting around requires patience, persistence, common sense, and money. Be prepared. The weather is unpredictable and the pickup plane might be several days late. There are times when it rains for weeks straight in southeastern Alaska, snows even in the summer in the Arctic, and blows more than 100 knots on the Alaska Peninsula. In the Valley of Ten Thousand Smokes in Katmai National Park, winds can carry volcanic ash hundreds of feet into the air, knock hikers off their feet, and pit the plastic lenses of their eyeglasses.

S o why come here? Because when the sky opens up and the weather smiles, as John Muir witnessed, "the distant mountains, a vast host, seemed more softly ethereal than ever, pale blue, ineffably fine, with all angles and harshness melted off in the soft evening light."

Nearly 15 percent of this state is designated wilderness, compared with only 2 percent of the contiguous United States. There are 8 national parks, plus 10 national preserves, 4 national monuments, 16 national wildlife refuges, 26 national wild and scenic rivers, 2 national forests, and a state park system with more than 100 units (including parks, historic sites, and recreation areas).

Despite all this, natural Alaska is threatened on many fronts by commercial development and growth. Nearly every economic plan and political platform in the state rests on developing natural resources. The clear-cutting of Alaska's old-growth forests is financed at a loss by United States taxpayers, while the logs are shipped to Asia to make paper, chopsticks, cellophane, ice-cream binders, and disposable diapers. Every year commercial fishing lobbies try to raise quotas, recreational anglers crowd certain riverbanks shoulder to shoulder, and hatchery-reared salmon are released into wild stocks. Mining companies propose building slurry lines over glaciers and roads across the tundra. The oil industry fights for congressional approval to construct drilling platforms, airfields, roadways, desalinization plants, and a pipeline in the coastal plain of the Arctic National Wildlife Refuge.

This book touches on these issues, for natural Alaska—if it is to remain natural—can ill afford the avarice and short-sightedness that fenced, paved, and poisoned much of wild America. The same two Alaskas recognized a century ago by the Harriman Alaska Expedition— one for the taking, one for the saving—remain alive today. Their future—the future of natural Alaska—is uncertain. In a shrinking world burdened with an exploding human population, Alaska is both a tonic and a temptation. Its greatest attribute is space—vast, roadless, unpopulated space where the single adventurer, or group of adventurers, can discover wild plants and animals living together from one distant horizon to another. It is a land shared by all and dominated by none. Yet this space—all that land, all those resources—is also Alaska's greatest seduction. Will we succumb beneath the weight of our own arrogance, and slowly change Alaska—a road here, a pipeline there, clear-cut here, oil well there? The future of Alaska, like the earth, is in our hands.

RIGHT: *A 3 A.M. summer sunrise burnishes the braided channels of the north-flowing Toklat River in Denali National Park. Near the Arctic Circle, Denali receives 21 hours of daylight in summer, 3 in winter.*

SOUTHEASTERN ALASKA

I f there is any place where land and sea have become one, intertwined like clasping hands, each firmly locked into and dependent upon the other, it is southeastern Alaska. Although some call this region—a narrow stretch of coastline southeast of the body of the state, squeezed between British Columbia, Canada, and the Pacific Ocean—the panhandle, most Alaskans simply call it "Southeast." From Misty Fjords to Yukatat Bay—almost 600 miles in a straight line— southeastern Alaska contains more than ten million acres of forest, 10,000 miles of shoreline, and 1,000 islands. More wet than cold, more green than white, this is home to the Inside Passage, the famous coastal waterway composed largely of north-south-running canals, inlets, and straits that is protected by islands and popular with summertime cruise ships. It is also home to the Tongass National Forest, the largest of 156 national forests in the United States.

The moderating influence of the sea—its surface temperatures warmer than the surrounding air in winter, cooler than the surrounding air in summer—creates a maritime climate with fairly heavy precipitation. Rainfall in some of the wettest areas in southeastern Alaska, such as Misty Fjords, at the bottom of the panhandle, typically exceeds 150

LEFT: *In Muir Inlet, icebergs stranded by the outgoing tide bejewel a beach in Glacier Bay National Park. White Thunder Ridge, behind, along with much of Glacier Bay, was buried in ice as recently as 200 years ago.*

inches per year, sometimes 200 inches. Other areas, such as Lynn Canal, in the rain shadow of Glacier Bay, receive less than 50 inches per year.

When the sun shines, however, the scenery is breathtaking, as icy summits scythe the sky and crystalline glaciers stand majestically beside deep green forests. Even overcast days have their beauty, as tendrils of fog wrap around the fjords and tree-lined slopes, and the glacial ice turns cobalt blue.

Glaciers are common in southeastern Alaska, for when it rains at sea level, it snows at higher elevations, usually every month of the year. The snow accumulates, compresses into dense, glacial ice, and flows slowly yet steadily downslope in the form of glaciers. During the Ice Age, about 2 million to 10,000 years ago, glaciers covered all but the highest contours in the panhandle. The waterways that define the region today—wide storm-tossed canals, twisting fjordlike inlets, placid bays and coves—were carved by glaciers thousands of feet thick that once filled them. Today about 70 glaciers occupy southeastern Alaska, some of them more than ten miles long and a mile wide, all of them a mere fraction of what they once were.

Roughly 10 percent of this region is covered by ice and snow, 45 percent by forest, and the rest by alpine areas (snow-free in summer), marshy estuaries, and river valleys. Tides in southeastern Alaska rise or fall as much as 18 vertical feet in six hours, creating currents so loud and rapid (up to ten knots) that visitors mistake them for rivers. This tremendous ebb and flow stirs nutrients and plankton through the sea from top to bottom and alternately inundates and exposes vast areas of beach, headland, and tidal flat called the intertidal zone. Life here is stratified into ecological niches dictated by competition for food and space. Barnacles, the life-form most resistant to desiccation when the tide is out, form a white band at the top of the zone. Below them live purple-blue mussels, and below them, mottled starfish. Green sea urchins inch along the bottom. And long stalks and blades of kelp—a species of brown algae—grow as much as a foot a day, creating forests under the sea. So abundant and varied are the organisms here, the Tlingit used to say, "When the tide is out, our table is set."

Two major ecosystems—terrestrial and marine—encompass southeastern Alaska. The area supports approximately 350,000 Sitka black-tailed deer, 25,000 black and brown bears, 15,000 bald eagles (the

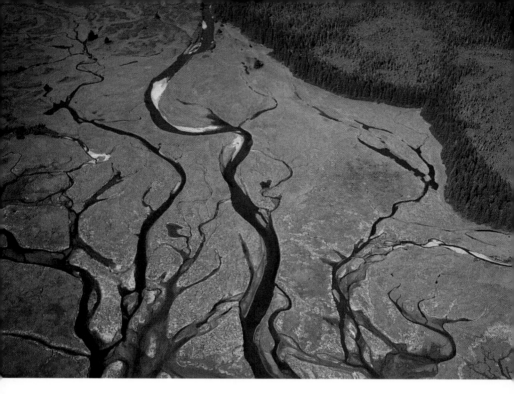

largest population in the world), 12,000 mountain goats, whose range extends from alpine meadows down to rocky shores, 700 wolves, and only 70,000 people. Wolves and bears are mutually exclusive: where one is found the other is not. Admiralty Island has brown bears but no wolves, for example, while Prince of Wales Island has wolves but no bears. Rounding out the wildlife panoply are wolverines, red foxes, beavers, mink, and marten onshore, and harbor seals, Steller sea lions, porpoises, dolphins, and whales offshore. All five species of Pacific salmon—king (chinook), silver (coho), sockeye (red), chum (dog), and humpback (pink)—migrate through the seas and rivers of the panhandle every year. Other fish include Dolly Varden, steelhead, and rainbow trout, halibut, and numerous smaller species.

Because of the abundant year-round supply of food on land and sea, life was good for the native people of southeastern Alaska: Tlingit in the north, Haida in the south, and, at a later date, Tsimshian on Annette Island, in the south near Ketchikan. They lived comfortably, built permanent villages and summer fishing camps, developed a sea-going culture with cedar canoes, and maintained a rigid social structure along kinship lines. Master storytellers and artisans, they carved totem poles and made blankets and baskets of exquisite design often dominated by the family crests of eagle and raven. They considered the animals they caught gifts, not property. After eating a salmon, a Tlingit might return the bones to the stream where the fish's life began; thus a spiritual bond would come full circle, and Tlingit and salmon would respect one another.

More than 300 species of birds occur in southeastern Alaska, some solitary, some social. Snow buntings, a type of finch, flit about the surface of snowfields and glaciers. Black oystercatchers live along the shore and use their long, red bills to pry open clams and mussels. Great rafts of phalaropes rise off the water in swirling vortices of beaks and wings, then settle down again to feed. Ravens call in a guttural vernacular as they flap overhead. Hermit thrushes sing their fluted forest melodies to attract mates, and belted kingfishers chatter on the wing and plunge into the water to catch fish.

More than three fourths of the land in southeastern Alaska lies within the 16.8-million-acre Tongass National Forest, created in 1907. Throughout the 1980s, logging and road building proceeded at an accelerated rate here, as mandated in 1980 by the Alaskan congressional delegation. Critics nationwide claimed it was a travesty economically and ecologically, and in 1990 the mandate was repealed with passage of the Tongass Reform Act. Nearly 300,000 acres of wilderness were added to the forest, and today the Tongass contains 5.9 million acres of officially designated wilderness in 17 areas. Logging continues elsewhere in the Tongass—it probably always will—yet an ever-enlightened public questions with a louder voice whether trees have more value felled or left standing. The Tongass is an old-growth temperate rain forest, one of the rarest biomes in the world, and although trees are a renewable resource, an old-growth forest is not.

Most southeastern towns contain limited

ABOVE: *Rattles inspired by the black oystercatcher were used by Tlingit shamans to cure witchcraft-related illnesses.*

LEFT: *Tendrils of brackish water reach across a tidal flat on Chichagof Island, part of a temperate rain forest that is one of the rarest biomes in the world.*

OVERLEAF: *A green and gold spruce-hemlock rain forest flourishes in Barlett Cove, at Glacier Bay National Park.*

networks of roads, but travel among them must be done by boat and plane. The Alaska State Ferry System (called the Alaska Marine Highway) has a fleet of ferries that connects major southeastern towns and runs as far south as Bellingham, Washington. Commercial jets fly daily between Seattle and Juneau and on to Sitka. Charter boats and planes are available in several southeastern towns (Juneau, Sitka, Ketchikan, Petersburg, Wrangell, Skagway, Haines, and Gustavus), and regularly scheduled flights (via small plane) also connect these communities. Ferry reservations for passengers and vehicles should be made early.

SOUTHERN PANHANDLE

Located just east of the fishing and timber town of Ketchikan, **Misty Fjords National Monument❖** can be entered along Behm Canal, whose forested shores give way to magnificent granite walls with waterfalls plunging thousands of feet into Rudyerd Bay. Glaciers carved these fjords thousands of years ago, but volcanism also played its hand at Misty Fjords. A towering erosion-resistant volcanic plug called **New Eddystone Rock,** so named by Captain George Vancouver for its resemblance to a lighthouse off the coast of England, rises like a pillar from the sea. Lava flows have occurred here (near the Blue River) as recently as the 1920s.

Commercial flights from Seattle and Juneau service Ketchikan daily, where summer tour boats depart for the monument. Cruise ships usually feature Misty Fjords as the magnificent finale to the thrilling trip through the Inside Passage. During the passage in, the boat proceeds into growing silence and solitude, for this is the largest designated wilderness area in Alaska's national forests. One can hear the trill call of the varied thrush, the cry of a bald eagle, the whoosh of air as a harbor porpoise surfaces, breathes, dives again. Of the 2.3 million acres that constitute Misty Fjords, only 142,757 are not wilderness, sacrificed to the mining of molybdenum, a metallic element used as a hardening agent in steel alloys.

The Misty Fjords rain forest is dominated by an ecological triumvirate of spruce, hemlock, and cedar, with a shaded, tierlike understory of alder, willow, huckleberry, blueberry, devil's club, lichens, and mosses. Hardly a patch of bare ground is exposed; the mosses appear to cover everything, even the lower trunks and limbs of the trees. Stretched out on this moss, soft as a bed, one can watch the crowns of the trees 200 feet above, swaying and murmuring in the wind.

Twenty air miles west of Ketchikan lies **Prince of Wales Island,** at 2,731 square miles the second largest island in Alaska (after Kodiak Island). Unlike most of Alaska, Prince of Wales has an extensive road system, created primarily by the timber industry. Small plane traffic services the island daily from nearby Ketchikan, as do state-run ferries.

Despite extensive clear-cuts, patches of wilderness do survive here, such as the 91,000-acre **South Prince of Wales Wilderness Area❖,** home to an old-growth forest of Sitka spruce, western hemlock, Alaska cedar, and western red cedar. The best way to experience the area is by sea kayak, paddling along the shore to discover favorable places to camp. There are no maintained trails or facilities. About 200 wolves live on the island, and the surrounding shore offers some of the best sea-otter habitat in southeastern Alaska.

Paralleling the Inside Passage to the east, the continental Coast Range climbs into impressive peaks 6,000 to 10,000 feet above nearby inlets and islands. Snow may fall at the higher elevations nearly every month of every year while rain falls at the lower elevations. This is the birthplace of the **Stikine** and **Juneau Icefields❖,** vast areas of ice from which glaciers flow like rivers from a lake. From the air, the icefields appear as snowy, white blankets rimmed by distant jagged summits. Only 100 air miles north of Ketchikan, and 50 miles east of Petersburg, the Stikine Icefield feeds the deeply crevassed LeConte Glacier, the southernmost tidewater glacier in North America.

Ski-planes and helicopters land on the icefields and deposit adventurers for days or weeks of cross-country skiing and mountaineering. Both can be chartered from Juneau, Wrangell, and Petersburg.

Due east of Petersburg and west of the LeConte Glacier, the coast opens to the mighty **Stikine River❖,** a proposed national wild and scenic river that flows 335 miles from its headwaters in British Columbia through two Canadian provincial parks and the Coast Range before emptying into the sea. Stikine is Tlingit for "great river," a fitting name for this broad, brown waterway that drains an area of 20,000 square miles and has only two towns, Telegraph Creek and Glenora, along its entire length. The area is accessible only by water. Visitors must rent a boat or paddle a kayak from the town of Wrangell. Every spring hundreds of thousands of shorebirds, mostly western sandpipers, feed on the tidal flats at the river's mouth during their migration to breeding grounds in northern and western Alaska. The area also serves as the gathering place for the second largest concentration of bald eagles in North America; here, they feast on hordes of spawning smelt.

CENTRAL PANHANDLE

North of Petersburg and the mouth of the Stikine River, narrow waterways open into **Frederick Sound❖** and **Stephen's Passage.** Whether from a state-run ferry, fishing boat, or kayak, these are prime areas to see humpback whales, among the most celebrated summer residents of southeastern Alaska. After spending winters in their calving waters off the coasts of Mexico and Hawai'i, the whales return every summer to feed in these cool waters rich in nutrients, plankton, and fish. They often travel in pods with an older female as their leader. Humpback whales, which measure up to 50 feet long and weigh as much as 50 tons, have no teeth. Their mouths are pleated with comblike rows of baleen (made of keratin, like human fingernails) that sift out seawater and retain their preferred food—herring, krill, capelin, and sand lance. The whales practice a sophisticated feeding technique called bubble netting, wherein one or even a whole pod of whales dives below a school of fish and ascends in a spiral. While ascending, they release air bubbles that concentrate and corral the fish on the surface. In unison, the whales rise through the middle of the "net" with mouth and baleen wide open, swallowing hundreds of fish at once.

ABOVE: *A sea otter's fur coat contains more than 300,000 hairs per square inch, insulating it from cold Alaskan waters. The otter often does a comfortable back paddle while enjoying a leisurely snack of urchins, chitons, mussels, snails, clams, octopuses, crabs, sea stars, fish, or abalone.*

RIGHT: *The early-morning light illuminates the snowcapped peaks at Walker Cove in Misty Fjords, one of two large national monuments (the other is Admiralty Island) in the Tongass National Forest.*

Midway up Stephens Passage, boaters can turn in to Tracy Arm or Endicott Arm, two fingers of sea that reach into the mainland Coast Range. (Floatplanes charted out of Juneau also bring visitors here.) Part of the 653,179-acre **Tracy Arm–Fords Terror Wilderness Area❖**, each of these arms is a deep, narrow fjord about 30 miles long that ends with the vertical, icy blue terminus of a tidewater glacier. Many people think the rock-ribbed scenery of Tracy Arm rivals, or even exceeds, that of Glacier Bay. Fords Terror, off Endicott Arm, is a bottleneck opening into a small fjord. It was named for a crewman who rowed a boat into the tight canyon at slack tide in 1889 and then spent six terrifying hours trapped there in a vortex of rushing, swirling tidal currents.

Admiralty Island National Monument❖, accessible only by boat or plane, lies to the immediate west of Tracy Arm and Endicott Arm and due south of Juneau. Daily flights connect Juneau and Angoon, the only permanent settlement on the island, and state ferries service

Angoon, though less frequently. Kayaks and canoes provide the most flexible way to see the island itself, where approximately 90 percent of the land (all but the northern end) is a national monument.

This island takes its name from the British Admiralty, so given by Captain George Vancouver, who sailed through southeastern Alaska in 1794. The names he chose for the landscapes he encountered, like those of most early navigators, were colored more by nationalism than by the physical, biological, or cultural attributes of the land itself.

The Tlingit of southeastern Alaska called this island Kootznawoo, meaning "fortress of the bears." It is a better name—more descriptive, more poetic, and vastly more appropriate, for an estimated 1,700 Alaskan brown bears live on the island, an average of one per square mile. Their presence is pervasive: bear tracks in the mud, bear scat in the grass, and bear scratchings in the forest, sometimes on spruce trunks nine feet off the ground.

The Alaskan brown bear is the same species as the grizzly, but typically lives within a hundred miles of the coast, eats more meat (especially salmon), and grows to a greater size. Whereas an average-sized adult male Alaskan brown bear male measures 46 inches at the shoulder and weighs 500 to 600 pounds, his inland grizzly counterpart reaches only 40 inches at the shoulder and weighs just 350 to 400 pounds.

Although Admiralty is a stronghold for bears, their numbers cannot be taken for granted. Females do not begin breeding until age seven and often average only one litter of two cubs in four years. Cub mortality in the first year can reach 20 to 30 percent. The bears typically live 15 to 25 years, but with only 7 percent of the monument—the areas contained in the **Pack Creek** and **Mitchell Bay Bear Reserves**—closed to bear hunting, many don't live that long. In addition, logging interests have stripped portions of the northern end of the island, outside the national monument, of old-growth forest, a habitat important to the survival of the bears.

Bald eagles—the national symbol of the United States—have also found a fortress at Admiralty, and this one small island contains more bald eagles than the entire contiguous United States. Biologists have discovered more than 800 nests here, most of them in old-growth spruce and hemlock within 200 yards of shore. The eagles mate for life and often use the same nest year after year, building on until it reaches magnificent proportions, upwards of 12 feet wide and 6 feet deep. The eagles perch in the trees with regal definition and in striking contrast to the evergreen foliage. Their name comes from the Old English word "balde," meaning white, in reference to their handsome white heads, which are attained only upon sexual maturity, about four years of age. The younger birds have darker, mottled heads.

Like the bears of Admiralty, the eagles struggle in the wake of man's ignorance and presumptuousness. From 1917 to 1953 more than 128,000 were shot by bounty hunters for two dollars per bird, under the mistaken impression that they competed with fishermen for fish. They do not: Eagles primarily eat salmon that have spawned and are dying, not prime salmon. Today their numbers have rebounded, yet biologists with the U.S. Fish and Wildlife Service have discovered what they call a "direct and inverse relationship" between man's development and the nesting density and survival success of eagles.

Due west of Admiralty Island across Chatham Strait, **Baranof Island❖** and **Chichagof Island❖** rise defiantly against the maritime storms that blow off the Gulf of Alaska. Crowned by snowy summits and cloaked in evergreen forests of hemlock and spruce, these islands both contain several small towns serviced regularly by plane and ferry. On Baranof Island commercial jets fly into Sitka, the old Russian capital that still retains some of its Slavic flavor from 200 years ago; fishing boats or kayaks can be rented here for further exploration. The islands lie in the shape of an arrowhead, with Chichagof directly above Baranof, separated by Peril Strait. Both face the open Gulf of Alaska, where wild surf cuts and etches the shore to create misty, phantasmagoric headlands in some places, quiet coves in others. This coast is a favorite habitat of playful sea otters. They float on their backs with whiskers alert and crack open Dungeness crabs by cradling them on their bellies while pounding them with a rock.

Although both islands contain impressive stands of old-growth forest, the northeastern corner of Chichagof has been heavily logged and laced with roads, mostly to satisfy demands for jobs in the nearby town of Hoonah and an appetite for raw wood in Asia.

Forty air miles east of Hoonah lies picturesque Juneau, Alaska's capital city. Reachable by plane and boat (commercial flights from Seattle and Anchorage; smaller planes from outlying communities; and frequent

171

state ferries), Juneau sits on the mainland beneath tall, snowy mountains next to Gastineau Channel. Roads connect Juneau with Douglas Island across Gastineau Channel and with the Mendenhall Valley, 15 miles north opposite the Juneau airport, and **Mendenhall Glacier❖**, the most accessible glacier in southeastern Alaska. A visitor center on the shore of a meltwater lake across from the glacier offers a fine view. Even better is the view from the West Glacier Trail, which climbs 1,000 feet above the glacier's deeply crevassed surface. Perhaps the greatest views of all are from the airplane and helicopter flight-seeing trips offered every day in summer (weather permitting) over the glacier and sometimes up to the Juneau Icefield.

Over the centuries, outwash from the glacier has created a large tidal estuary, wherein lies the 3,000-acre **Mendenhall Wetlands State Game Refuge❖**, home to 140 species of birds (at various times of the year), 12 species of mammals, and 8 species of fish. Amid the noise of Juneau's aircraft and automobile traffic (the airport is built on part of the

LEFT: *With an eight-foot wingspan, a bald eagle soars past a mountainous backdrop. Eagles mate for life and hunt with eyesight six times more powerful than a human's.*

173

wetlands), one can hear the quacking and cackling of ducks and geese, especially in April and May when they stop over en route to nesting grounds farther north. This is one of the few places in Alaska to see redheads, ring-necked ducks, blue-winged teals, and cinnamon teals, all in strikingly handsome plumage.

NORTHERN PANHANDLE

Eighty air miles northwest of Juneau, the hamlet of Haines sits where the Chilkat River empties into a large fjord called **Lynn Canal.** Accessible by small plane or state ferry from Juneau, or by highway from Anchorage, Fairbanks, or Whitehorse (in Canada's Yukon Territory), Haines is the southern terminus of the Haines Highway, which connects with the Alaska Highway (also called the Alcan, short for Alaska–Canada) inland at Haines Junction. Many travelers put their cars on the Alaska State Ferry in Bellingham, Washington (90 miles north of Seattle), travel up the Inside Passage, disembark at Haines, and drive into interior Alaska.

Leaving Haines, the highway follows the Chilkat River and passes through the **Alaska-Chilkat Bald Eagle Preserve❖**, home to the largest concentration of bald eagles in the world. Warm, upwelling water delays the Chilkat River from freezing over, enabling a late run of spawning chum salmon to enter the river and thus attract as many as 3,500 bald eagles along a 20-mile section every October, November, December, and January. In some years the numbers of salmon are larger than in others, yet the eagles are always there, perched in giant cottonwoods along the shore, as many as 3 to a limb and 20 to a tree. They lift their white heads into the sky and call in high-pitched cries that pierce the cold winter air. Beyond the eagles to the west, on a clear day one can see the snowy Chilkat Mountains, behind which lies Glacier Bay (most easily reached via commercial flight from Juneau).

GLACIER BAY

Two hundred years ago Glacier Bay did not exist; the entire bay—

RIGHT: *An aqua tidewater glacier rises near the rocks it has scoured in Glacier Bay. Whereas most glaciers in Glacier Bay National Park continue to retreat, a few in the West Arm area have begun to readvance.*

ABOVE: *An Alaskan bull moose sheds velvet from his antlers as the annual challenge of the autumn rut (mating season) approaches. The largest members of the deer family, moose can weigh up to 1,600 pounds.*

today 65 miles long and pulsing with whales, bears, seals, and birds—was filled by a single, massive glacier more than 10 miles wide (in some places) and thousands of feet thick. From the deck of a boat in the upper bay, one can see the rounded shoulders and summits of 15,000-foot mountains, shaped by the grinding mass of ice that buried them only two centuries ago.

The entrance to **Glacier Bay National Park and Preserve❖** lies 60 air miles due west of Juneau. Commercial jets depart daily in summer for the small town of Gustavus, next to the park, where buses leave to follow a gravel road ten miles to Glacier Bay Lodge and Bartlett Cove Campground, in the park on the shore of the bay. Boats depart from the lodge daily for tours up the bay; visitors can also explore other parts of the park by ski-plane, rented boat, or on foot.

This dynamic bay represents the fastest known glacier retreat on record; the story begins with Captain George Vancouver in July 1794.

Dropping anchor of HMS *Discovery* at Cross Sound (just north of Chichagof Island), Vancouver ordered two lieutenants to push long-boats eastward through the floating ice of Icy Strait. Stepping ashore at or near what is today Point Carolus, the lieutenants observed a solid wall of blue, glacial ice in the misty distance ahead. Astounded, they reported back to Vancouver, who described in his logbook a wild shoreline whose waterways terminated in "compact solid mountains of ice, rising perpendicularly from the water's edge, and bounded to the north by a continuation of the united lofty frozen mountains that ex-tend eastward from Mount Fairweather."

The lieutenants had seen the tidewater terminus—hundreds of feet high and probably 5 miles wide—of the single, massive glacier that filled what would someday be Glacier Bay. Vancouver's map showed a bay not 65, but 5 miles long, just beginning to open.

Eighty-five years later the indefatigable naturalist John Muir arrived in southeastern Alaska to see it for himself. He had heard rumors about Glacier Bay, and together with four Tlingit and a Presbyterian minister, paddled into it in a dugout canoe on a cold, rainy day in October 1879. For Muir, who would later describe himself as an "author and student of glaciers," this bay was a holy land emerging from beneath retreating blue ice. He could climb into the clouds, cross crevasses, and test his theories about glaciation. Muir wrote of "far spreading fields of ice, and the ineffably chaste and spiritual heights of the Fairweather Range...making a picture of icy wildness unspeakably pure and sublime."

By 1879 the glacier that had filled the bay in Vancouver's time had re-treated 30 miles and split into a **Y** to form two main tributaries: the Grand Pacific Glacier in the west arm of the bay and what would later be called the Muir Glacier in the east arm of the bay. Since then, another 30 to 40 miles of retreat have opened the complete length of Glacier Bay, and most of the ice has stabilized. More than a dozen tidewater glaciers—rivers of ice that flow into the sea—are now sequestered at the heads of their respective inlets in the upper bay. Their blue, vertical faces rise out of the sea upwards of 300 feet. Weakened by salt water and the tides, the glaciers pop and groan as they move and occasionally drop car-sized chunks of ice that hit the water with a sound like cannon fire. Infrequently, a massive shard of ice falls away from the glacier like a pillar and hits the sea with a tremendous explosion the Tlingit called "white thunder." The spray shoots up hundreds of feet, waves ripple down the inlet, and countless icebergs are born.

With the glacier's retreat the bay came alive. Wind-borne plants pioneered bare ground, and mosses, flowering dwarf fireweed, and mountain avens arrived. As each plant community established itself, fixing nitrogen from the air, laying down a thin veneer of soil, it paradoxically prepared the ground for another plant community that a few decades later would displace it. In this remarkable process called plant succession, a plot of bare ground can become a mat of pioneering flowers, then a thicket of alder, and eventually a forest of spruce and hemlock.

Each new plant community in turn represents new habitat for wildlife that migrate into the landscape. Today in Glacier Bay National Park mountain goats explore the vertical cliffs and alpine meadows, and moose feed in thickets of willow. Black bears inhabit the forested southern part of the bay, while brown bears roam inlet shores up to the glaciers. Both bears swim, and individuals have been seen huffing their way toward islands and across inlets. Humpback whales arrive in the bay every summer to feed. Thousands of harbor seals give birth to their young on icebergs next to tidewater glaciers. Black-legged kittiwakes—a type of gull—nest on the cliffs near Margerie Glacier and raise their voices in a din above the rumble of ice. Deep within the forest hermit thrushes and ruby-crowned kinglets interweave their summer songs.

A journey up Glacier Bay today is more than a passage through sea and land; it is a journey through time, beginning in the green forest of the present and ending in the blue ice of the past, face to face with the towering tidewater glacier Vancouver's lieutenants encountered in 1794.

Immediately to the west of the bay lies the **Brady Icefield,** a great white plain of ice that feeds several of the glaciers—Hugh Miller, Reid, Lamplugh—in the west arm of the bay. Above the icefield stand the icy, rocky battlements of the Fairweather Range, crowned with the 15,300-foot summit of Mount Fairweather, the highest point in southeastern Alaska. On the western, windward side of the range, the outer coast faces the open Gulf of Alaska and greets the sea with rocky headlands, hidden coves where commercial fishermen drop anchor, and open beaches covered in driftwood thrown ashore during winter storms.

LaPerouse Glacier, Alaska's only tidewater glacier that flows into the open ocean (rather than a protected fjord or inlet), cascades down

ABOVE: *A hiker approaches the entrance to a cave that has formed beneath remnant glacial ice in the Chilkat Mountains. Although beautiful, ice caves should be explored with extreme caution—and never alone.*

the mountains here like a rippled white ribbon. Just north of LaPerouse the coast opens into Lituya Bay, where in 1958 an earthquake set loose an enormous landslide, creating a wave that sloshed 1,700 feet up a forested mountainside, stripped off the trees, rebounded off the back of the bay, and raced back out to sea as a solid wall of water.

The area from Glacier Bay north to Icy Bay is a stronghold for the remarkable, gunmetal-blue phase of black bear called the glacier bear. Thousands of years ago when glaciers covered much of the area, black bears survived in places surrounded by ice. Unable or unwilling to migrate, they interbred in small, isolated populations in a dynamic land that was a prescription for accelerated genetic change. Thus, a new race of bear evolved. Glacier bears have since interbred with their numerous and genetically dominant black cousins, but some glacier bears still exist. It's a thrill to see them, their blue-gray fur rippling into silver as they walk.

The northern boundary of Glacier Bay National Park and Preserve is delineated by the **Alsek and Tatshenshini Rivers❖,** which meet a lit-

179

tle ways inland in British Columbia. These two rivers, which slice through the Saint Elias Mountains and skirt glaciers, have been ranked among the best in the world for offering untouched scenery and wilderness experiences. Sadly, that ranking may not last: The mining industry claims that a mountain near the confluence of the two rivers contains the largest known undeveloped copper deposit in North America. The industry proposes building a 70-mile road into the area and digging an open pit mine to retrieve the ore. Fifty environmental groups have merged to form Tatshenshini International, with the establishment of a wilderness preserve in the watershed as its primary objective. Both sides have dug in; it promises to be a long, hard fight. Access to the area today is usually with guided float trips that begin in Haines Junction in Canada's Yukon Territory; trips can be arranged by Juneau-based adventure-travel companies.

YAKUTAT BAY REGION

About 150 miles northwest of Glacier Bay the Fairweather Range joins the Saint Elias Mountains, and the coastline opens into mountain-rimmed Yakutat Bay. The bay's southeastern coast is the northwestern extreme of the **Tongass National Forest❖**. The easiest route to the forest is to take a commercial flight to Yakutat (daily from Juneau and Anchorage) and charter a small plane or boat from there.

North along Yakutat Bay (often included in cruise-ship itineraries), snowy peaks stand straight ahead, etched by ice and as sharp as fangs. At the head of the bay the shoreline doglegs at the blue 300-foot-high tidewater terminus of **Hubbard Glacier,** and opens into **Russell Fjord.** In times past, most recently in 1986, Hubbard Glacier has surged forward at the dogleg and created an ice dam that has blocked the fjord from the bay. The fjord then becomes a lake, isolated from the sea for months as it fills with fresh water from the surrounding slopes. As the lake level rises, pressure builds on the ice dam, and on one spectacular day it suddenly breaks. A wall of water surges into the bay, the glacier fractures into millions of pieces, and the fjord settles down to sea level on a massive, wondrous scale that is fittingly Alaskan.

RIGHT: *In the Russell Fjord Wilderness Area, yellow paintbrush, red dwarf fireweed, and blue Nootka lupine brighten the shore of iceberg-filled Harlequin Lake, in the Tongass National Forest near Yakutat.*

SOUTH-CENTRAL ALASKA AND THE ALEUTIAN ISLANDS

A laska's south-central coast embraces the Gulf of Alaska in a glorious salutation of land and sea. Great mountains challenge the sky in a sweeping arc; the first rays of dawn and the last of dusk anoint the snowy peaks in rose quartz alpenglow. Glaciers and volcanoes abound here, and thousands of seabirds swirl through the air and plummet into the water to catch fish. Steller sea lions cruise the mouths of rivers in pursuit of salmon—tens of millions of salmon, of five species—that return to fresh water each year. Mountain goats negotiate vertical cliffs, and black and brown bears investigate tidal flats, forests, meadows, and any other habitat suited to their omnivorous diet. Brown bears dig for clams, and black bears gnaw on barnacles against a backdrop formed by the mighty profiles of the Saint Elias, Wrangell, Chugach, and Aleutian ranges.

Temperature and precipitation gradients here are steep, primarily because of the high coastal mountains. Anchorage, for example, averages 20 inches or more of precipitation annually, while Whittier, only 50 air miles away on the other side of the mountains in Prince William Sound, averages 174 inches. Residents diligently shovel walkways that look more like tunnels than paths by the end of winter. Most of this

LEFT: *Serpentine medial moraines (ridges of rock and sediment) pattern the snow- and ice-clad surface of Russell Glacier as it flows from the Saint Elias Mountains in Wrangell–Saint Elias National Park.*

BERING

SEA

PACIFIC

OCEAN

BRISTOL BAY

ALASKA PENINSULA

LAKE CLARK
NATIONAL
PRESERVE

*Telaquana
Lake*

*Turquoise
Lake*

Mulchatna River

Chilikadrotna R

*Twin
Lakes*

*Lake
Clark*

Port
Alsworth

WOOD-
TIKCHIK
STATE
PARK

Nushagak River

Dillingham

*Naknek
Lake*

NPS VISITORS
CENTER

KATMAI
NAT PARK &
PRES

WALRUS ISLANDS
STATE GAME
SANTUARY

King Salmon

Brooks
Camp

BECHAROF
NWR

Griggs
Volcano

Martin
Volcano

Katmai
Vol

*Becharof
Lake*

*Amalik
Bay*

Mt Peulik

Mt
Becharof

Novarupta

Pribilof Islands

St Paul

ALASKA
MARITIME
NATIONAL
WILDLIFE
REFUGE

Mt
Ugashik

Valley of
10,000 Smokes

Paule Bay

Shelikof

KODIAK
NWR

*Surprise
Lake*

Port Heiden

*Black
Lake*

ANIAKCHAK
NAT MON
& PRESERVE

ALASKA
PENINSULA
NWR

ALASKA

*Chignik
Lake*

IZEMBEK
NWR

Cold
Bay

ALASKA-PENINSULA NWR

Unimak I

Shishaldin Volcano
9372

ALEUTIAN
ISLANDS
NWR

Shumagin Islands

Fairbanks

DALTON HWY
TRANS-ALASKA OIL PIPELINE

③

②

C A N A D A
Y U K O N   T E R R I T O R Y

DENALI
NATIONAL PARK &
PRESERVE
Denali
(Mt McKinley)
20320

ALASKA   RANGE

GEORGE PARKS HWY

DENALI
STATE
PARK

BYERS LAKE
CAMPGROUND

DENALI
HWY ⑧

Tok

ALASKA

②

Paxson

TANGLE LAKES
ARCHAEOLOGICAL
AREA

①

Talkeetna
Range

Talkeetna

NANCY LAKE
STATE REC AREA
③

WRANGELL-ST ELIAS

Wrangell   Range

NATIONAL PARK &

HWY

Glenallen

Matanuska   Valley

Copper
Center

Copper

①

PALMER HAY FLATS
STATE GAME REF

Harriman
Fjord

College
Fjord

Chugach

Kennicott
McCarthy

Chitina   River

LAKE
CLARK

NATIONAL

PARK

Anchorage

ANCHORAGE
COASTAL W R

Turnagain   Arm

CHUGACH
SP

Columbia
Glacier

Valdez

Range

PRESERVE

St Elias   Mts

Portage Lake

Miners
Lake

RICHARDSON HWY

Kenai

KENAI
NWR

Whittier

CHUGACH

Mt St Elias
18008

Soldotna

Prince   William

Cordova

NATIONAL

⑩

Bering   Gl

Argent Range

SEWARD
HWY

Portage
Glacier

Sound

FOREST

Iliamna Vol
x 10016

Harding
Icefield

⑨

Malaspina
Glacier

STERLING HWY

①

Seward
Resurrection
Bay

Hartney   Bay

Kayak I

Cape Suckling

Icy   Bay

Yakutat   Bay

Cook   Inlet

Homer

Kachemak
Bay

Kenai   Range

Aialik
Bay

Exit
Glacier

Copper River Delta

Cape St Elias

NEIL RIVER
ATE REFUGE
GAME
NCTUARY

KACHEMAK BAY
SP & WILDERNESS
PARK

KENAI
FJORDS
NAT PARK

Chiswell
Islands

kak
y
Ban I
Afognak I
nik I

Kodiak

G U L F   O F   A L A S K A

Kodiak
Island

SOUTH-CENTRAL
ALASKA
AND THE
ALEUTIAN ISLANDS

50   0   50 Miles

50   0   50 Kilometers

precipitation falls as rain in summer at lower elevations and as snow year-round at higher elevations.

The constant high-altitude snowfall, which can total hundreds of inches annually, has created an enormous subpolar ice mass, a great glaciated mountain arc with a center lying roughly in the Saint Elias Mountains. Standing out there on a windless winter day, before spring arrives and avalanches begin, one experiences absolute silence. This ice mass, in turn, has given birth to more than 150 glaciers, several of which are more than 20 miles long and reach tidewater. The age of the ice in the glaciers could be decades or centuries old, depending on the size and rate of flow of the glacier. A great, yawning crevasse might reveal ice that formed from snow that fell during the American Civil War or when Columbus sailed the Atlantic.

Whereas high precipitation characterizes the Saint Elias region, constant winds characterize the lower Alaska Peninsula and the Aleutian Islands. People who live here joke about the day the wind stopped blowing and everyone fell down. The Aleutian chain is an inclement, treeless place, one of the most remote in Alaska. Getting there is expensive, and parts of the archipelago are closed by military restrictions.

Cradled above the Aleutians is the Bering Sea, a relatively shallow, fish-rich body of water that contains the Pribilof Islands, known as the "Galápagos of the North." Islands farther north in the Bering Sea and the Bering Strait are discussed in the following

ABOVE: *A common year-round resident in the coastal forests of southern Alaska, the raucous but provident Steller's jay stores food when it is abundant and retrieves it when it is not.*
RIGHT: *Turbid with suspended sediments and thundering with rolling boulders, the Kuskulana River cascades down the glacier-scoured flanks of Mount Blackburn, in Wrangell–Saint Elias National Park.*

186

chapter along with the description of interior Alaska.

Most of the south-central region, as is usual in Alaska, is roadless and accessible by plane and boat only. A few inviting exceptions include Turnagain Arm, the Kenai Peninsula, the Matanuska Valley, and portions of Prince William Sound and Wrangell–Saint Elias National Park and Preserve, all reachable by highway from Anchorage, Alaska's largest city (population 250,000), located at the top of Cook Inlet in the middle of the south-central coast. Anchorage has a modern international airport with regularly scheduled commercial flights to many towns and communities around the state, including Cordova, Valdez, Seward, Kenai, Soldotna, Homer, and Kodiak in south-central Alaska, and Port Alsworth, King Salmon, Dillingham, Port Heiden, Cold Bay, and Dutch Harbor on the Alaska Peninsula and the Aleutian Islands.

WRANGELL–SAINT ELIAS NATIONAL PARK AND PRESERVE

In size and ruggedness, **Wrangell–Saint Elias National Park and Preserve**❖ is everything Alaskan: wild, immense, and breathtaking. If the Ice Age hasn't really ended, but has only gone into hiding, waiting to advance again over northern latitudes, then this is probably where it resides. From the heart of the park, every horizon runs seemingly forever in a vast, unbroken vista of an angular world of rock, ice, and snow, broken only here and there by verdant valleys and alpine slopes. There's no need for exaggeration, hyperbole, or mythology here; this landscape can match almost any myth. A single glacier in this park, the Bering, is larger than the state of Rhode Island, and another, the Malaspina, is a close second to the Bering. They spread across the land like seas of ice, fractured with blue crevasses and surfaced with meltwater pools. Inviting one minute, intimidating the next, it is a landscape that evokes both desire and fear, for many visitors find themselves drawn into the vastness and the raw beauty of mountains beyond mountains, glaciers after glaciers, and rivers flowing into rivers.

Rangers who have flown small planes over this park for ten years still occasionally find themselves piloting up a valley they have never seen before. At 13.2 million acres, Wrangell–Saint Elias is the largest unit in the U.S. National Park Service system. Six Yellowstones would fit into it.

The third highest mountain in North America, after Denali (Mount

McKinley) and Mount Logan, **Mount Saint Elias** rises 18,008 feet above the sea. Only 22 miles from the coast of Icy Bay, this peak crowns the Saint Elias Mountains, the highest coastal range in the world, where precipitation is constant, and snow and ice accumulations are many thousands of feet thick.

The Wrangell–Saint Elias region contains remarkably diverse geological features. Ten thousand years ago this land was buried in ice, with only the highest peaks rising above like naked islands in a frozen sea. Today, those peaks are joined by knife-edged ridges, called aretes, sharpened by glaciers. Ridgelike kame terraces are slapped against mountainsides where they formed at the interface of land and ice. Kettle ponds, created from abandoned chunks of retreating glacier, now glimmer with aquamarine meltwater. Recessional moraines stand in crooked rows where the retreating ice deposited them. Bedrock faces grimace with deep striations where glaciers powered over them, grinding rock against rock. Wrangell is especially intriguing in that it features glaciers, particularly in **Chitistone Canyon,** that continue to reshape the landscape; in Wrangell, glaciers still hang, scour, and form.

Four major mountain ranges converge here: the Alaska, Wrangell, Saint Elias, and Chugach. With those mountains converge the habitats of animals. In the upper Chitina drainage in the Wrangell Mountains, for example, Dall sheep and mountain goats can be seen grazing on the same summer slopes. Both climb the cliffs nimbly on padded hooves, but the mountain goat wears a longer, shaggier coat than the short-haired Dall sheep. Bison can also be found in the park; one herd roams the upper Chitina River Valley, the other wanders near the Copper River between the Dadina and Kotsina rivers. Spruce grouse, ruffed grouse, and Alaska's three species of ptarmigan can be spotted in the tundra throughout Wrangell–Saint Elias.

Black bears, brown bears, and grizzly bears also live here. Brown and grizzly bears are the same species, *Ursus arctos*; those within a hundred miles of the coast are commonly called brown bears, those found farther inland are grizzlies. Because they eat more fish—predominantly spawning salmon—and therefore have a higher protein diet, brown bears attain a greater height and weight than grizzly bears.

Large mammals are not the only attractions here. Size can be charming on a small scale, too, as tiny wildflowers open across alpine slopes

189

each summer. The upper tundra hosts white mountain avens and yellow arnicas that nod in the rain, as well as cream-colored diapensia and pink woolly louseworts. Higher still, among the rocky outcrops, bloom yellow arctic poppies, which track the sun like radar, purple mountain saxifrage, and Scammon's spring beauty, isolated on slopes of igneous rock. These plants attest to hard-won fights for adaptation and survival, hugging the barren ground like a living skin, surviving in microclimates of warmer, relatively wind-free air.

Thousands of rivulets pour off the slopes and join rivers that run tumbling and turbid down long valleys. Weather permitting, one can fly into the park, or over it, by small charter plane out of Valdez, Glenn-allen, Gulkana, McCarthy, or Tok. One can also drive in along one of the two unpaved roads that enter the park. The Slana –Nabesna Road enters from the north and offers majestic views of the Wrangell Mountains as it travels 42 miles through spruce forest and tundra to the old mining town of Nabesna. From the route, lovely scenes of the high country above Jacksina Creek are visible. The Chitina–McCarthy Road enters from the west and runs 61 miles along an old railroad bed to the Kennicott River, passing ponds where loons and grebes nest, and at the end of the road a hand tram provides access across the river to the colorful community of McCarthy. From McCarthy, a road runs five miles up a gentle slope to the old mining site of Kennicott, once one of the richest copper mines in the world

ABOVE: *Wild iris (or flag) brightens a meadow in Portage Valley at the end of Turnagain Arm in Chugach National Forest. An early bloomer, the showy blue-flowered perennial may have originated in Siberia.*

LEFT: *Growing beneath a storm-gnarled forest near Prince William Sound, yellow skunk cabbage is an important food for Steller's jays, Canada geese, and black bears.*

and today one of the most photogenic historic building sites in Alaska.

Although there are no maintained trails or manmade river crossings in Wrangell–Saint Elias, the park offers boundless opportunities to explore and savor true Alaskan wilderness. Mountain climbing, fishing, river running, backpacking, and cross-country skiing are all possible here, but careful planning is absolutely necessary.

Chugach National Forest and Prince William Sound

Skirting Wrangell–Saint Elias National Park, the Copper River curves south, parallel to the highway from Slana to Copper Center. It then slices through the Chugach Mountains to reach the Gulf of Alaska, where sediment washed out by the river has spread and settled with the tides here for thousands of years. The result is the broad **Copper River Delta❖**, an estuary and tidal flat up to 5 miles wide and 45 miles long, running from the mouth of the river west to Cape Whitshed. This is an extremely important staging area for birds migrating along the Pacific Flyway, especially in April and May when the waterfowl and shorebirds arrive. It is not unusual to see 100,000 western sandpipers at a time, winging through the air in magical synchrony, flying, turning, and wheeling together as if the entire flock were a single organism. They flash white from their undersides and dark from their backsides, like a sheet snapping in the wind, then settle onto the tidal flat and call in a tremulous chorus.

Bound for nesting grounds along Alaska's western coast, they stop at the delta to replenish their fat stores. Three dozen species of shorebirds spend at least part of their year here, and biologists have estimated that as many as 20 million individuals use the delta to feed and rest.

Early May is the peak time to observe the spectacle of migrating shorebirds. Take a commercial flight from Juneau or Anchorage to nearby Cordova or travel to Cordova by Alaska State Ferry from Whittier or Valdez. From Cordova it is a seven-mile drive south to Hartney Bay, where the birds gather.

Down the coast, about 35 miles southeast of the Copper River Delta, lies **Kayak Island❖**, its southwest promontory crowned by Cape Saint Elias. It was here that a small, wooden packet boat, the *St. Peter*, dropped anchor in July 1741. At the helm was Danish explorer

Vitus Bering, and beside him was the German physician and naturalist Georg Wilhelm Steller, sailing under the Russian flag. Although they didn't have an exact idea of where they were, they suspected that they had landed on the northwestern coast of North America. Bering sent Steller ashore, where he found a species of bird he had never seen before, a blue bird with a dark crest and a raucous disposition. Steller reported that the discovery of a bird so different could only confirm their speculation that they had reached a separate continent, North America. The bird came to be known as the Steller's jay, and Steller's observations became the first known written record of the natural history of Alaska. Today Steller's jays still populate this remote island, which can only be reached by charter seaplane from Yakutat or Cordova on a calm day or by boat.

The 5.8-million-acre **Chugach National Forest❖** extends over Kayak Island and Cape Suckling, opposite, on the mainland. It continues northwest between the Gulf of Alaska and the Saint Elias, Chugach, and Kenai mountain ranges, wrapping around Prince William Sound to the northeastern corner of the Kenai Peninsula. Roughly the size of New Hampshire, the Chugach is one of only two national forests in Alaska (the other is the Tongass, in southeastern Alaska). It is a verdant forest, largely coastal, dominated by mature stands of Sitka spruce and western hemlock. More than 200 miles of hiking trails run through the forest and lead to backcountry cabins, fishing spots, and ski areas. Portions of the forest are reachable by highway from Anchorage and from the smaller communities of Seward, Valdez, and Cordova.

Prince William Sound❖ entered the collective American conscience on Friday, March 24, 1989, when the single-hulled supertanker *Exxon Valdez* ran aground on Bligh Reef and hemorrhaged 11 million gallons of crude oil that washed as a sticky, toxic tide onto hundreds of miles of shoreline. It was Alaska's Black Friday: the day environmentalists had always feared and oil industrialists had always dismissed.

The cold, nutrient-rich waters of Prince William Sound support a varied marine pyramid of phytoplankton, zooplankton, intertidal life, mammals, and fish, including all five species of Pacific salmon. Steller sea lions feed on salmon and other fish and patrol the mouths of rivers to catch them. Harbor seals prey on a variety of seafood, and are preyed

193

upon in turn by orcas (killer whales). Playful sea otters, insulated by fur rather than blubber, must eat constantly to maintain body heat; an adult male five feet long and weighing 80 pounds might consume as many as 14 Dungeness crabs per day. The humpback whales that frequent Prince William Sound feed primarily on small fish such as herring and sand lance. Humans also make a good living here, as this is one of Alaska's richest commercial fisheries. (A rented fishing boat, in fact, is a good way to explore the sound; many fish and mammals can also be spotted from cruise ships and state-run ferries between Whittier, Cordova, and Valdez.)

The sound's marine pyramid was no doubt altered by the *Exxon Valdez* spill, but to what extent is unknown. At least half a million birds died, plus some 5,500 sea otters and 200 harbor seals. The oil, although it has been cleaned off the surfaces of most beaches, still lingers in the coastal substrates and water column with a toxicity that may never be fully measured or understood.

Twenty-five years to the day before the spill, on March 27, 1964, the strongest recorded earthquake in North America shook Prince William Sound for nearly five minutes. Centered next to the sound just west of Columbia Glacier under Miners Lake, it measured 8.6 on the Richter scale. Some parts of the sound subsided 6 feet while others rose nearly 40 feet, drowning trees, altering streams, and creating new beach lines. Entire clamming areas were destroyed, small, local fishing businesses were threatened, and

ABOVE: *The setting sun highlights the plumage of a short-billed dowitcher at Potter Marsh, in the Anchorage Coastal Wildlife Refuge.*
LEFT: *As low tide and sunset coincide, thousands of western sandpipers and dunlins feed in Hartney Bay, near the hamlet of Cordova in eastern Prince William Sound. For a few days each May, great clouds of shorebirds wing through the area, en route to summer breeding grounds far to the north.*

195

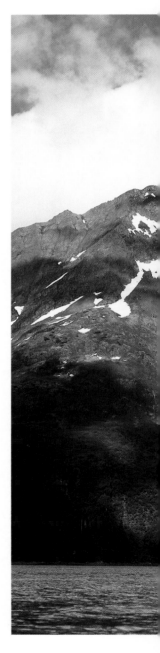

countless animals perished. The most visible testimony to the earthquake today are the intermittent stands of dead trees along the shore, killed when the land dropped and saltwater invaded the roots.

The sound eventually recovered from the earthquake, as it may someday from the spill. Yet both earthquake and oil spill could be mere preludes to the final destruction of Prince William Sound: clear-cut logging. With passage of the Alaska Native Claims Settlement Act of 1971, more than a quarter million acres of forest inholdings were selected by Native Alaskan regional and village corporations in the sound as candidates for logging in the coming decades. The logging has already begun, and there is no end in sight.

The sound was named by Captain James Cook in 1778 in honor of the 13-year-old son of England's King George III. At 15,000 square miles and 100 miles in diameter, it is roughly 15 times larger than San Francisco Bay. It contains 19 major islands, 150 minor islands, and hundreds of sea stacks, rocks, reefs, inlets, bays, coves, fjords, and tidewater glaciers. In the northwestern corner of the sound, more than a dozen tidewater glaciers flow into College and Harriman fjords. Harriman Fjord was not encountered by white explorers until the Harriman Alaska Expedition steamed into the iceberg-filled waters in 1899.

KENAI PENINSULA
West of Point Bainbridge, where Prince William

RIGHT: *A sailboat navigates through the scenic Nuka Passage at the southwestern end of Kenai Fjords National Park. Humpback whales frequent these waters in the summer, feeding on shrimp and small fish; orcas, or killer whales, prey on northern fur seals, too.*

Sound ends, Alaska's gulf coastline veers inland at Resurrection Bay (which extends to the town of Seward) and **Kenai Fjords National Park❖**. Although it is the smallest of eight national parks in Alaska, Kenai Fjords packs a variety of landscapes and wildlife into its 580,000 acres. Mountains rising abruptly from the sea capture snow and form glaciers, and the sea itself harbors whales, sea lions, and great colonies of nesting birds. People drive here from Anchorage (130 miles via the Seward Highway) and take a boat tour of the fjords, a hike to Exit Glacier, or a flight-seeing trip out of the town of Seward.

Crowning the park is the 300-square-mile **Harding Icefield,** vast and white and punctuated on the skyline by nunataks, the peaks of mountains rising above the ice. Storms from the Gulf of Alaska drop more than 400 inches of snow on the icefield every year. As it accumulates, the snow compresses at the lower depths from the overlying pressure of successive snow accumulations and then recrystallizes into dense, glacial ice. Under the influence of gravity, it finds the path of least resistance and flows downslope as a river of ice, slowly yet inexorably undercutting mountains and grinding rock into silt. Thus glaciers have shaped and continue to shape most of the Alaska coast from the bottom of the southeastern panhandle, up through Prince William Sound and Kenai Fjords, and west to the Alaska Peninsula toward the Aleutian Islands. The fjords, inlets, and arms that mark the coastline today were filled with glaciers thousands of years ago during the Ice Age. The glaciers sequestered at the heads of fjords and inlets today are indeed impressive and powerful, but they are shrunken shadows of what they once were.

Thirty-four glaciers flow from the Harding Icefield in Kenai Fjords. The trailhead for a short, easy hike to one of them, **Exit Glacier,** begins nine miles from Seward, via a dirt road. More challenging is the trail that climbs 3,000 feet from the terminus of the glacier to the Harding Icefield. Mountain goats inhabit the rocky terrain along the way, and if the weather cooperates the views of the icefield are magnificent.

Boats depart Seward every day of summer (unless the winds and seas are too rough) for tours of Kenai Fjords. The usual itinerary includes a visit to a tidewater glacier in Aialik Bay, where the boat skipper kills the engine so all can hear the popping and rumbling of the moving ice. Kittiwakes, puffins, and other seabirds fly past bow and stern en route to feeding and nesting areas. Another stop is a Steller sea lion colony in the nearby **Chiswell Islands,** a small offshore archipelago. The sea lion bulls gather harems, and all of them—bulls, cows, and little pups—bask on rocky shores bellowing and yelling in a salty vernacular uniquely their own. The large bulls (up to ten feet long and weighing 2,200 pounds) prop themselves up on their fore flippers and survey their coastal domain like Ottoman sultans. Although the sea lions appear awkward and lumbering on land, they swim with great agility and can easily dive 100 feet in search of prey.

The numbers of Steller sea lions in the Gulf of Alaska and the Bering Sea have dropped by nearly 90 percent in the last ten years, alarming biologists and conservationists. The exact reasons are difficult to isolate, but the answer might lie in the increased human demand for pollock, an important fish for sea lions. As human fishing for pollock has spiraled upward, the sea lion populations have spiraled down. The sea lions are listed as threatened and may soon be listed as an endangered species. Humpback whales and orcas also inhabit these waters, but their numbers thus far appear to be in no danger of collapse.

Immediately west of Kenai Fjords is **Kachemak Bay State Park and Wilderness Park❖.** Kachemak Bay is 30 miles long and averages 7 miles wide. Captain Cook explored this bay in 1778, and the Russians arrived soon after, in 1795. Homer, one of the most picturesque hamlets in Alaska, sits at the opening to the bay (225 miles via the Sterling Highway from Anchorage) on a 5-mile-long spit that juts out into the water. In the park, across the bay opposite Homer, glaciers tumble down the Kenai Mountains to meet lush spruce and hemlock forests at the edge of the sea. In summer boats travel daily across the bay from Homer to the park.

To the north of Kenai Fjords and Kachemak Bay, lying in the heart of the Kenai Peninsula, is **Kenai National Wildlife Refuge and Wilderness❖,** 1.97 million acres of mountains tapering into rolling hills, forests, rivers, wetlands, and lakes. In this broad area of the western Kenai Peninsula, calm, windless summer days can be warm but thick with mosquitoes. Fish and wildlife abound, especially salmon, bald eagles, and moose. Major wildfires in 1947 and 1969 created a matrix of vegetation types rich in willow, a post-fire pioneering plant and favorite browse of moose. Thus moose have prospered, sometimes to the point of becoming pests, blocking residents' driveways and back patios. (Before 1980 the refuge was named the Kenai National Moose Range.) The Sterling Highway (connecting Anchorage and the Kenai Peninsula) runs through the refuge and provides access to numerous campgrounds, picnic sites, hiking trails, and boating opportunities, including canoeing and kayaking.

ANCHORAGE AND ENVIRONS

North of the Kenai Peninsula is a broad inlet called Turnagain Arm. While exploring Alaska in 1778, Captain Cook hoped this inlet would be an entrance to the fabled Northwest Passage, but it was not. As with so many disappointments before, he had to "turn again." Turnagain Arm contains the second strongest tides in North America (after Canada's Bay of Fundy), rising or falling as much as 35 feet in six hours. The tide sometimes floods so rapidly it creates a vertical wall of water two or three feet high and moving several knots. Called a bore tide, it stirs small organisms to the surface, which attracts clouds of hungry gulls, feeding and calling on the wing. Bald eagles also partake of the bore-tide feast. A good view can be found by driving along the Seward Highway.

Anchorage rests on an outwash plain immediately north of Turnagain Arm. It is a large, modern, sprawling city with accommodations and opportunities suited for visitors any time of year. On a clear day mountains are visible on every horizon: the Chugach immediately to the east; the Kenai to the south; the Chigmit to the southwest (part of Lake Clark National Park, including Redoubt and Iliamna volcanoes); the Talkeetna to the north; and Denali (Mount McKinley) and Mount Foraker beyond the Talkeetna, crowning the Alaska Range, 130 miles north-northwest of downtown Anchorage.

East of the city rise the Chugach Mountains, location of **Chugach State Park❖.** One of the largest state parks in the United States, this half-million-acre bastion of glacial topography and serrated peaks is home to brown bears, black bears, moose, Dall sheep, wolves, wolverines, lynx, red foxes, porcupines, and numerous species of birds. Several roads lead from the city into the park; where the roads end, the trails begin, offering excellent summer hiking and winter cross-country skiing.

Anchorage's backyard also encompasses **Anchorage Coastal Wildlife Refuge❖,** just south of town along the Seward Highway and Turnagain Arm. Straddling the highway with Potter Marsh on one side

ABOVE: *Two climbers tempt fate on the crevassed surface of Matanuska Glacier near Anchorage. The two should be roped together, carrying ice axes, and trained in mountaineering safety and methods of self-arrest.*

and tidal flats on the other, this is critical waterfowl habitat during spring and fall migrations. More than 130 species of birds have been recorded here. Some are more bashful than others: While Canada geese paddle the waters in full view with a string of goslings in tow, grebes and loons inhabit the more hidden, heavily vegetated areas. A parking lot and boardwalk provide excellent viewing opportunities.

Beyond Potter Marsh at the end of Turnagain Arm are **Portage Lake and Portage Glacier❖**. Only one hour southeast of Anchorage

in Chugach National Forest, this is one of Alaska's most popular tourist destinations. Despite the summer crowds and bus traffic, it is worth the visit. Massive icebergs often come to rest in shallow water near shore, right next to the visitor center. Thrusting 30 feet into the sky, they melt into phantasmagoric tones of icy blue. A daily boat tour departs from near the visitor center and travels the length of the lake to the terminus of the glacier.

Northeast of Anchorage about 20 miles via the Glenn Highway, the Chugach and Talkeetna mountains frame the windy, riverine flats of **Matanuska Valley** and **Palmer Hay Flats State Game Refuge❖**. Established in 1975 and expanded in 1985, the refuge provides important habitat for tens of thousands of surface-feeding (dabbling) ducks and diving ducks. April and May are the best months to visit, when the birds arrive to rest on their journeys north.

Sixty-seven miles north of Anchorage along the George Parks Highway (which branches off the Glenn Highway) is **Nancy Lake State Recreation Area❖**, encompassing terrain that was buried under glaciers thousands of years ago. Today 130 lakes lie amid rolling hills covered in birch and spruce. The Nancy Lake area is noted for its abundance of rainbow trout, as well as the northern pike, first noted in Red Shirt Lake in 1980. Canoeing here is excellent, with the sights enriched by sunlight on the water, and the sounds garnished with the fluted calls of loons.

To the north, from mile 132 to mile 170, the George Parks Highway runs through **Denali State Park❖**. Created in 1970, this park is crossed by hiking trails, including a favorite that climbs up Kesugi Ridge and on clear days culminates with breathtaking views of Denali (Mount McKinley) and the Alaska Range. If Denali National Park feels too crowded (as it easily can in the middle of summer), this is a good place to visit. Byers Lake Campground offers boating and hiking but fills daily in summer, so get there early.

From Cantwell (mile 210 on the George Parks Highway) the Denali Highway runs 130 miles east to Paxson. The highway, most of it gravel, winds past glacial moraines and kettle ponds and even along the top of a

---

LEFT: *With the Chugach Mountains providing a fittingly dramatic backdrop, a summer rainstorm and 10 P.M. sunset conspire to create a technicolor rainbow over a nameless pond in the Matanuska Valley.*

sinuous glacial ridge called an esker, laid down as sediment in a meltwater river beneath the ice thousands of years ago. The snowy ramparts of the Alaska Range guard the horizon to the north, while the distant Talkeetna Mountains stand to the south. Near Paxson the highway passes the **Tangle Lakes Archaeological Area❖,** where evidence of Athabascan occupation reaches back more than 10,000 years. Boating on the lakes is pleasant, but beware of sudden winds sweeping off the nearby mountains. Tangle Lakes is also known for its profusion of berries, including crowberries, cranberries, and red currants; many people come here specifically to pick the glorious blueberries. Visitors who want to experience the scenic and natural pleasures of the Delta wild, scenic and recreational River can take out their canoe or kayak off the Richardson Highway. From Paxson the Richardson Highway can be followed north to Delta Junction and Fairbanks or south to Glennallen and Anchorage.

One hour west of Anchorage by small plane, across Cook Inlet and into the Chigmit Mountains, is **Lake Clark National Park and Preserve❖**, a geographical and biological microcosm of the state that has been called "Alaska's epitome."

This park and preserve offers excellent tundra hiking in the Telaquana, Turquoise, and Twin Lakes region, and the rivers that drain these lakes—the Telaquana, Mulchatna, and Chilikadrotna—make for good float trips (raft, kayak, or canoe). The tundra is wet and spongy in some low-lying areas but mostly dry and solid on the ridges and open slopes above. Some visitors fly by air taxi from Anchorage to the community of Port Alsworth, on the shore of 50-mile-long Lake Clark, then take a charter flight from there. Others charter out of Anchorage and fly directly to their destination.

Two active volcanoes, Iliamna and Redoubt, stand guard over the southern flanks of the park, where the Aleutian Range begins. Redoubt erupted in 1966 and 1989–90, dusting Anchorage in ash, and threatens to do so again at any time. Both volcanoes occasionally emit plumes of steam and ash.

Katmai Country

Sixty miles southwest down the coast from Lake Clark National Park is one of the most famous wildlife-viewing areas in the world, **McNeil River State Game Refuge and Sanctuary❖**. In midsummer more than

60 Alaskan brown bears gather at McNeil Falls to fish for migrating salmon, while not far away a group of lucky people watch in awe. Admission to McNeil is by lottery only, and the odds at having one's name selected are less than 10 percent. To apply, contact the Alaska Department of Fish and Game in Anchorage.

Directly to the south of McNeil River lies **Katmai National Park and Preserve❖,** established in 1918 as Katmai National Monument and enlarged and renamed in 1980. Steaming volcanoes form the vertebrae of this park, while the state's largest protected population of brown bears patrols the slopes, valleys, and coastline below. The winds can be strong and unrelenting, stirring up whitecaps on the lakes.

Although Katmai encompasses 4.1 million acres of inviting wilderness terrain, nearly all of which has seldom, if ever, felt the tread of human feet, almost every visitor here aims for **Brooks Camp,** next to the mouth of Brooks River on the shore of Naknek Lake. On a sunny day in July it can appear as if every person, bear, fish, boat, and plane in Katmai has crowded into this one small place at the same time. Because the brown bear viewing opportunities are excellent at Brooks Camp, visitation has soared here in recent years, and a lodge and campground reservation system has been introduced. Plan ahead and make early reservations, especially for July when the bears are most plentiful.

A short trail leads from the Brooks Camp and Brooks Lodge (clustered together with a National Park Service visitor center) to Brooks River, where sockeye salmon school together before leaping through the air to ascend Brooks Falls and swim upstream to spawn in July. Not surprisingly, Alaskan brown bears congregate here to feed on salmon. The bears stand atop the falls and catch the fish in midair, or plunge into the pools below, or work the river banks and shallow riffles. All the bears have individual fishing methods, often learned from their mothers when they first visited the river as cubs.

A bear-viewing platform has been constructed at the end of the trail next to the falls. A second run of salmon occurs in Brooks River in early September. By October, after the lodge has closed, the bears work the river mouth and lakeshore, feeding on fish that have spawned.

Commercial jets fly daily from Anchorage to King Salmon, 250 miles to the southwest. In summer air taxis fly 35 miles into the park from King Salmon, usually to Brooks Camp and Brooks Lodge and the

ABOVE: *Having beaten great odds to get this far, a spawning sockeye (red) salmon, beats them again as it leaps past the snapping jaws of an Alaskan brown bear at Brooks Falls in Katmai National Park.*

National Park Service visitor center and information station.

Daily bus/van tours from Brooks Camp follow a 23-mile road (the only road in the park) to the **Valley of Ten Thousand Smokes,** one of the most unusual landscapes in Alaska. Once a verdant valley of forests and beaver ponds, today it is a volcanic terra incognita filled with ash and pumice. The transition occurred suddenly, during a cataclysmic eruption in June 1912. When the summit of nearby Mount Katmai collapsed, a volcanic vent on the flank of the mountain, called Novarupta, blew out a volume of ash and rock estimated at 100 times greater than that spewed in the 1980 eruption of Mount Saint Helens in Washington State. The valley was buried in a river of hot, incandescent ash that settled in places up to 700 feet thick.

In July 1916, Robert F. Griggs of the National Geographic Society came upon the valley: "The sight that flashed into view as we surmounted the hillock was one of the most amazing visions ever beheld by mortal eye. The whole valley as far as the eye could reach was full of hundreds, no thousands—literally tens of thousands—of smokes curling up from the fissured floor. From our position they looked as small as the little fumaroles near by, but realizing something of their distance we knew many of them must be gigantic. Some were sending up columns of steam which rose a thousand feet before dissolving."

Although the smoke eventually disappeared, the name did not, and the valley today remains largely free of vegetation and dominated by winds that can roar through Katmai Pass and across the valley at 100 miles per hour, lifting great plumes of ash into the air. In good weather the hiking is wonderful; in bad weather it can be a nightmare.

The road from Brooks Camp ends at a cabin at **Three Forks Overlook.** Daily tours spend about three hours here, time for a pleasant and rewarding hike down to the **Ukak River Gorge.** Visitors can opt to hike ten miles from Three Forks Overlook to Baked Mountain Cabin for overnight stays. Two miles beyond is Novarupta, the dark, domelike volcanic plug one-quarter mile in diameter and 200 feet high from which the ash and pumice ejected during the 1912 eruption.

Nearly every major mountain surrounding this valley—Mageik, Martin, Katmai, Griggs—is a volcano. These peaks are part of the Aleutian Range, a palisade that spans the length of the Alaska Peninsula and the Aleutian archipelago and includes some 80 active volcanoes and hundreds of inactive ones. This battlement of volcanoes forms the igneous spine of Katmai National Park and Preserve; the lake region lies to the west, and the seacoast to the east.

The Katmai coast is the least visited part of the park, and the people who know it best are probably the commercial fishermen who find salmon runs and safe harbor here every summer. Bald eagles and brown bears feed on the salmon, and nesting seabirds inhabit the steepest cliffs. During spring, hundreds of harlequin ducks and migrating geese gather in the quiet coves. This coast, among the wildest in Alaska, was corrupted in 1989 when oil from the ruptured supertanker *Exxon Valdez* traveled nearly 500 nautical miles from Prince William Sound and washed ashore as a thick, toxic mousse. Bears were sighted with

---

OVERLEAF: *Tall red fireweed brightens a hill near the Ukak River in the Valley of Ten Thousand Smokes. A cataclysmic volcanic eruption in 1912 desolated this once-verdant section of Katmai National Park.*

their heads smeared in oil; rafts of dead birds washed ashore; sea lions and seals took refuge wherever they could. The casualties were impossible to tally. They still are, although only a trained eye can find oil there today. On some headlands, for example, the oil has hardened into splotchy patterns that look and feel like conglomerate rock. In some quiet coves and bays, it probably seeped into gravel and sandy substrates. A statement from the National Park Service summarized the impact of the spill: "The true loss is not one of dollars or individual birds or mammals, but in a radical and uncertain alteration of ecosystems whose integrity had been as uncompromised as any in North America."

The Katmai coast can be reached by chartering a floatplane out of King Salmon, Homer, or Kodiak (Kodiak is perhaps best, because flights from King Salmon have to cross the Aleutian Range, where inclement weather is common). From the air, the coast spreads out in a rugged pattern of headlands, islands, cliffs, and coves, and culminates in volcanoes rising 7,000 feet above the sea. Kukak Bay and Amalik Bay, providing protection from prevailing storms in Shelikof Strait, offer some of the area's best sea kayaking. Amalik Bay has a cabin that is occasionally occupied by backcountry rangers in summer. Travelers in small boats and planes should be careful traveling from bay to bay, as good landing sites are rare, and storms can kick up quickly in Shelikof Strait, one of the most notorious bodies of water in Alaska.

KODIAK ISLAND

Thirty miles east across Shelikof Strait from the Katmai coast, and 250 air miles south of Anchorage, lies the forested, mountainous big-bear island called Kodiak. At 3,588 square miles it is the largest island in Alaska, and it forms the centerpiece of 16 islands in the Kodiak archipelago. The town of Kodiak sits on the island's northeastern coast and is home to one of the richest and largest fishing fleets in Alaska. Commercial jets arrive and depart here daily, and summer brings a brisk business of small planes coming and going. **Kodiak National Wildlife Refuge❖** covers 1.9 million acres on Kodiak, Uganik, Afognak, and Ban islands. Although the visitor center is just outside Kodiak town, the refuge itself is 25 miles away and accessible by plane or boat only. It was established in 1941 to protect wildlife, primarily the Kodiak brown bear, *Ursus arctos middendorfi*, the largest brown (or grizzly) bear in North America. Females weigh about 650 pounds, males reach up to 1,500 pounds. Because the islands are isolated and difficult for land mammals to colonize, the only other terrestrial mammals that occur naturally here are the red fox, river otter, short-tailed weasel, little brown myotis (a type of bat), and tundra vole. Birds, however, are another story: more than 210 species have been recorded. An estimated 2 million seabirds and 200,000 waterfowl winter in the protected bays and inlets, and 200 pairs of bald eagles—easily visible with their white heads and tails—nest in the refuge.

BRISTOL BAY

West of Kodiak Island and Katmai National Park, on the Alaska Peninsula's opposite shore, is Bristol Bay, a southeastern arm of the Bering Sea that is home to the richest sockeye salmon fishery in the world. Within this bay, some 250 miles southwest of King Salmon, are the islands of the **Walrus Islands State Game Sanctuary❖**, the most famous of which is **Round Island,** where up to 15,000 Pacific walruses haul ashore for the summer. Most are younger, nonmating bulls, who blanket the beach, snorting, snoring, and occasionally swinging their great tusks at one another. Steller sea lions also gather here, and red foxes den on the upper, grassy slopes. To gain access to the sanctuary you must register with the Alaska Department of Fish and Game. To get there, take a commercial flight from Anchorage to Dillingham, an air taxi to Togiak, and a charter boat across Bristol Bay to the island.

Due north of Bristol Bay, near Dillingham, the Nushagak River leads into the lake-studded, mountain-rimmed country of **Wood-Tikchik State Park❖**. Fish and wildlife abound here, including all five species of Pacific salmon, and the opportunities for canoeing, kayaking, and rafting are excellent, as many of the lakes are interconnected by rivers. The best route is to fly commercially from Anchorage to Dillingham and charter a small plane from there.

ALASKA PENINSULA

Immediately south of Katmai down the Alaska Peninsula lies **Becharof National Wildlife Refuge❖** (best reached by airplane from King Salmon), another casualty from the *Exxon Valdez* oil spill. Puale Bay, once famous for its thriving colonies of seabirds—among the largest on the Alaska Peninsula—was lathered in oil in 1989. Sea cliffs

211

once pulsated with the antics and aerobatics of puffins, murres, kittiwakes, and cormorants; vociferous harbor seals and sea lions hauled themselves up on the rocks below. All is relatively quiet today.

Inland, the 1.2-million-acre refuge is dominated by Becharof Lake, the second largest lake in Alaska (after Iliamna). The western side of this refuge is lake-filled lowlands, while the eastern side, toward the coast, is crowned by the Aleutian Range. As many as 115,000 caribou migrate through the refuge and winter here, and salmon streams attract brown bears every summer and fall.

On a clear day, which is a rare occurrence here, the Becharof horizon is broken by three volcanoes: Mount Peulik, which erupted in 1814 and 1852, Mount Ugashik, and Mount Becharof. An unusual volcanic feature in the refuge is Ukinrek Maars, two huge steam explosion craters formed from a series of eruptions in 1977 near the south shore of Becharof Lake.

Most of the Alaska Peninsula south and west of Becharof is contained within the 4.3-million-acre **Alaska Peninsula National Wildlife Refuge❖.** The Aleutian Range dominates the refuge with active volcanoes, while the surrounding topography comprises lakes, rivers, tundra, and a rugged stretch of coast. Mount Veniaminof, midway down the length of the refuge, last erupted in 1993 with a light dusting of ash and could erupt again at any time. High winds and fluctuating temperatures characterize this area, and severe storms occur year-round. The pristine, glacial-fed Black and Chignik lakes buzz with activity in July and August, when hundreds of bears arrive to gorge on swarms of salmon. The entire refuge plays host to a welter of large and beautiful fish, including northern pike, Arctic grayling, and Dolly Varden; catch-and-release fishing is recommended, so others can enjoy the wonders of these Alaskan fish. The refuge also supports strong populations of other wildlife, including staging waterfowl on their way to and from nesting grounds in the Arctic. The world's entire population of emperor geese—an estimated 100,000 birds with handsome white heads and black throats—migrates through here every year. The area is accessible by scheduled and small charter flights from Anchorage to Port Heider and Cold Bay.

RIGHT: *Horned puffins, versatile seabirds that use their wings to swim as well as fly, survey the waves and rocky cliffs of Bristol Bay's Round Island, in the Walrus Island State Game Sanctuary.*

ABOVE: *Conservationist Henry W. Elliott, who campaigned for 40 years to stop the slaughter of northern fur seals in the Pribilof Islands, depicted himself amid a thriving seal colony in this 1872 self-portrait.*

Splitting the Alaska Peninsula National Wildlife Refuge in two is **Aniakchak National Monument and Preserve❖**, 10 miles east of Port Heiden and 150 miles southwest of King Salmon. The focal point here is the 6-mile-wide, 2,000-foot-deep **Aniakchak Crater,** a caldera that last erupted in 1931 and has been described as "a world within a world." Volcanic basalt and pumice texture the slopes inside, and warm springs color the rocks red with iron oxide. **Surprise Lake** reaches more than two miles across the caldera floor and sustains Dolly Varden char and sockeye salmon. Of the more than 300 units within the U.S. National Park Service system nationwide, Aniakchak is perhaps the least visited. In some years only a few hundred adventurers come here. The best access is to fly commercially to King Salmon or Port Heiden and take an air charter from there. The Aniakchak coast can be reached by boat from Kodiak or Chignik.

Near the southwestern tip of the Alaska Peninsula is **Izembek**

National Wildlife Refuge❖: 320,000 acres of glacial-capped volcanoes, tundra uplands, nameless streams, trackless sand dunes, barrier
islands, and, most important for wildlife, lagoons. Izembek Lagoon, the
largest of several in the refuge, contains an 84,000-acre eelgrass bed
that feeds hundreds of thousands of geese on their southbound migrations every fall. Nearly the entire population of black brant, 120,000 to
150,000 birds, stops here to feed on the eelgrass, as do an estimated
50,000 Canada geese and 80,000 emperor geese. By November most
of the geese have gone, and a new wave of birds has arrived: mostly
sea ducks here to spend the winter in the lagoons, protected from
storms on the Bering Sea. Izembek can be reached by flying from
Anchorage to Cold Bay and traveling overland a few miles by road
from there.

ALEUTIAN AND PRIBILOF ISLANDS

The **Aleutian Islands** swing like a mammoth's tusk 1,200 miles from
the end of the Alaska Peninsula, near Izembek NWR, toward the
Kamchatka Peninsula and the Russian Far East. The longest archipelago of small islands in the world, it is actually made up of the summits
of volcanoes rising above the surface of the North Pacific. Mount
Shishaldin, 9,372 feet above sea level and 34,472 feet from the sea
floor, is the highest.

This is inclement, treeless, volcanic country where a featureless
fetch of sea breaks its back on remote shores. It rains or snows here
more than 200 days a year. Of the 124 islands in the chain, all but 5
are part of the **Alaska Maritime National Wildlife Refuge❖,** which
consists of 2,400 parcels of land (most of them in the Aleutians) reaching from Forrester Island in southeastern Alaska to Cape Lisburne in
the Chukchi Sea, 150 miles north of the Arctic Circle. Roughly 75 percent of Alaska's seabirds—15 million to 30 million individuals belong-
ing to 55 species—nest, feed, or rest in this refuge.

The Aleutian unit of the Alaska Maritime NWR pulsates in summertime with nesting seabirds, primarily murres, cormorants, auklets,
puffins, and kittiwakes. **Unimak Island,** at the beginning of the archipelago near the Alaska Peninsula, marks the western natural limit of
caribou, brown bears, wolves, wolverines, ground squirrels, and
weasels. Nearly all the mammals that occur beyond here were intro-

215

duced by humans: rats, sheep, cattle, foxes, and horses. The results have been less than beneficial, as rats and foxes have ravaged some bird nesting areas, eating unprotected chicks and eggs. Wildlife biologists have begun to eradicate the introduced animals in the most sensitive nesting areas, and the results are slow but promising.

Commercial flights regularly connect Anchorage and Dutch Harbor, the busiest town in the Aleutians, where planes and boats can be chartered to other areas. A state ferry, the MV *Tustumena*, runs between Seward and Homer (on the Kenai Peninsula) and Dutch Harbor every summer, stopping at settlements on the Alaska Peninsula along the way.

Cradled above the Aleutian chain is the Bering Sea, a relatively shallow, storm-tossed area from which millions of tons of fish and crab are removed every year by commercial fishing. The bounteous conditions would remain if the fishing industry were properly policed and the quotas maintained at safe margins, but greed prevails. Thus an industry that could be stable is not, and the entire Bering Sea ecosystem—including its fish, seabirds, and marine mammals—remains endangered.

Anchored in isolation 250 miles north-northwest of Dutch Harbor are the **Pribilof Islands.** The sea cliffs and shores of the Pribilofs are not only alive with birds and seals, they are approachable, too. Commercial flights three times a week in summer connect Anchorage with Saint Paul, the largest town on the largest island in the archipelago, from which tour buses travel dirt roads to the bird colonies and seal rookeries.

The Pribilof Islands, also part of the Alaska Maritime NWR, are a volcanic cluster rather than a chain of islands. The jagged rocks have been worn smooth by the shuffling of northern fur seals that have hauled out here every summer for hundreds, perhaps thousands of years. Their grunts and growls fill the salty, misty air as the bulls fight for females, and the pups bellow for their mothers. The future here is uncertain, however, since major changes in the Bering Sea fishery could threaten the birds and seals that depend on those fish—and the people of the Pribilofs as well.

RIGHT: *Northern fur seal bulls, cows, and pups congregate on a bouldered beach of Saint Paul Island in the Pribilofs. The bulls defend their harems, challenging all intruders (note the male in the lower center).*

INTERIOR ALASKA

Interior Alaska is the broad, riverine foreland in central Alaska that lies between the Alaska Range to the south and the Brooks Range to the north. It is a land dominated by subtle contours more than dramatic ones. Winter brings pastel dusks at midday, popping river ice at minus 50 degrees Fahrenheit, curtains and spirals of northern lights, and caribou haloed by their own breath. With summer comes the gift of light as night becomes day. Fairbanksans play softball past midnight, birds sing across green tundra, and rivers flow freely again.

The state's largest river, the Yukon, begins in Canada and enters eastern Alaska near the town of Eagle, then runs 1,265 miles westward through the interior before emptying into the Bering Sea. The interior contains Alaska's other largest rivers as well—the Porcupine, Koyukuk, Kuskokwim, Tanana, and Innoko—wide and turbid waters running past forests of birch, aspen, and spruce.

This is a region of tundra and taiga. *Tundra,* a word synonymous with the north, is treeless and windswept with moisture-retaining soils that freeze and thaw seasonally. Three types of tundra—wet, moist, and alpine—support low-growing vegetation composed of woody shrubs, such as willow and dwarf birch, and delicate wildflowers, mosses, and

---

LEFT: *Dall sheep rams rest above the lower Sanctuary River in Denali National Park. While these sheep enjoy relative safety, others in Alaska fall victim to trophy hunters, some of whom hunt in parks illegally.*

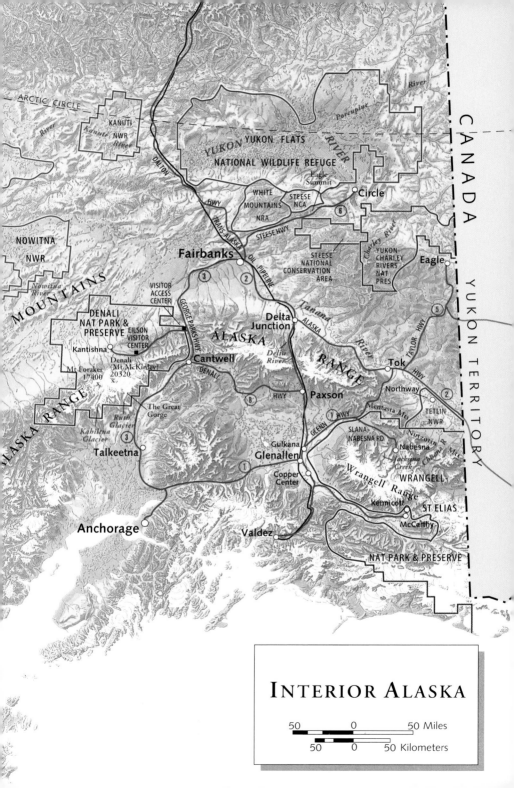

INTERIOR ALASKA

50   0   50 Miles

50   0   50 Kilometers

lichens. *Taiga,* a Russian word that means "land of little sticks," refers to the vast boreal forests of white and black spruce common throughout the region (and in parts of south-central Alaska as well). The more robust white spruce grows in drier soils, while thin and spindly black spruce—almost sickly in appearance—lives in wetter soils.

A continental climate prevails over the interior, with extreme temperatures reaching 80 to 90 degrees Fahrenheit in summer and minus 50 to minus 60 degrees Fahrenheit in winter. Because this region is so far north and so cold, the tree line averages only 1,500 to 2,500 feet above sea level. Annual precipitation averages 12 inches.

Surprisingly, vast portions of the interior were not glaciated during the end of the Pleistocene epoch, or Ice Age, 10,000 to 25,000 years ago. Massive glaciers covered much of Alaska then, grinding mountains and sharpening ridges to the south and north while the interior remained largely ice-free. Thus, older landscapes exist here, with intermittent communities of plants that represent Pleistocene Alaska. They are islands in time, what ecologists call "refugia." In the Bering Land Bridge and Yukon–Charley Rivers national preserves, for example, these refugia of remnant Ice Age vegetation occur as arctic steppe and tundra, and in some places refugia contain species of woody and flowering plants found nowhere else in the world.

Fire also plays a dominant role in the ecology of the interior. In years of heavy burning, more than 500 separate fires can ignite more than one million acres in this region, with some 80 percent of the fires resulting from summer storms and lightning. The fires help in cycling nutrients through the tundra and taiga, creating a matrix of habitat types and new browse for wildlife.

The centerpiece of this chapter, and of much of Alaska's tourism, is Denali National Park and Preserve, formerly Mount McKinley National Park. Despite its popularity and growing crowds, Denali has an enduring ability to lift one's gaze—and spirits—to the frozen spires of the Alaska Range, down the twisting rivers of sweeping valleys, and across the tundra, where caribou, moose, grizzlies, and wolves ap-

---

RIGHT: *Sunrise warms the shoreline grasses in Tetlin National Wildlife Refuge, near Tok. Waterfowl nest here in huge numbers each summer and fly south for the winter, leaving the refuge cold, white, and silent.*

pear. The clouds roll in and out; but look again, the highest of them might not be a cloud at all, but 20,320-foot Mount McKinley, the tallest mountain in North America, more properly called Denali, the native Athabascan word meaning "the high one."

Whereas most of the places discussed in this chapter are reachable only by boat or plane in summer, or by snowmobile, dogsled, or skiplane in winter, Denali is an exception, accessible via the George Parks Highway.

This chapter begins in the east with Tetlin National Wildlife Refuge (along the Alaska-Canada boundary) and moves westward, ending with Alaska's western and Bering Sea coasts, including Nunivak Island, most of which lies within Yukon Delta National Wildlife Refuge.

EASTERN ALASKA

The 730,000-acre **Tetlin National Wildlife Refuge❖,** created in 1980, contains the broad basins and twisting tributaries of the Chisana and Tanana rivers, plus marshes, lakes, foothills, and some of the Nutzotin and Mentasta mountains. It is a diverse, variegated landscape, rendered dark green by spruce, light green by aspen and birch, whitened in winter, and patterned with waters both flowing and still.

From this refuge the Tanana River flows 400 miles to the Yukon River, which continues another 600 miles to the Bering Sea. This thousand-mile journey takes the water approximately six days. Salmon make the trip every year, and northern pike and whitefish also swim these waters. Within the refuge nesting and migrating waterfowl are common, with some parts of the refuge containing as many as 600 nesting ducks—of 17 species—per square mile. Watch for them from the Alaska Highway, which parallels the Tanana. More than 300,000 sandhill cranes rest and feed here during migration, spiraling up and down in great, gray clouds, calling on the wing in high, rhapsodic trills. Since the creation of the refuge the resident trumpeter swan population has risen from approximately 50 to 350. Lynx, the only wildcats in Alaska, also make a good living here. With broad feet, high hips, and long back legs, they are well adapted for bounding after snowshoe hares, their preferred prey. Beavers, black and grizzly bears, and moose live here as well, and Dall sheep cavort in the mountains.

The Tetlin region is one of the coldest places in Alaska, with winter

224

temperatures often lingering at minus 40 degrees Fahrenheit and sometimes plunging to minus 70. To reach the heart of the refuge requires a
boat or plane in summer (air charter from the nearby town of Tok) or
dogsled, snowmobile, or ski-plane in winter. At Northway Junction,
highway mile 1,264, a dirt road branches south and runs nine miles
into the refuge to the village of Northway. Although much of the surrounding land is owned by the Tetlin Indians and may not be entered
without permission, the road itself is open to the public and offers
good views of ponds and forests.

At mile 1,301.7, the Taylor Highway (usually open from April to
October) branches north off the Alcan Highway and runs 161 miles to
Eagle, a hamlet of independent people colorfully recorded in John
McPhee's 1976 book *Coming into the Country*. Eagle sits on the Yukon
River, which in turn flows northwest and enters nearby **Yukon
–Charley Rivers National Preserve❖**, a 2.5-million-acre wilderness
watershed that preserves both human and natural history. Decaying
mining cabins and rusting dredges can be found throughout the area
from the turn-of-the-century heyday of Klondike stampeders.

The heart of this preserve is its showpiece: the Charley River and watershed. Because this area produced no valuable ore and stirred little interest among miners, it is one of the most pristine river systems in
Alaska, an officially designated wild and scenic river. The Charley glides
and riffles northbound past tundra, muskeg, and hills and mountains
cloaked in spruce. In autumn the tundra turns red, while riverside birch-
es and cottonwoods turn gold. The clear waters of the Charley join the
brown of the Yukon, then flow northwest through the top of the preserve, passing below towering bluffs more than a thousand feet high.

Although lynx, moose, black bears, brown bears, wolves, wolverines, Dall sheep, and beavers live in the preserve, the most noteworthy
resident is the peregrine falcon. Victimized by DDT and other pesti-
cides, it has rebounded from darker days and established a secure
home here. The riverside bluffs offer good nesting habitat from which
the adults can dive at more than 200 miles per hour at their prey: primarily birds, plus small mammals and fish.

Ecologically, this preserve stands out as a refugium because it was
spared by the most recent tide of continental glaciation that buried
much of northern North America (including Alaska) as recently as

ABOVE: *The distinctive silhouettes of sandhill cranes fill the skies of Denali National Park each fall during their migration south from nesting areas*

10,000 years ago. There are no granite monoliths or deep blue glaciers here, but rather mysteries and half-hidden eloquences revealed in subtle patterns of vegetation, permafrost, and soil chemistry.

Fire plays a major role here, changing and cycling the plant community's composition of trees, shrubs, and herbs, and modifying the underlying layer of permafrost. But although fire is important, it occurs best on its own natural timetable. In the summer of 1990, U.S. Air Force jets dropped hot flares into the preserve during low-flying com-

in northern Alaska and Siberia. One of the oldest bird species in the world, cranes mate for life and fly at elevations greater than 10,000 feet.

bat training runs and ignited a fire that accidentally destroyed 30,000 acres, including peregrine habitat. Furthermore, the sonic booms from the jets flushed birds off their nests. A subsequent inquiry asked how much of our natural heritage must be sacrificed to maintain our national defense. The answers are pending.

Although the Yukon River has a lot of motorized traffic, visitors can take float trips on it through the preserve (trips begin in Eagle). Charter flights to the quiet Charley River can be arranged out of Eagle, Circle,

Tok, or Fairbanks. Besides Eagle, those with cars can also drive to Circle, on the western, downriver side of the preserve, by taking the Steese Highway 162 miles out of Fairbanks. (Both the Taylor and Steese highways are unpaved.)

Due west of the Yukon-Charley area, beyond the town of Circle, the Steese Highway skirts the edges of **Steese National Conservation Area❖** and **White Mountains National Recreation Area❖.** The Bureau of Land Management (BLM), which administers both areas, permits commercial mining, and the resulting physical, chemical, and biological damage is significant in some places. Yet throughout the areas one can still find large sections of pristine country: rolling mountains blanketed in spruce, quiet tundra meadows, windswept ridges, and serpentine streams.

Every February, when the land is whitened with snow, mushers and huskies travel over nearby Eagle Summit during the Yukon-Quest International Sled Dog Race, a thousand-mile wilderness epic that runs between Fairbanks, Alaska, and Whitehorse, in Canada's Yukon Territory. (The race also follows the Yukon River between Circle and Eagle, through Yukon–Charley Rivers National Preserve).

The Steese National Conservation Area straddles the Steese Highway and contains a portion of the Tanana-Yukon uplands, where the spruce forest thins into single, isolated trees that eventually surrender to alpine tundra. The dark trees punctuate the scene nicely, especially in autumn when the tundra turns burnt red. In the forested valleys, eroded stream banks sometimes expose sections of permafrost and the fossil remains of mastodons and other Pleistocene mammals. The **Pinnell Mountain National Recreation Trail** is the best access into the uplands here, at mile 85.6 and mile 107 on the Steese Highway. Displays of alpine wildflowers here are stunning in June, as red, pink, white, yellow, and blue blossoms create a botanical rainbow across the tundra. In the summer months, such birds as Lapland longspurs, Baird's sandpipers, water pipits, and northern wheatears visit the area.

Rising above 3,500 feet, the White Mountains form a rampart of limestone pinnacles and rounded, eroded shoulders. Whereas the upper elevations are windblown and treeless, the valleys below contain spruce forests with open patches of wet, treeless, subarctic bogs. Eighteen miles of hiking trails and 200 miles of skiing and snowmobile trails run through the area—some of them to cozy log cabins, which offer some breathtaking, moonlit views. Many of the trails are reachable via the Steese Highway from Fairbanks.

Due north of the White Mountains, the physical geography flattens out and opens to the Yukon River and the 8.63-million-acre **Yukon Flats National Wildlife Refuge❖**, one of the most productive waterfowl areas on the continent. The refuge contains more than 400 lakes and countless meandering streams that are home to the densest concentrations of nesting ducks in Alaska. Practically any lake, pond, or marsh is a summer home and nursery for the many species that come here to raise families. Scaup and pintails are the most abundant, and 10 percent of North America's canvasbacks breed here. The mighty Yukon bends and bows beneath a great dome of blue sky in summer and freezes solid in winter, the ice more than five feet thick. Come the warmth of spring, the ice pops and thunders as the current moves below it, then a piece suddenly breaks apart and washes downriver, melting as it goes. The refuge turns blue and green again, and the ducks return. Air taxi operators can bring visitors into the refuge from Fairbanks and Fort Yukon. Boaters can access the refuge from Circle and from the Dalton Highway, which runs from Fairbanks up along the refuge's western side.

DENALI NATIONAL PARK AND PRESERVE
Southwest of Fairbanks, situated in the middle of the state, is the focal point on the maps and minds of practically everyone interested in Alaska, **Denali National Park and Preserve❖**. At six million acres, it is roughly the size of Massachusetts (you could explore a thousand acres a day, every day for 16 years, and still not cover it all). A handsome blend of multihued tundra and taiga extends over the open valleys and broad vistas, lifting at its edges into the icy, crenulated peaks of the Alaska Range. Most visitors experience Denali from a bus tour on the road, and this in itself can be a fulfilling journey. Yet stronger hearts believe the true park experience—the Denali wilderness—occurs away from the road, across the tundra, and up the treeless ridges where the sights and sounds of people and buses give way to the chatterings of arctic ground squirrels, the melodies of white-crowned sparrows, the clicking of caribou hooves, the aerobatics of gyrfalcons,

the sudden and heart-pounding glimpse of a grizzly bear.

Hiking in the park is excellent, and ranger-led "discover" hikes (three to six hours long) occur every day in summer. Well-developed trails are rare, but the tundra generally offers solid, dry footing (except after a rain), and one can usually see what routes are available up ahead. Backpackers headed into the backcountry for overnight stays must register at the Visitor Access Center; so must visitors wishing to stay in the park's designated campgrounds. The crowds at the park entrance can be daunting, but they're manageable—and Denali is worth it.

Because it is the most accessible, well known, and heavily visited national park in the state, Denali has become the Yellowstone of Alaska. Nearly every visitor comes here to see the "wildlife grand slam"—grizzly bear, Dall sheep, caribou, moose, and wolf—and the highest mountain in North America, Mount McKinley, all in one day. To see a mountain that big, however—a mountain that makes its own weather—requires a clear day, and the odds for that in summer are only about 30 percent. The best rule for visiting Denali is to allow at least three days to explore the options, beat the crowds, and take advantage of the mercurial weather.

The entrance to Denali is at mile 237.3 on the George Parks Highway between Anchorage and Fairbanks. In summer, public transportation makes the trip every day, as does the historic, colorful, and comfortable Alaska Railroad. In the 1920s and 1930s, a 90-mile stretch of dirt road was built through the park to the mining settlement of Kantishna. Back then, the only way to reach the park entrance was by railroad. That changed in 1972 with the completion of the George Parks Highway, and annual visitation jumped that year from 44,000 to 88,000. Today an average of 250,000 people visit the park annually.

To minimize traffic and maximize driver safety and wildlife sightings along the road, the National Park Service oversees a shuttle bus system that runs from the Visitor Access Center (VAC, at mile 0.7 on the park road) to Eielson Visitor Center (VC, at mile 66) and beyond to the end

---

LEFT: *In Denali National Park, a shuttle bus carries visitors over 3,700-foot Polychrome Pass, above the braided rivers on the Plains of Murie.*

OVERLEAF: *Seen from 30 miles away at Wonder Lake, Denali —or Mount McKinley—rises to 20,320 feet, the highest point in North America.*

of the line at Wonder Lake (mile 86.1), five miles shy of Kantishna. The round-trip journey from the VAC to Eielson VC takes eight hours, to Wonder Lake ten and a half hours. Bus drivers use elaborate hand signals to tell each other what wildlife they have seen and where. Buses regularly stop for five or ten minutes to watch Dall sheep cross the road, or a moose browse on willow, or a grizzly eat berries or chase an arctic ground squirrel. Should the squirrel dash down one of its burrows, the bear will dig after it, sometimes excavating a pit three feet deep and five feet wide.

About a thousand people make the journey to Eielson every summer day, and roughly 95 percent see grizzly bears, Dall sheep, and caribou. Approximately 250 grizzly bears live in the park, some of them Toklat grizzlies, a strikingly handsome blond variety of bear. The incidence of problematic bear-human encounters has been extremely low since overnight backpackers have been required to carry their food in bear-resistant containers (available at the VAC).

Roughly 80 percent of visitors see moose and 15 percent see wolves, or a single wolf, as pack hunting in winter gives way to solitary hunting in summer. Some 30 percent of summer visitors to the park are treated to a clear view of Denali, "the great one," also known as Mount McKinley. Thirty-three air miles due west of Eielson Visitor Center, it rises like a citadel of ice, rock, and snow, gleaming in sunshine and brooding clouds, 20,320 feet above sea level.

As many as a thousand moun-taineers test their mettle on Denali and its satellite peaks each year, usually from April to June; about half reach the summit. Most begin in Talkeetna, a small town south of the park, from which they fly in small wheeled ski-planes to the 7,200-foot-level of the Kahiltna Glacier, one of 17 major rivers of ice that flow down the flanks of Denali. From the Kahiltna the long climb begins. The average time up and back is three weeks, although storms can trap climbers for many days. More than 60 mountaineers are known to have died on the mountain, and half of those are still up there, entombed in ice.

The air taxis of Talkeetna em-ploy some of the best glacier pilots in the world, and a flight-seeing trip with them is an exhilarating

ABOVE: *Preeminent symbol of wilderness in Alaska, a grizzly bear stands amid dwarf birch and blueberries in autumn color in Denali National Park.*

LEFT: *A sure sign of summer, tall red fireweed blankets a meadow in southeastern Denali National Park, home to more than 300 species of flowering plants.*

experience. A 90-minute charter flight will sweep you over the broad tun-dra forelands, past the icy spires of the Alaska Range, into the granite canyons of the Ruth Glacier and Great Gorge—a rock-ribbed vault of ver-tical granite walls and hanging glaciers—and perhaps even land on the ice at 5,500 feet in the Don Sheldon Amphitheater.

To ease trip preparations, contact the Alaska Public Lands

Information Center in Anchorage or Fairbanks months before planning to arrive in Denali.

THE SOLAR BASIN REFUGES

Northwest of Denali, the Alaska Range melts into lowlands of rivers, lakes, marshes, and wet tundra. Here the mighty Yukon River flows like a great, brown sheet, heavy with suspended sediment, more than a mile wide in some places. It skirts the edges of **Nowitna National Wildlife Refuge❖** and **Innoko National Wildlife Refuge❖,** and nearly touches **Koyukuk National Wildlife Refuge❖.** Farther to the north lies **Kanuti National Wildlife Refuge❖.** Each is within a solar basin: an area of encircling hills with light winds, little rain, long, dark, severe winters, and warm summers blessed with 24-hour sunlight.

Waterfowl thrive in the wetlands of each of these refuges. In Nowitna NWR northern pike and sheefishes spawn up the Nowitna River, while black bears, marten, and mink inhabit the forests. Innoko NWR is roughly 80 percent wetlands, providing good nesting grounds for a quarter million geese and ducks. Beavers are especially abundant here; some years 40 percent of all beavers trapped in Alaska are caught in this refuge. Koyukuk NWR contains 14 rivers and hundreds of creeks, plus one of only two actively shifting sand-dune fields in Alaska: the 10,000-acre **Nogahabara Dunes,** created from windblown deposits 10,000 years ago. (Alaska's other dunes are in Kobuk Valley National Park in the Arctic). Kanuti NWR, straddling the Arctic Circle, contains important waterfowl habitat and supports 16 species of fish.

Each of these refuges is roadless, remote, and lightly visited by people, most of whom come to hunt, trap, or fish. All four can be accessed by charter flights and boats (all are named for the rivers that flow through them). Contact refuge offices or the nearest town for information.

Selawik National Wildlife Refuge❖ lies directly northwest of Koyukuk NWR. A world of water, Selawik's wetlands, lakes, estuaries, river deltas, and tundra slopes provide valuable nesting sites for migratory birds from North and South America, Asia, and even Australia. The western Arctic caribou herd migrates through here as well, feeding on the lichen-covered hills. The Selawik River twists and winds through the center of the refuge. To get here, take a commercial flight from Anchorage to Kotzebue, then fly by small plane into the refuge. Selawik is also reachable by boat from Kotzebue, though it requires crossing Hotham Inlet (Kobuk Lake), which can be treacherous in strong winds.

SEWARD PENINSULA–YUKON DELTA AREA

Due west of Kanuti and Koyukuk refuges, the **Seward Peninsula** challenges the Bering Sea as it juts westward to within 50 miles of the Russian Far East. The northern flank of this peninsula touches the Arctic Circle and contains the 2.8-million-acre **Bering Land Bridge National Preserve❖**. This preserve sits on the coast of the Bering Strait, which today separates Asia from North America. But 10,000 to 25,000 years ago, when sea level was lower (because more of the earth's water was invested in continental glaciers), the Bering Strait did not exist. In its place was a bridge of land—a broad causeway, in fact—connecting Alaska and Siberia. Where whales and seals now swim people once walked across dry land to become the first North Americans.

Besides its anthropological significance, the preserve also contains sea cliffs where birds of prey nest, lagoons where waterfowl nest, and granite promontories rising above carpets of red Kamchatka rhododendrons. Lava beds betray a volcanic past here, as does Serpentine Hot Springs, a favorite among visitors, where 140-degree water is piped into a covered pool. Bering Land Bridge National Preserve can be accessed by charter plane from Kotzebue and Nome (both are serviced daily by commercial flights from Anchorage).

Due south of the Seward Peninsula and across Norton Sound, the Alaskan landscape spreads out in a seemingly endless maze of water and tundra where the mighty Yukon River empties into the Bering Sea to form one of the largest deltas in the United States. Just south of the Yukon, the Kuskokwim, another great river, meets the sea. The 19.6-million-acre **Yukon Delta National Wildlife Refuge❖** encompasses the final stretch of both rivers, and their deltas, and everything in between, including the center of today's Yupik Eskimo culture. Forty-two villages punctuate this refuge, comprising the largest concentration of Eskimo in Alaska. Airplane navigational charts of this refuge list "many small lakes," and flying over it shows that description to be an understatement: There are more than 40,000.

The largest wildlife refuge in the world, it was created in 1980, and is immeasurably valuable for waterfowl. More than 20 million migratory

237

birds use it each year. Arriving and departing, they create great feathered clouds calling on the wing and skirting the sky. But once on the ground, or on the lakes and in the marshes, they assume quieter profiles, raising their young in grassy nests. The world's entire population of cackling Canada geese nest here, as do 90 percent of the Pacific Flyway's greater white-fronted geese, 50 percent of the world's bristle-thighed curlews, 80 percent of the Pacific Flyway's tundra swans, 80 percent of the world's emperor geese, and 50 percent of North America's black brants. From a small plane, the swans below, arrayed in pairs—they mate for life—stand out like white pearls on a canvas of blue water and green marsh. More than 170 species of birds (including all 4 species of eiders, one of which is threatened) and 43 species of mammals occur here regularly.

The easiest access to the refuge is by commercial jet from Anchorage to Bethel and by small plane from there. Much of the land within the refuge is owned by the Yupik Eskimo. It is important to check with refuge headquarters in Bethel before planning a trip.

ABOVE: *An estimated 7,000 wolves range throughout Alaska; amid great controversy, some have recently been culled by the state.*

RIGHT: *Volcanic spires punctuate the windswept tundra close to Serpentine Hot Springs, near the Bering Land Bridge preserve.*

A final treat is **Nunivak Island,** just off the coast of the refuge, with its volcanic cones, sea cliffs, and saltwater lagoons accessible by air via Anchorage and Bethel. Most noteworthy is the island's population of musk oxen: shaggy-haired animals with high shoulders and sweeping horns that form a line, shoulder to shoulder, to protect their young when approached. Wiped out by hunters in 1865, musk oxen were reintroduced in Alaska from Greenland around 1930 and are thriving today. Like every other species, they add an important brush stroke to the wilderness canvas of Alaska, standing on the edge of land and sea, past and present.

ARCTIC ALASKA

If any part of Alaska is a land of extremes, it is the Arctic. Sweeping across the northern fifth of the state, it dwells in total darkness for three months during winter and basks in 24-hour daylight for three months during summer. January finds it frozen and dormant; June finds it bursting with life.

"There was a peculiar feeling about this mild and melting spring landscape that made an impression upon me," wrote Danish explorer Knud Rasmussen about Alaska's Arctic. "Without being able to explain why, I had ever the presentiment that I would meet something I had never seen before. Over the meadows there was the song of thousands of birds, one continuous tremulous tone of joy and life. I saw geese, ducks and eider ducks swimming about in all the lakes, and every time I approached they rose noisy and cackling, only to drop into the next lake. The swamps were full of wading birds building their nests and laying eggs, and all these voices from the thousands of birds joined into one great chorus singing that once again the earth lived."

Indeed, for those who truly appreciate wilderness, the earth lives in the Arctic. There are no containing walls here. The land rises in the weathered and broken vertebrae of the Brooks Range, an ancient bat-

---

LEFT: *Caribou antlers whiten in the russet, autumnal tundra at Onion Portage in Kobuk Valley National Park. Eskimos gather here to harvest caribou during their annual migration south from arctic calving grounds.*

tlement of peaks that form the northernmost mountain range in North America and run the width of the state, 650 miles east to west, across the Arctic. The Brooks Range is also the continental divide; every river flowing off its southern side empties into the Bering Sea, part of the Pacific Ocean; every river flowing off its northern side empties into the Beaufort Sea, part of the Arctic Ocean.

The rivers themselves are among the wildest and most pristine in the world. Gates of the Arctic National Park and Preserve, straddling the heart of the Brooks Range, contains six nationally designated wild and scenic rivers. The Noatak, which begins in Gates of the Arctic and flows some 400 miles west through Noatak National Preserve, is the largest wilderness river basin in the world; it is largely unpeopled and rimmed by distant mountains that have seldom felt the tread of human feet.

While the relatively moist southern side of the Brooks Range supports trees, the dry northern side does not. Here the land descends from the mountains into the North Slope, and ultimately flattens out to form the broad, flat coastal plain. Most geographers consider this region a desert because it receives less than ten inches of precipitation a year. Strictly speaking, they are correct. But when flying over the North Slope and Arctic coastal plain in summer one sees water everywhere: pooled in bogs, lakes, and lagoons; in moist, spongy tundra; meandering in rivulets, streams, and rivers. Although little precipitation occurs here, what does fall tends to stay awhile. Cool temperatures minimize evaporation, and underlying permafrost—a matrix of ice and rock that begins just below the surface and continues as deep as 2,000 feet—creates an impervious layer in the ground, trapping water near the surface each summer.

The wind can blow for days on end in this part of Alaska. Temperatures can drop below freezing anytime, and fog blowing on-shore from the Arctic Ocean can chill campers to the bone. Hiking can be downright frustrating in tufted, ankle-twisting mounds of vegetation called tussocks that form through cycles of freezing and thawing. Arctic Alaska is not a gentle landscape.

"A flat, crummy place," an Alaskan oil executive once called the coastal plain of the Arctic National Wildlife Refuge, adding that, "only for oil would anybody want to go there." How wrong he was. Asked to de-scribe the same area, an environmentalist said it was beyond description,

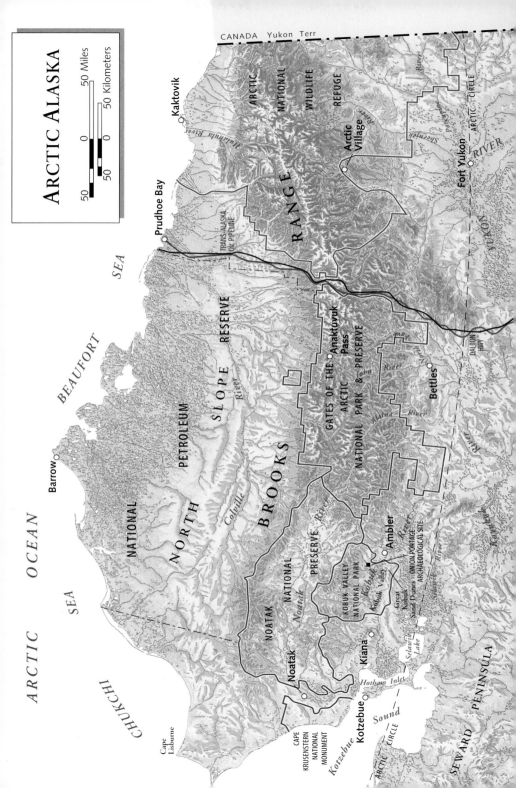

like "the smile on the Mona Lisa."

Every year more and more people raft the rivers, climb the mountains, and hike the tundra of this refuge and other wild places in the Arctic. They discover a difficult land, but a land of magic and serendipity as well. Here the midnight sun glides along the northern horizon, casting cinnabar light across the tundra, tempting visitors to stay up until four o'clock in the morning, when the sun is low and the light warm, and sleep until noon. Musk oxen, grizzly bears, foxes, and wolves roam the landscape while plovers, sandpipers, horned larks, and other birds—some from as far away as Central America and Asia—nest on the open tundra, practicing the art of inconspicuousness. Occasionally snowy owls and golden eagles come into view. Intrepid visitors might find themselves in the midst of a caribou herd, mesmerized as thousands of animals walk by, flowing around them in a great, braided river of antlers, legs, and hooves. It has been said that when the caribou pass, the whole earth appears to move; when they run, the earth rumbles.

Caribou are to Arctic Alaska what bison once were to the Great Plains: They define the magnitude of the wilderness and are extremely important to the native people, the Iupiat Eskimo, who live throughout the region. Three distinct herds—the western Arctic herd, the central Arctic herd, and the

LEFT: *Caribou from the Porcupine herd migrate on the coastal plain of the Arctic National Wildlife Refuge, an American Serengeti next to the Beaufort Sea.*

Porcupine herd (named for the Porcupine River in Canada, where they spend the winter)—occupy Arctic Alaska, migrating between winter feeding grounds and summer calving grounds. Their numbers are highly cyclic. The western Arctic herd, for example, which contained about 75,000 animals in the early 1970s, grew to some 500,000 animals in the early 1990s. The other herds also expanded during that time. But as surely as their numbers go up, they come down, and no one is certain what exactly causes the cycles. As the Eskimo say, "No one knows the ways of the wind or the caribou."

Most visitors to the Arctic arrive by small charter plane. In summer, daily scheduled flights depart Fairbanks for Fort Yukon, Bettles, Arctic Village, Anaktuvuk Pass, Prudoe Bay, and Kaktovik (Barter Island). From any of these areas charter flights can be arranged into the Arctic National Wildlife Refuge and Gates of the Arctic National Park. Farther west, the Arctic can be accessed via Kotzebue (commercial flights operate daily from Anchorage), where scheduled flights leave daily for Ambler and Noatak. Charter flights can also be arranged out of Kotzebue and Ambler to reach Noatak National Preserve, Kobuk Valley National Park, and Cape Krusenstern National Monument.

Hiking is good in many of these areas, as long as one avoids tussocks. Recommendations are available from whatever agency or office administers the particular park, preserve, monument, or refuge you plan to visit. Don't overlook the possibility of a float trip (via raft, kayak, or canoe) down a river, especially a trip that allows time for day hiking as well as floating. Several wilderness guide companies offer these fun, safe introductions into a part of Alaska that can be beautiful if one is fully prepared—and frightening if one is not.

THE BROOKS RANGE

In the north-central reaches of Alaska is **Gates of the Arctic National Park and Preserve❖,** a bastion of jagged spires, wild rivers, and roadless, peopleless, nameless valleys. Of the eight million acres in this park and preserve, seven million are designated wilderness. Six nation-

---

RIGHT: *Autumn-tinted bearberry brightens the slopes of Boreal Mountain above the North Fork of the Koyukuk River where it flows through "the Gates" in Gates of the Arctic National Park.*

al wild and scenic rivers—the Alatna, John, Kobuk, Noatak, Tinayguk, and the North Fork of the Koyukuk—flow wholly or partially within the park. A thin mantle of life survives here, with alpine tundra on the mountain slopes and ridges, and birch, willow, alder, and spruce in the south-side river drainages.

Black bears, moose, and marten haunt the lowland forests, as do mink and porcupines. Beavers often swim the rivers and nearby ponds. Snowshoe hares dash for cover, and chattering red squirrels might be seen or heard amid the spruce. Grizzlies, wolverines, foxes, and wolves also inhabit river valleys, but they climb higher as well, forever in search of food. The highest alpinists of all are the majestic Dall sheep, foraging the summer alpine pastures and climbing narrow ledges and scree slopes thousands of feet above rivers. It takes a fine blend of patience and persistence to find wildlife here, for animals in the mountains and riverside vegetation are not as easily seen as those on the open coastal plain. Just because you don't see them doesn't mean they don't see you. River rafters can glide past a motionless moose 30 feet away in thick willows and not see it.

Gates of the Arctic was named by Robert Marshall, cofounder of the Wilderness Society, a hiker and bon vivant who explored here in 1929. Traveling with pack horses up the valley of the North Fork of the Koyukuk River, he recalled cresting a hill: "The view from the top gave us an excellent idea of the jagged country toward which we were heading. The main Brooks Range divide was entirely covered with snow. Close at hand, only about ten air miles to the north, was a precipitous pair of mountains, one on each side of the North Fork. I bestowed the name Gates of the Arctic on them, christening the east portal Boreal Mountain and the west portal Frigid Crags." (The Eskimo name for these mountains translates into "fingers of an outstretched hand.") Marshall dreamed of a wilderness park that would encompass and protect all of Alaska's Arctic, and although he and his colleagues didn't succeed on that scale, the park eventually established here is impressive.

The best access to Gates of the Arctic is via scheduled flight from Fairbanks to Bettles or Anaktuvuk Pass and by charter plane from there into the park, landing on whatever river bar or lake the pilot feels is safe. One can also drive north from Fairbanks on the Dalton Highway to Galbraith Lake and hike into the park from there.

With its headwaters in the western end of Gates of the Arctic National Park, the Noatak River flows west for 400 miles through wild, pristine Alaska, never dipping below the Arctic Circle. The centerpiece of **Noatak National Preserve❖**, the river riffles past rolling tundra, through two canyons and a forested floodplain, and finally empties into Kotzebue Sound, part of the Chukchi Sea. Knowing that a river such as this exists—that somewhere out there is a place still untouched, what author-historian Wallace Stegner called a "geography of hope"—can enrich a soul.

Except for about 700,000 acres of the lower river around the village of Noatak, this entire 6.6-million-acre preserve is designated wilderness. Many tributary rivers and streams join the Noatak, and migrating caribou follow the gentle contours in their annual migration between summer calving grounds to the north and winter feeding grounds to the south. Brown (grizzly) bears and black bears live here, as do moose, wolves, wolverines, and foxes, leaving their tracks in the mud and the sand along the river. The western, more mountainous end of the preserve, near the river's headwaters, contains Dall sheep.

As with most of the Arctic, the most popular time to visit here is June, July, and August. Fall colors, which can be brilliant reds, oranges, and yellows, usually peak in mid-August in the eastern, high elevation part of the preserve and late August in the western part. Access is gained via plane from Kotzebue (serviced by commercial flights daily from Anchorage) and Bettles (serviced by flights from Fairbanks). The most popular method of travel within the preserve is raft or kayak on the river.

South of the Noatak basin is another great river, the Kobuk, flowing through 1.7-million-acre **Kobuk Valley National Park❖**. Because this park is nestled on the south side of the Brooks Range—where precipitation is higher, and southern exposures gather more sunlight and warmth—trees are more numerous. The river itself averages four to five miles an hour in its quiet journey through the park, meandering past sandbars, oxbows, and handsome blends of spruce, birch, and open tundra.

Two features give this park special significance: the Great Kobuk Sand Dunes and the Onion Portage archaeological site. The **Great Kobuk Sand Dunes,** located just south of the Kobuk River midway between the villages of Ambler and Kiana, appear out of the boreal

ABOVE: *The Arctic explodes with wildflowers every June and July as it basks in nearly 24-hour sunlight. Blossoms fill the Jago River Valley, deep in the heart of the Brooks Range in the Arctic National Wildlife Refuge.*

forest like a little Sahara. Together with a smaller field of dunes only a few miles away, they cover 25 square miles, with the largest dunes reaching more than 100 feet high. This is the largest actively shifting dune field in Arctic North America. It can be reached by floating the Kobuk River to its confluence with Kavet Creek, then hiking a couple of miles along the creek to the dunes. Upriver from the dunes is **Onion Portage,** one of the most significant archaeological sites in Alaska. Here the Kobuk River makes a wide, six-mile-long loop that nearly doubles back on itself. By walking across the neck of the loop,

RIGHT: *Glistening after a summer thunderstorm, yellow arnica and blue lupine are part of a varied wildflower community that is important for feeding insects, birds, and other denizens of the Arctic.*

early travelers shortened their journeys on the river. The name comes from the small, edible wild onion, a distant cousin to commercial onions, that grew there. Evidence suggests that native peoples have used Onion Portage for more than 10,000 years, hunting caribou that migrate down from the north every fall and swim the river en route to wintering grounds to the south. Even today the river provides important access for Eskimo who travel by motorboat and hunt caribou with high-powered rifles. Subsistence hunting—an ancient way of life practiced with a modern twist—is permitted in this park and several others in Alaska.

The best way to experience the Kobuk Valley is via raft, kayak, or canoe, floating down the Kobuk River for a week from Ambler to Kiana. Several flights per day connect these villages with the town of Kotzebue (which in turn receives commercial flights daily from Anchorage). From mid-June to early September is the best time to visit, although insects can be bothersome from late June through July. Autumn colors peak the first week of September, at which time caribou can be seen swimming across the river. This is also when native villagers hunt caribou, a remarkable sight that some people find objectionable. Check with the National Park Service office in Kotzebue before planning a trip.

THE NORTHWEST COAST

Due west of the Kobuk Valley, not far above Kotzebue where Arctic Alaska meets the Chukchi Sea, the coastline sweeps to the northwest in a series of beach ridges, lagoons, lakes, and low hills that make up **Cape Krusenstern National Monument❖;** it is reachable by charter boat or plane from Kotzebue. Summer splashes the land with Kamchatka rhododendrons, yellow cinquefoils, and cream-colored rock jasmine. The ground is marked with wolves' tracks the size of a large human fist and the tracks of red foxes, small and evenly spaced, made by an animal almost always trotting, hunting, and on the move. Shorebirds, such as plovers and sandpipers, arrive to nest at water's edge. But it is archaeology, not natural history, that distinguishes this area. Like Onion Portage in Kobuk Valley, Cape Krusenstern is an open book on Alaska's past. The beach sand ridges—a total of 114 of them—spread out like pages parallel to the shore, one next to the other, in linear sequence, and contain artifacts from every known Eskimo occupation of North America. Through the millennia, great storms deposited ridges at the cape (adding a new ridge about every 75 years), and with the creation of each new ridge came its occupation by people who preferred to hunt and fish near the sea. Thus was created a horizontal chronology of human survival as exciting as any found in the Arctic.

Times have changed on Cape Krusenstern. The Red Dog Mine has been constructed just to the east, creating a new generation of Eskimo lead and zinc miners, rather than subsistence hunters and fishermen. A road to the mine has been built through the monument, and some native elders have asked the same question that has been asked throughout America for a long time: "Will the legacy we create today be better or worse than the one we inherited?"

ARCTIC NATIONAL WILDLIFE REFUGE

Sequestered high in the northeastern corner of Alaska is the **Arctic National Wildlife Refuge❖.** Its 19 million acres straddle the Brooks Range and reach north to the coastal plain of the Beaufort Sea, east to the international boundary with Canada, south to Yukon Flats National Wildlife Refuge, and west to within a few miles of the Dalton Highway and the Trans-Alaska Oil Pipeline. It is the northernmost and second largest wildlife refuge in the United States and is the only conservation unit in the nation that contains a complete array of undisturbed arctic ecosystems.

More than 140 species of birds—some from as far away as Japan and Russia—fly here to nest each year. Dall sheep inhabit the craggy slopes of the mountains, and wolves, wolverines, and grizzly bears go wherever they please. Hikers might find grizzly tracks on the coastal plain, or, just as likely, atop a mountain ridge in the heart of the Brooks Range. Polar bears hunting for seals (their preferred food), patrol the northern sea ice in summer and move along the coast in winter.

In June and July, the tundra is splashed with colorful wildflowers—blue forget-me-nots, yellow arnica, pink phlox, purple mountain saxifrage, white dryas—but the air can be thick with mosquitoes as well. August finds the colors of autumn encroaching up on the mountain slopes and temperatures falling below freezing. With September comes winter, with darkening nights and better opportunities to see the northern lights: those dancing, pulsating rays, arcs, or curtains of green, white, and red light created by solar wind charging the earth's atmosphere.

The refuge's coastal plain, running between the Brooks Range and the Beaufort Sea, serves as the calving ground for the Porcupine caribou, a herd 180,000 strong that follows ancient routes through the mountains and across the rivers to bring forth yet another generation. Born in late May and early June, the calves start out on wobbly legs, but in a world of predator and prey, fitness or death, they develop rapidly and can run swiftly in a week. The caribou migrate through the refuge each year never following exactly the same route as before, but

253

ABOVE: *An arctic fox studies its own reflection in a melting spring lagoon. Fleet-footed and a perpetual hunter, it makes a good living in the harshest of environments.*

BELOW: *The ermine, or short-tailed weasel, is a bold predator of mice and voles; its white winter coat turns brown in spring.*

instead weaving and meandering, diverging and converging as they steadily make their way between summer calving grounds on the refuge and winter feeding grounds in Canada.

Although the Arctic NWR is isolated in geography, it has not escaped controversy. In the early 1980s, the oil industry targeted the refuge's coastal plain as a potential petroleum bonanza. Environmentalists crossed their arms and said, "Stay out," and battle lines have been drawn and filibusters fought to determine the future—development or designated wilderness—of the last, best place in wild North America. It so happens that oil development looks most promising right in the middle of the Porcupine caribou calving grounds.

The development argument is simple: The United States is an oil-dependent nation. Unless promising reserves are explored within its borders, the United States will slide deeper and deeper into dependence on oil from other countries, primarily those in the politically unstable Middle East. Developing the coastal plain of the Arctic NWR will create jobs and improve national security.

ABOVE: *Hunters of seals, swimmers of the frigid seas, travelers of a frozen realm, polar bears inhabit the entire arctic coastline of Alaska and occasionally venture into Eskimo villages, from Kaktovik to Barrow.*

On the other side, environmentalists claim the time has come to begin serious energy conservation. The United States holds 5 percent of the world's population but burns 25 percent of the world's energy—and the time has come to save what few wild places we have left. In the long run these places will be far more valuable, spiritually, socially, and economically, than a quick meal of oil for the United States's energy appetite. If the refuge contains 3.2 billion barrels of oil, as scientists predict, it would be enough to sustain the United States for 200 days at present consumption levels—nothing more. Oil in the Arctic is no more than an economic narcotic, while the Arctic itself, open, quiet, and free from industrial intrusion, refreshes every soul that appreciates wilderness.

Most visitors come to the refuge in June, July, and August, and enjoy the refuge by rafting one of its rivers, most popularly the Sheenjek, Kongakut, or Hulahula. Guided trips are usually safe but expensive, and the advertised fares are most often based on beginning and ending in

Fairbanks. The best access into the refuge is by flying from Fairbanks to Fort Yukon, Arctic Village, or Kaktovik (Barter Island) and continuing by charter plane into the refuge from there.

THE NORTH SLOPE

Due north of Noatak National Preserve sprawls the 23-million-acre **National Petroleum Reserve❖**. Created in 1923 as one of four naval petroleum reserves, which the secretary of the Navy was charged to "explore, protect, conserve, develop, use, and operate"—a seemingly impossible combination of tasks—the area was redesignated the National Petroleum Reserve–Alaska in 1977, and jurisdiction was transferred to the secretary of the Interior. In 1981, Congress authorized a competitive leasing program that has since resulted in land sales and some active drilling. Yet the area still contains great vistas of unspoiled North Slope terrain. The Colville River—at 428 miles, the seventh-longest river in Alaska—flows past numerous bluffs where peregrine falcons nest. The surrounding tundra is home to many other species of nesting birds, including snowy owls and Pacific black brant. The area also boasts 75 percent of the world's speckled eider population, and 100 percent of its Steller's eider population. The town of Barrow sits at the top of the reserve, on the Arctic coast. It is the northernmost settlement in the United States and the largest Inupiat Eskimo village in Alaska. Daily flights connect Anchorage and Barrow, a good jumping-off point into the reserve.

The promises and dreams of Alaska are usually as big and wild and diverse as the land itself. New adventures begin here every day, most of them anchored in the undistilled excitement of having hundreds of miles of America's purest wilderness waiting, like a gift, to be opened and enjoyed. Hike the tundra, run the rivers, kayak the fiords, take the bad weather with the good, and go lightly and with respect, for experiencing Alaska is largely a matter of attitude. This is indeed natural America, a flagship of wild geographies.

LEFT: *With majesty, poetry, and power, massive herds of caribou have traveled throughout Arctic Alaska for countless centuries. They flow like great rivers, neither fully understood nor understandable.*

FURTHER READING ABOUT ALASKA

Alaska Wilderness Milepost. Portland, OR: Alaska Northwest Books, 1994 (updated yearly). An excellent guide to the hows, whens, and wheres of traveling in Alaska.

ARMSTRONG, ROBERT H. et al. *The Nature of Southeast Alaska.* Portland, OR: Alaska Northwest Books, 1992. A good traveling companion for anyone interested in the natural history of southeastern Alaska.

BOHN, DAVE. *Glacier Bay: The Land and the Silence.* Anchorage: Alaska Natural History Association, 1967. A strong narration of the human history and environmental concerns in Glacier Bay National Park.

BROWN, WILLIAM E. *This Last Treasure.* Anchorage: Alaska Natural History Association, 1982. A compelling summary of Alaskan National Park Service areas, written by a former historian with the National Park Service.

GOETZMANN, WILLIAM H., AND KAY SLOAN. *Looking Far North.* New York: Viking Press, 1982. The story of the 1899 Harriman expedition to Alaska that shaped impressions still alive today.

HEACOX, KIM. *Alaska's National Parks.* Portland, OR: Graphic Arts Center Publishing, 1990. A coffee-table book (photos by Fred Hirschmann) that offers a synopsis of Alaska's national parks, preserves, and monuments.

———. *In Denali.* Santa Barbara, CA: Companion Press, 1992. Winner of the Benjamin Franklin Nature Book Award; a photographic essay and conservation-oriented text on Alaska's most famous national park.

HEDIN, ROBERT, AND GARY HOLTHAUS. *Alaska: Reflections on Land and Spirit.* Tucson: University of Arizona Press, 1989. A collection of essays on Alaska's natural and human history.

JANS, NICK. *The Last Light Breaking.* Portland, OR: Alaska Northwest Books, 1993. A beautifully written account of living among the Inupiat in northwestern Alaska.

LOPEZ, BARRY. *Arctic Dreams.* New York: Charles Scribner's Sons, 1986. Winner of the National Book Award; a vivid and poetic look at life in the Arctic.

MCPHEE, JOHN. *Coming into the Country.* New York: Farrar, Strauss and Giroux, 1976. Considered to be one of the most eloquent nonfiction accounts of life in Alaska.

MICHENER, JAMES A. *Alaska.* New York, Random House, 1988. A fictional, sweeping epic of life in Alaska, based largely on actual historical events.

NELSON, RICHARD. *The Island Within.* San Francisco: North Point Press, 1989. Winner of the John Burroughs Medal for excellence in nature writing; one man's account of living on an island near Sitka in southeastern Alaska.

WEEDEN, ROBERT B. *Promises to Keep.* Boston: Houghton Mifflin, 1978. A thorough look at Alaska's approach to natural resources, written by a former professor from the University of Alaska.

FURTHER READING ABOUT HAWAI'I

ABBOT, ISABELLA AIONE. *La'au Hawaii: Traditional Hawaiian Uses of Plants.*
Honolulu: Bishop Museum Press, 1992. An elaborately illustrated guide to
traditional uses of native plants for food, medicines, cloth, weapons,
tools, canoes, and more.

BALL, STUART M., JR. *The Hiker's Guide to Oahu.* Honolulu: University of
Hawaii Press, 1993. An up-to-date guide to the many hiking trails of
Hawai'i's most populous island.

BERGER, ANDREW J. *Birdlife in Hawai'i.* Aiea, HI: Island Heritage, 1983. An
illustrated guide to the endemic and introduced birds of the Hawaiian Islands.

BIER, JAMES A. *Reference Maps of the Islands of Hawai'i.* Honolulu, HI:
University of Hawaii Press. Excellent, finely detailed maps, essential for
exploring back roads and natural areas.

CANHAM, ROD. *Hawaii Below: Favorites, Tips and Secrets of the Diving Pros.*
San Diego: Watersport Books, 1991. An illustrated site-by-site guide to underwater flora and fauna, with much educational material about Hawaiian sea life.

CARLQUIST, SHERWIN. *Hawaii: A Natural History.* Lawai, Kauai: Pacific
Tropical Botanical Garden, 1980. The seminal primer on the evolution of
the natural environment in Hawai'i.

CHISOLM, CRAIG. *Hawaiian Hiking Trails.* Lake Oswego, OR: The Fernglen
Press, 1991. An illustrated hiking guide to some of the best trails on the
islands, with maps.

CULLINEY, JOHN L. *Islands in a Far Sea: Nature and Man in Hawaii.* San Francisco: Sierra Club Books, 1988. A beautifully written account of the interplay
between native and introduced species—including humans—in the islands.

LONDON, JACK. *Stories of Hawaii.* New York: Appleton, 1965. Tales of true
adventure in old Hawai'i.

MACDONALD, G. A., AND A. T. ABBOT. *Volcanoes in the Sea: The Geology of
Hawaii.* Honolulu: University of Hawaii Press, 1970. A classic introduction to the geological evolution of the islands.

MICHENER, JAMES. *Hawaii.* New York: Random House, 1959. An exciting
fictional account incorporating many details of Hawaiian history.

SCOTT, SUSAN. *Plants and Animals of Hawaii.* Honolulu: Bess Press, 1991.
Written for the general reader, this illustrated book concentrates on the
native and introduced species visitors are likely to encounter.

SMITH, ROBERT. *Hiking Kauai.* Long Beach, CA: Hawaiian Outdoors
Adventures Publication, 1989. Illustrated guide to the best trails on the
Garden Isle by the acknowledged expert on Hawaiian hiking.

SOHMER, S. H., AND ROBERT GUSTAFSON. *Plants and Flowers of Hawaii.*
Honolulu: University of Hawaii Press, 1987. Full-color photographs illustrate this guide to the botany of the Hawaiian Islands.

GLOSSARY

ALASKA

arete sharp-crested ridge

biome ecological community type composed of a distinctive group of plants and animals

boreal refering to the northern biotic area characterized especially by dominance of coniferous forests

bore tide a frothing wall of water (one to two feet high) formed by a strong, flooding tide forced through a narrow area (best in Alaska: Turnagain Arm, near Anchorage)

breaching vertical leap of a whale out of the sea

break up springtime melt of solid surface ice; broken pieces then float downstream

calving process of a glacier dropping ice off its terminus or edge

estuary region of interaction between ocean waters and rivers, where tidal action and river flow mix fresh and salt water

fjord narrow inlet of the sea between cliffs or steep slopes

glacier river of ice that moves slowly downslope under the influence of gravity and its own weight; capable of radically altering landscapes

icefield vast, mountainous basin filled with ice often thousands of feet thick; usually creates glaciers

intertidal referring to the shoreline zone between the highest high tide and lowest low tide

kame cone-shaped hill of rock debris deposited by glacial meltwater

moraine debris (rock, sand, gravel, silt, and clay) carried by a glacier and left behind along its sides or terminus wherever it paused or retreated

nunatak top of a mountain protruding above an icefield

permafrost permanently frozen mixture of ice, soil, and rock that can extend from just below the surface to as deep as 2,000 feet

relict persistent remnant of an otherwise extinct species

staging the activity of birds resting and feeding while migrating

taiga from the Russian meaning "land of little sticks," the subarctic region dominated by spruce and fir that begins where tundra ends

tidewater glacier glacier that terminates in the sea, usually at the head of a fjord, inlet, or arm

tundra treeless region of arctic or subarctic regions dominated by lichens, mosses, and low-growing vascular plants

tussock a clump or tuft of raised solid ground in a bog or marsh held together by roots of low-growing vegetation

HAWAI'I

Native Hawaiian words appear in roman type.

'a'a rough, broken lava

ahu altar or shrine; cairn or trail marker

aiguille sharp pinnacle of rock

ali'i chief, ruler; Hawaiian ruling class

alluvium silt, gravel, or other material deposited by running water

anchialine pools inland pools of brackish water where a singular community of flora and fauna thrive; sunk in porous substrate such as lava, the pools are invisibly connected to the sea

atoll coral island consisting only of a reef surrounding a lagoon

'auwai aqueduct, ditch

caldera crater formed by collapse of

the center of a volcano

coralline of or resembling coral

cycad tropical plants that reproduce by means of spermatozoids

endemic having originated in and restricted to one particular environment

epiphyte plant that usually grows on another plant and derives its moisture and nutrients from the rain and air

hala pandanus tree that grows at low altitudes; female trees bear pineapple-shaped fruit; male trees bear fragrant flowers

hapu'u tree fern endemic to Hawai'i

hau type of hibiscus tree; its sap was formerly used for medicine

heiau shrine, place of worship

hinahina silvery gray plants that include silverswords, native heliotropes, native geraniums, and other native plants

honeycreeper family of birds endemic to Hawaii; marked by curved bills

indigenous having originated in and occurring naturally in a particular environment but also growing elsewhere

Kahiki, or **Tahiti** Polynesian for "the sky," islands from which ancestors of modern Hawaiians emigrated

kahuna healer, sorcerer; wise person

kapu ancient taboo; strict Hawaiian prohibitions

kiawe common, thorny legume tree; also called algaroba or mesquite

kipuka oasis, especially a clear place within a lava bed where vegetation grows

koa largest of native Hawaiian forest trees, with white flowers and crescent-shaped leaves; valuable lumber source (*Acacia koa*)

kukui candlenut tree; used as symbol of enlightenment, as its kernels were formerly used for lights

leeward facing away from the wind

littoral of or on a shore, especially a seashore

makai toward the sea

mamane native Hawaiian leguminous tree with distinctive yellow flowers; it thrives at high altitudes

mauka toward the mountains; inland

menehune legendary Hawaiian "little people" who built fishponds, according to folklore

mo'o water or lizard spirit, enchanter

naupaka native Hawaiian shrub bearing white berries and white flowers; both mountain-growing and seashore varieties are common

nene rare native Hawaiian goose, protected on Maui and the Big Island

'ohi'a native Hawaiian tree, with red flowers that resemble pompons

pahoehoe satiny, unbroken lava

paka lolo marijuana; literally, "numbing tobacco"

pali cliffs, steep hills, or slopes

petroglyph figure carved or scratched on a rock

protea evergreen shrubs grown for their dense flower heads

scarp line of steep cliffs formed by erosion

seamount submarine mountain that rises above the sea floor but does not reach the surface

taro plant grown for its edible starchy rootstocks and its ornamental value

tsunami large, potentially destructive ocean wave produced by submarine geological movements or by volcanic eruption

ulu breadfruit tree grown for its edible fruits

windward facing the direction from which the wind is blowing; into the wind

LAND MANAGEMENT RESOURCES

The following public and private organizations are among the important administrators of the preserved and protected areas described in this volume. Brief explanations of the various legal and legislative designations of these areas follow.

MANAGING ORGANIZATIONS

Bureau of Land Management (BLM) Department of the Interior
Administers nearly half of all federal lands, some 272 million acres. Resources are managed for multiple uses: recreation, grazing, logging, mining, fish and wildlife, and watershed and wilderness preservation.

National Park Service (NPS) Department of the Interior
Regulates the public's use of national parks, monuments, and preserves. Resources are managed to protect landscape, natural and historic artifacts, and wildlife. Administers historic and natural landmarks, national seashores, wild and scenic rivers, and the national trail system.

The Nature Conservancy (TNC) Private organization
International nonprofit organization that owns the largest private system of nature sanctuaries in the world, some 1,300 preserves. Its aim is to preserve significant and diverse plants, animals, and natural communities. Some areas are managed by other private or public conservation groups, some by the Conservancy itself.

U.S. Fish and Wildlife Service (USFWS) Department of the Interior
Principal governmental agency responsible for conserving, protecting, and enhancing the country's fish and wildlife and their habitats. Manages national wildlife refuges and fish hatcheries as well as programs for migratory birds and endangered and threatened species.

U.S. Forest Service (USFS) Department of Agriculture
Administers more than 190 million acres in the national forests and national grasslands and is responsible for the management of their resources. Determines how best to combine commercial uses such as grazing, mining, and logging with conservation needs.

DESIGNATIONS

International Biosphere Reserve
Protected area set aside to help solve problems associated with the effects that human impact over time has upon natural ecosystems. Managed by the U.S. Man and the Biosphere Program.

Marine Life Conservation District
Protected area designed to preserve marine resources; some recreational uses are permitted, although removal of coral and rocks is prohibited. Managed in Hawai'i by the Hawaii Division of Aquatic Resources.

National Conservation Area
Special area set aside by Congress to protect specific environments; may be used for recreation or other specific purposes. Managed by the BLM.

National Forest

Large acreage managed for the best use of forests, watersheds, wildlife, and recreation by the public and private sectors. Managed by the USFS.

National Historic Site

Land area, building, or object preserved because of its national historic importance. Managed by the NPS.

National Monument

Nationally significant landmark, structure, or object, or an area of scientific or historic importance. Managed by the NPS.

National Natural Landmark

Nationally significant natural area that is a prime example of a biotic community or a particular geological feature. Managed by the NPS.

National Park

Primitive or wilderness area with scenery and natural wonders so outstanding it has been preserved by the federal government. Managed by the NPS.

National Preserve

Area that protects specific natural resources; hunting, fishing, and mining may be permitted. Managed by the NPS and local or state authorities.

National Recreation Area

Site established to conserve and develop for recreational purposes an area of national scenic, natural, or historic interest. Hunting, fishing, boating, mountain biking, and off-road vehicles may be permitted. Managed by the NPS.

National Wildlife Refuge

Public land set aside for wild animals; protects migratory waterfowl, endangered and threatened species, and native plants. Managed by USFWS.

Natural Area Reserve

Protected land or water area in Hawai'i that supports communities of natural flora and fauna or is an important geological site. Managed by the Hawai'i Division of Forestry and Wildlife.

Special Ecological Area

Area within Hawai'i Volcanoes National Park that is intensively managed because it has been least damaged by the introduction of alien plant and animal communities; these areas contain whole spectrums of native plant and animal species and represent Hawai'i at its most pristine.

Wild and Scenic River System

National program set up to preserve selected rivers in their natural free-flowing condition; stretches are classified as wild, scenic, or recreational, depending on the degree of development on the river, shoreline, and adjacent lands. Management shared by BLM, NPS, and USFWS.

Wilderness Area

An inviolate area that by law must retain its primeval character and influence, without permanent improvements or human habitation; recreational use is permitted, subject to regulation. Designation was created by the Wilderness Act of 1964. Managed by the BLM.

NATURE TRAVEL

The following is a selection of national and local organizations that sponsor nature-related travel activities from extended tours to day trips and ecology workshops.

National Audubon Society
700 Broadway
New York, NY 10003
(212) 979-3000
Offers a range of ecological field studies, tours, and cruises throughout America

National Wildlife Federation
1400 16th Street N.W.
Washington, DC 20036
(703) 790-4363
Offers training in environmental education for all ages, wildlife camp and teen adventures, conservation summits involving nature (walks, field trips, and classes)

The Nature Conservancy
1815 North Lynn Street
Arlington, VA 22209
(703) 841-5300
Offers excursions based out of regional and state offices. May include hiking, backpacking, canoeing, horseback riding. Contact above number to locate offices

Sierra Club Outings
730 Polk Street
San Francisco, CA 94109
(415) 923-5630
Offers tours of different lengths for all ages throughout the United States. Outings may include backpacking, hiking, biking, skiing, and water excursions

**Smithsonian Study Tours
and Seminars**
1100 Jefferson Drive S.W.
MRC 702
Washington D.C. 20560
(202) 357-4700
Offers tours, cruises, research expeditions, and seminars in the United States

ALASKA

Alaska National Park Service
Concessions Branch
2525 Gambell Street
Anchorage, AK 99503

(907) 257-2594
Regulates tour vendor contracts, permits, and visitor services. Maintains lists and brochures for specific tour operators and types of travel throughout state

**Alaska Public Lands
Information Center**
605 West 4th Avenue, Suite 105
Anchorage, AK 99501
(907) 271-2737
Central visitor information center for state's public lands and parks. Assists in visitor planning, recreational activities, and travel and highway information

**American Museum of Natural History
Discovery Cruises**
Central Park West at 79th Street
New York, NY 10024
(212) 769-5700
Offers yearly cruises and tours to Alaska that are guided by naturalists from the Museum of Natural History

HAWAI'I

Hawai'i Audubon Society
212 Merchant Street, #320
Honolulu, HI 96813
(808) 528-1432
Local chapter offers a variety of day trips,. including birding trips, outings, nature walks, and tidal pool studies

Hawai'i Trail and Mountain Club
PO 2238
Honolulu, HI 96804
(808) 734-5515
Offers hikes varying in distance, duration, and type of terrain, including ridge, valley, and stream

Hawai'i Visitors Bureau
2270 Kalakua Avenue
Honolulu, HI 96815
(808) 923-1811
Provides information on tours, cruises, outfitters, travel and transportation

HOW TO USE THIS SITE GUIDE

The following site information guide will assist you in planning your tour of the natural areas of Alaska and Hawai'i. Sites set in **boldface** and followed by the symbol ❖ in the text are here organized alphabetically by state and, within Hawai'i, by island. Each entry is followed by the mailing address (sometimes different from the street address) and phone number of the immediate managing office, plus brief notes and a list of facilities and activities available. (A key appears on each page.)

Information on hours of operation, seasonal closings, and fees is not listed, as these vary from season to season and year to year. Please also bear in mind that responsibility for the management of some sites may change. Call well in advance to obtain maps, brochures, permits, and up-to-date information that will help plan your Pacific or northern adventures.

Each site entry in the guide includes the address and phone number of its immediate managing agency. Many of these sites are under the stewardship of a forest or park ranger or are supervised from a small nearby office. Hence, in many cases, sites will be difficult to contact directly, and it is preferable to call the managing agency.

The following umbrella organizations can provide general information for individual natural sites, as well as the area as a whole:

Alaska Department of Fish and Game
PO 25526
Juneau, AK 99802
(907) 465-4100

Alaska Department of Natural Resources
400 Willoughby, 5th Fl.
Juneau, AK 99801
(907) 465-2400

Alaska State Division of Tourism
PO Box 110801
Juneau, AK 99811
(907) 465-2010

National Audubon Society, Alaska Regional Office
308 G Street, Suite 217
Anchorage, AK 99501
(907) 276-7034

Hawai'i Audubon Society
212 Merchant Street, #320
Honolulu, HI 96813
(808) 528-1432

Hawai'i Botanical Society
c/o Botany Dept.
University of Hawai'i
3190 Maile Way
Honolulu, HI 96822
(808) 956-8072

Hawai'i Department of Land and Natural Resources
PO 621
Honolulu, HI 96809
(808) 587-0400

Hawai'i Division of Aquatic Resources
1151 Punchbowl Street
Honolulu, HI 96813
(808) 587-0100

Hawai'i Division of Forestry and Wildlife
1151 Punchbowl Street
Honolulu, HI 96813
(808) 587-0166

Hawai'i Division of State Parks
PO 621
Honolulu, HI 96809
(808) 587-0300

Hawai'i Visitors Bureau
2270 Kalakaua Ave.
Suite 801
Honolulu, HI 96815
(808) 923-1811

Nature Conservancy of Hawai'i
1116 Smith Street, #201
Honolulu, HI 96817
(808) 537-4508

ALASKA

ADMIRALTY ISLAND NATIONAL MONUMENT
U.S. Forest Service Headquarters
PO 21628, Juneau, AK 99802
(907) 586-8790
> Access via boat or plane only; public-use cabins available—advance permit necessary; includes Mitchell Bay Bear Reserve [(907) 788-3166], Pack Creek Bear Reserve, Cross-Admiralty Canoe Route **BW, C, CK, F, H, I, L, MT, TG**

ALASKA-CHILKAT BALD EAGLE PRESERVE
Alaska Dept. of Natural Resources
400 Willoughby Ave., 3rd floor
Juneau, AK 99801
(907) 465-4563
> Access via boat or plane only; primitive camping **BW, C, CK, F, H, RA, TG, XC**

ALASKA MARITIME NATIONAL WILDLIFE REFUGE
U.S. Fish and Wildlife Service
2355 Kachemak Bay Dr., Suite 101
Homer, AK 99603
(907) 235-6961
> Access via boat or plane only; most islands restricted by military **BW, C, CK, F, GS, H, I, L, RA, TG, XC**

ALASKA-PENINSULA NATIONAL WILDLIFE REFUGE
U.S. Fish and Wildlife Service, PO 277
King Salmon, AK 99613
(907) 246-4250
> Access via boat or plane only; primitive camping; includes Mt. Veniamanof, Mt. Chiginagak **BW, C, CK, F, H, TG, XC**

ALSEK RIVER/TATSHENSHINI RIVER
National Park Service
Glacier Bay National Park
PO 140, Gustavus, AK 99826
(907) 697-2230
> Permit required; primitive camping **C, CK, F, H, TG**

ANCHORAGE COASTAL WILDLIFE REFUGE
Alaska Dept. of Fish and Game
333 Raspberry Rd.
Anchorage, AK 99518
(907) 344-0541
> Includes Potter Marsh Boardwalk **BT, BW, I, XC**

ANIAKCHAK NATIONAL MONUMENT AND PRESERVE
National Park Service, PO 7
King Salmon, AK 99613
(907) 246-3305
> Access via plane only; primitive camping; one very primitive public-use cabin available; experienced backcountry campers only; includes Surprise Lake, Aniakchak River **BW, C, CK, F, H, I, L, TG**

ARCTIC NATIONAL WILDLIFE REFUGE
U.S. Fish and Wildlife Service
Federal Bldg. Box 20
101 12th Ave.
Fairbanks, AK 99201
(907) 456-0250
> Access via plane only; primitive camping; includes Kongakuk River, Hulahula River, Sheenjek River **BW, C, CK, F, H, I, TG**

BARANOF ISLAND
U.S. Forest Service
Tongass National Forest
Sitka Ranger District
201 Katlian, Suite 109
Sitka, AK 99835
(907) 747-6671/(907) 586-8751
> Access via boat or plane only; weather is very rigorous; public-use cabins available; includes South Baranof Wilderness Area, Goddard Hot Springs, Kruzof Island **BT, BW, C, CK, F, H, I, L, MT, PA, RC, S, T, TG**

BECHAROF NATIONAL WILDLIFE REFUGE
U.S. Fish and Wildlife Service, PO 277
King Salmon, AK 99613
(907) 246-4250
> Access via boat or plane only; primitive camping; includes Becharof Lake, Mt. Peulik, Gas Rocks Hot Springs, Ukinrek Maars **BW, C, CK, F, GS, H, I, TG**

BERING LAND BRIDGE NATIONAL PRESERVE
National Park Service, PO 220
Nome, AK 99762
(907) 443-2522
> Access via boat or plane only; primitive camping; includes Serpentine Hot Springs **BW, C, CK, F, H, XC**

BT Bike Trails	**CK** Canoeing, Kayaking	**F** Fishing	**HR** Horseback Riding
BW Bird-watching	**DS** Downhill Skiing	**GS** Gift Shop	**I** Information Center
C Camping		**H** Hiking	

CAPE KRUSENSTERN NATIONAL MONUMENT
National Park Service, PO 1029
Kotzebue, AK 99752
(907) 442-3890
Access via boat or plane only; primitive
camping   **BW, C, CK, F, GS, H, I, TG**

CHICHAGOF ISLAND
U.S. Forest Service
Tongass National Forest
Hoonah Ranger District, PO 135
Hoonah, AK 99829
(907) 945-3631
Access via boat or plane only; primitive
camping; vehicles can be brought by
ferry; includes West Chichagof-Yakobi
Island Wilderness Area
   **BW, C, CK, F, H, I, L, MT,
PA, S, TG, XC**

CHUGACH NATIONAL FOREST
U.S. Forest Service
3301 C St., Suite 300
Anchorage, AK 99503
(907) 271-2500
Year-round recreation available; in-
cludes Portage Glacier, Prince William
Sound, Begich Boggs Visitor Center,
Columbia Glacier, Kayak Island
   **BT, BW, C, CK, F, GS, H, HR, I, L, MT,
RA, T, TG, XC**

CHUGACH STATE PARK
Alaska Div. of Parks and Outdoor Recreation
HC 52, PO 8999, Indian, AK 99540
(907) 345-5014
Includes Eagle River Visitor Center,
Beluga Point, Windy Corner
   **BT, BW, C, CK, F, GS, H,
HR, I, MT, PA, RA, RC, TG, XC**

COPPER RIVER DELTA
U.S. Forest Service, Chugach National Forest
Cordova Ranger District
PO 280, Cordova, AK 99574
(907) 424-7661
   **BW, C, CK, DS, F, GS, H, I, L
MT, PA, RC, T, TG, XC**

DENALI NATIONAL PARK AND PRESERVE
National Park Service, PO 9
Denali Park, AK 99755
(907) 683-2294/(907) 683-1266
Includes Mount McKinley, Eielson Visitor
Center, Kahiltna Glacier, Ruth Glacier
   BW, C, H, I, L, MT, PA, T, TG, XC

DENALI STATE PARK
Mat-Su/Valdez–Copper River Area
Alaska Div. of Parks and Outdoor Recreation
Copper Basin Office, HC 32, PO 6706
Wasilla, AK 99687
(907) 745-3975
Includes Byers Lake Campground,
Veterans Memorial
   **BW, C, CK, F, H, I, L, MT,
PA, RA, S, TG, XC**

FREDERICK SOUND
U.S. Forest Service Headquarters, PO 21628
Juneau, AK 99802
(907) 586-8790
Access via boat or plane only; boaters
must keep distance from marine mam-
mals; primitive camping
   BW, C, CK, F, TG

**GATES OF THE ARCTIC NATIONAL PARK
AND PRESERVE**
National Park Service, PO 74680
Fairbanks, AK 99707
(907) 456-0281
Access via boat or plane only; primitive
camping
   BW, C, CK, F, GS, H, I, RC, TG, XC

**GLACIER BAY NATIONAL PARK AND
PRESERVE**
National Park Service, PO 140
Gustavus, AK 99826
(907) 697-2230
Some areas close intermittently; permits
required for boaters; includes Glacier Bay
Lodge, Bartlett Cove Campground, Brady
Icefield, Mount Fairweather, Hugh Miller
Glacier, Reid Glacier, Laperouse Glacier,
Margerie Glacier   **BW, C, CK, F, GS,
H, I, L, MT, RA, T, TG, XC**

INNOKO NATIONAL WILDLIFE REFUGE
U.S. Fish and Wildlife Service, PO 69
McGrath, AK 99627
(907) 524-3251
Access via plane only; primitive camping
   BW, C, CK, F, GS, I, L, TG

IZEMBEK NATIONAL WILDLIFE REFUGE
U.S. Fish and Wildlife, PO 127
Cold Bay, AK 99571
(907) 532-2445
Includes Izembek Lagoon
   BT, BW, C, F, H, I, L, RA, T, TG

JUNEAU ICEFIELD
U.S. Forest Service
Tongass National Forest
Juneau Ranger District
8465 Old Dairy Rd.
Juneau, AK 99801
(907) 586-8751
  Access via boat or plane only; experience in glacier travel recommended; primitive camping   **C, H, TG**

KACHEMAK BAY STATE PARK AND WILDERNESS PARK
Alaska Div. of Parks and Outdoor Recreation
PO 1247, Soldotna, Alaska 99669
(907) 262-5581
  Access via boat or plane only; public-use cabins available; includes Halibut Cove Lagoon, China Poot Bay, Poot Peak, Sadie Cove, Tutka Bay
                    BW, C, CK, F, H, I, L, MT, PA, RC, T, TG, XC

KANUTI NATIONAL WILDLIFE REFUGE
U.S. Fish and Wildlife
101 12th Ave., PO 11
Fairbanks, AK 99701
(907) 456-0329
  Access via boat or plane only; primitive camping   **BW, C, CK, F, I, L, XC**

KATMAI NATIONAL PARK AND PRESERVE
National Park Service, PO 7
King Salmon, AK 99613
(907) 246-3305
(907) 246-4250
  Access via boat or plane only; year-round recreation; includes Brooks Camp and Lodge [reservations req'd (800) 544-0551], National Park Service Visitor Center, Valley of Ten Thousand Smokes, Three Forks Overlook, Ukak River Gorge, Novarupta
                    BW, C, CK, F, GS, H, I, L, PA, RA, T, TG, XC

KAYAK ISLAND
U.S. Forest Service
Chugach National Forest
Cordova Ranger District, PO 280
Cordova, AK 99574
(907) 424-7661
  Access via boat or plane only; primitive camping

KENAI FJORDS NATIONAL PARK
National Park Service
PO 1727
Seward, AK 99664
(907) 224-3175
  Public-use cabins available; includes Exit Glacier, Harding Icefield, Chiswell Islands, and coastal fjords
                    BW, C, CK, F, H, I, L, MT, PA, RA, T, TG, XC

KENAI NATIONAL WILDLIFE REFUGE AND WILDERNESS
U.S. Fish and Wildlife Service
PO 2139
Soldotna, AK 99669
(907) 262-7021
  Boaters must contact Visitor Center in Soldotna; includes canoe trail route system, Skilak Wildlife Recreation Area
                    BW, C, CK, F, GS, H, I, MT, PA, RA, T, TG, XC

KOBUK VALLEY NATIONAL PARK
National Park Service
PO 1029
Kotzebue, AK 99752
(907) 442-3890
  Access via boat or plane only; primitive camping; caribou migration in August; includes Great Kobuk Sand Dunes, Onion Portage Archaeological Site, Salmon Wild River
                    BW, C, CK, F, GS, H, I, TG

KODIAK NATIONAL WILDLIFE REFUGE
U.S. Fish and Wildlife Service
1390 Buskin River Rd.
Kodiak, AK 99615
(907) 487-2600
  Access via boat or plane only; public-use cabins available; interior not accessible December–April; rain gear recommended
                    BW, C, CK, F, I, T

KOYUKUK NATIONAL WILDLIFE REFUGE
U.S. Fish and Wildlife Service
Koyukuk/Nowitna Refuge Complex
PO 287
Galena, AK 99741
(907) 656-1231
  Access via boat or plane only; primitive camping; includes Koyukuk River
                    BW, C, CK, F, H, TG

BT	Bike Trails	**CK**	Canoeing, Kayaking	**F**	Fishing	**HR**	Horseback Riding
BW	Bird-watching	**DS**	Downhill Skiing	**GS**	Gift Shop	**I**	Information Center
C	Camping			**H**	Hiking		

**LAKE CLARK NATIONAL
PARK AND PRESERVE**
National Park Service
4230 University Dr., Suite 311
Anchorage, AK 99508
(907) 271-3751
Access by plane only; includes Iliamna
Volcano, Redoubt Volcano
BW, C, CK, F, H, I, L, RC, T, TG, XC

**MCNEIL RIVER STATE GAME
REFUGE AND SANCTUARY**
Alaska Dept. of Fish and Game
333 Raspberry Rd., Anchorage, AK 99518
(907) 267-2179
Permit required; includes McNeil River
Falls   **BW, C, CK, F, H, I, RA, T**

MENDENHALL GLACIER
U.S. Forest Service
Tongass National Forest
Juneau Ranger District, 8465 Old Dairy Rd.
Juneau, AK 99801
(907) 586-8751/(907) 586-8800
Access via boat or plane only; rain gear
recommended   **BW, C, F, H, I, L, MT,
PA, RA, T, TG, XC**

**MENDENHALL WETLANDS
STATE GAME REFUGE**
Alaska Dept. of Fish and Game
PO 240020, Douglas, AK 99824
(907) 465-4290
Bring rubber boots
BT, BW, CK, F, H, MT, XC

MISTY FJORDS NATIONAL MONUMENT
U.S. Forest Service
Tongass National Forest
3031 Tongass Ave.
Ketchikan, AK 99901
(907) 225-2148
Access via boat or plane only; public-
use cabins require reservations; includes
New Eddystone Rock
BW, C, CK, F, GS, H, I, L, MT, S

NANCY LAKE STATE RECREATION AREA
Alaska Div. of Parks and Outdoor
Recreation, Finger Lakes Office
HC 32, Box 6706, Wasilla, AK 99687
(907) 745-3975
Public-use cabins available
**BW, C, CK, F, H, L, MT,
PA, S, T, TG, XC**

NATIONAL PETROLEUM RESERVE
Bureau of Land Management
Arctic District
1150 University Ave.
Fairbanks, AK 99709
(907) 474-2302
Extremely remote and undeveloped;
primitive camping   **C**

NOATAK NATIONAL PRESERVE
National Park Service, PO 1029
Kotzebue, AK 99752
(907) 442-3890
Access via boat or plane only; primitive
camping; caribou migration in August;
includes Noatak River
BW, C, CK, F, GS, H, I, TG

NOWITNA NATIONAL WILDLIFE REFUGE
U.S. Fish and Wildlife Service
Koyukuk/Nowitna Refuge Complex
PO 287, Galena, AK 99741
(907) 656-1231
Access via boat or plane only; primitive
camping; includes Nowitna River
BW, C, CK, F, H, TG

PALMER HAY FLATS STATE GAME REFUGE
Alaska Dept. of Fish and Game
333 Raspberry Rd.
Anchorage, AK 99518
(907) 344-0541
Primitive camping; includes Scout Ridge
Trail   **BW, C, CK, F, H, XC**

PORTAGE LAKE AND PORTAGE GLACIER
U.S. Forest Service
Chugach National Forest
3301 C St., Suite 300
Anchorage, AK 99503
(907) 271-2500
Wheelchair access; rain gear recom-
mended   **BW, C, CK, F, GS, H, I, MT,
RA, T, TG, XC**

PRINCE WILLIAM SOUND
U.S. Forest Service
Chugach National Forest
Glacier Ranger District
PO 129
Girdwood, AK 99587
(907) 783-3242
Access via boat or plane only; public-
use cabins available
BW, C, CK, F, H, L, MT, RC, TG

L	Lodging	**PA**	Picnic Areas	**RC**	Rock Climbing	**TG**	Tours, Guides
MT	Marked Trails	**RA**	Ranger-led Activities	**S**	Swimming	**XC**	Cross-country Skiing
				T	Toilets		

269

SELAWIK NATIONAL WILDLIFE REFUGE
U.S. Fish and Wildlife Service, PO 270
Kotzebue, AK 99752
(907) 442-3799
> Access via boat or plane only; primitive camping; very remote; winter travel is hazardous; includes Upper Selawik River, Waring Mountains Wilderness Area
> **BW, C, CK, F, H, I, XC**

SOUTH PRINCE OF WALES WILDERNESS AREA
U.S. Forest Service
Tongass National Forest Federal Building
Forest Supervisor's Office
Ketchikan, AK 99901
(907) 225-3101
> Access via boat or plane only; vehicles can be brought via ferry; includes Maurelle Island, Warren Island, Coronation Island, Karta Bay, El Capitan Caves
> **BW, C, CK, F, H, I L, MT, PA,T, TG, XC**

STEESE NATIONAL CONSERVATION AREA
Bureau of Land Management
Steese-White Mountains District Office
1150 University Ave.
Fairbanks, AK 99709
(907) 474-2352
> Accessible by highway vehicle; primitive camping; very remote; includes Pinnell Mountain National Recreation Trail, Birch Creek National Wild River
> **BW, C, CK, F, H, MT, XC**

STIKINE ICEFIELD
U.S. Forest Service
Tongass National Forest
Wrangell Ranger District
PO 51, Wrangell, AK 99929
(907) 874-2323
> Access via boat or plane only; primitive camping
> **C, RC, XC**

STIKINE RIVER
U.S. Forest Service
Tongass National Forest
Wrangell Ranger District, PO 51
Wrangell, AK 99929
(907) 874-2323
> Access via boat or plane only; river frozen solid in December
> **BW, C, CK, F, GS, H, I, L, MT, RC, S, T, TG, XC**

TANGLE LAKES ARCHAEOLOGICAL AREA
Bureau of Land Management
Glennallen District Office, PO 147
Glennallen, AK 99588
(907) 822-3217
> Accessible June–September only
> **BT, C, CK, F, H, PA, T**

TETLIN NATIONAL WILDLIFE REFUGE
U.S. Fish and Wildlife Service, PO 779
Tok, AK 99780
(907) 883-5312
> Access via boat or plane only
> **BW, C, CK, F, GS, HR, I, L, PA, RA, S, T, TG, XC**

TONGASS NATIONAL FOREST
U.S. Forest Service Headquarters
PO 21628, Juneau, AK 99802
(907) 586-8790/(907) 784-3359
> Access via boat or plane only; primitive camping; includes Hubbard Glacier, Russell Fjord
> **BW, C, CK, F, H, I, MT, PA, T, XC**

TRACY ARM–FORDS TERROR WILDERNESS AREA
U.S. Forest Service
Tongass National Forest
Juneau Ranger District
8465 Old Dairy Rd.
Juneau, AK 99801
(907) 586-8751/(907) 586-8800
> Access via boat or plane only; primitive camping
> **BW, C, CK, F, H, RA, TG**

WALRUS ISLANDS STATE GAME SANCTUARY
Alaska Dept. of Fish and Game
PO 1030, Dillingham, AK 99576
(907) 842-2334
> Access via boat or plane only; permit required for all visitors; primitive camping; open May–August
> **BW, C, H, MT, T**

WHITE MOUNTAINS NATIONAL RECREATION AREA
Bureau of Land Management
Steese-White Mountains District Office
1150 University Ave., Fairbanks, AK 99709
(907) 474-2352
> Accessible by highway vehicle; primitive camping; public-use cabins available; very remote; includes Eagle Summit, Beaver Creek National Wildlife River
> **BW, C, CK, F, H, L, MT, T, XS**

BT Bike Trails	**CK** Canoeing, Kayaking	**F** Fishing	**HR** Horseback Riding
BW Bird-watching		**GS** Gift Shop	
C Camping	**DS** Downhill Skiing	**H** Hiking	**I** Information Center

WOOD-TICHIK STATE PARK
Alaska Div. of Parks and Outdoor Recreation
PO 107001
Anchorage, AK 99510
(907) 762-2600
  Access via boat or plane only; public-
  use cabins available; includes Silverhorn
  Fjord, Goldenhorn Fjord, Agulukpak
  River, Tikchik River, Spires of the Wood
  River Mountains
            BW, C, CK, F, H, I, L, RC, S, TG, XC

WRANGELL–SAINT ELIAS NATIONAL PARK
National Park Service, PO 29
Glennallen, AK 99588
(907) 822-5234
  Primitive camping; may be inaccessible
  October–May; includes Bering Glacier,
  Malaspina Glacier
            BW, C, CK, F, GS, H, I, TG, XC

**YUKON–CHARLEY RIVERS
NATIONAL PRESERVE**
National Park Service
PO 167
Eagle, AK 99738
(907) 547-2233
  Primitive camping; public-use cabins
  available
            BW, C, CK, F, GS, H, I, L, T, TG, XC

**YUKON DELTA NATIONAL
WILDLIFE REFUGE**
U.S. Fish and Wildlife Service
PO 346
Bethel, AK 99559
(907) 543-3151
  Access via boat or plane only; primitive
  camping; very remote; includes Nunivak
  Island   **BW, C, CK, F, GS, H, I, XC**

**YUKON FLATS NATIONAL
WILDLIFE REFUGE**
U.S. Fish and Wildlife
Service Headquarters
101 12th Ave.
Box 14, Rm 110
Fairbanks, AK 99701
(907) 456-0440
  Access via boat or plane only, primitive
  camping   **BW, C, CK, F, G, I, L, TG, XC**

HAWAI'I

HAWAI'I: THE BIG ISLAND

'AKAKA FALLS STATE PARK
Hawai'i Dept. of Land and Natural
Resources
Div. of State Parks
Hawai'i District Office
PO 936, Hilo, HI 96721-0936
(808) 933-4200
  Includes Kahuna Falls and 'Akaka Falls
            H, MT, PA, T, TG

**HAKALAU FOREST
NATIONAL WILDLIFE REFUGE**
U.S. Fish and Wildlife Service
154 Waianuenue Ave.
Federal Building, Room. 219
Hilo, HI 96720
(808) 969-9909
  Special-use permit required; obtain at
  least 6 weeks in advance   **BW, H**

HAWAI'I VOLCANOES NATIONAL PARK
National Park Service
PO 52
Volcanoes National Park, HI 96718
(808) 967-7311 (person)
(808) 967-7977 (machine)
  Visitors with respiratory problems may
  be bothered by the sulfur in the air; in-
  cludes Halema'uma'u Crater, Visitors
  Center, Crater Rim Drive, Thurston Lava
  Tube, Pu'u Loa (petroglyphs), Ola'a
  Forest, Mauna Loa Strip Road
            **BW, C, GS, H, I,
            L, MT, PA, RA, T**

HYATT REGENCY WAIKOLOA
Waikoloa Beach Resort
HC02, PO 5500
Waikoloa, HI 96743
(808) 885-1234
  Anchialine pools on grounds
            GS, L, S, T

L	Lodging	**PA**	Picnic Areas	**RC**	Rock Climbing	**TG**	Tours, Guides
MT	Marked Trails	**RA**	Ranger-led Activities	**S**	Swimming	**XC**	Cross-country Skiing
				T	Toilets		

KA LAE
Dept. of Hawaiian Home Lands
Land Management Branch, PO 1879
Honolulu, HI 96805
(808) 586-3820
Permission needed to access Green
Sand Beach

**KALOKO-HONOKOHAU
NATIONAL HISTORICAL PARK**
National Park Service
73-4786 Kanalani St. #14
Kailua-Kona, HI 96740
(808) 329-6881
Includes Aimakapa Fishpond; bring
drinking water, sunscreen, sturdy
footwear, and hat; reserve for guided
tours in advance   **BW, H, MT, TG**

KALOPA STATE RECREATION AREA
Hawai'i Dept. of Land and Natural Resources
Div. of State Parks
Hawai'i District Office, PO 936
Hilo, HI 96721-0936
(808) 933-4200 (person)
(808) 775-7114 (on-site) **H, I, L, MT, PA, T**

KA'U DESERT
National Park Service, PO 52
Hawai'i Volcanoes National Park, HI 96718
(808) 967-7311

**KEALAKEKUA BAY STATE
UNDERWATER PARK**
Hawai'i Dept. of Land and Natural Resources
Div. of State Parks
Hawai'i District Office, PO 936
Hilo, HI 96721-0936
(808) 933-4200   **S, T**

KIPAHOEHOE NATURAL AREA RESERVE
Hawai'i Dept. of Land
and Natural Resources
Div. of Forestry and Wildlife
Hawai'i District Office, PO 4849
Hilo, HI 96720
(808) 933-4221

LAPAKAHI STATE HISTORICAL PARK
Hawai'i Dept. of Land
and Natural Resources
Div. of State Parks, PO 100
Kapaau, HI 96755
(808) 889-5566   **H, I, T, TG**

LAVA TREE STATE MONUMENT
Hawai'i Dept. of Land
and Natural Resources
Div. of State Parks
Hawai'i District Office, PO 936
Hilo, HI 96721
(808) 933-4200
Bring drinking water   **MT, PA, T**

MACKENZIE STATE RECREATION AREA
Hawai'i Dept. of
Land and Natural Resources
Div. of State Parks
Hawai'i District Office, PO 936
Hilo, HI 96721
(808) 933-4200
Bring drinking water   **C, F, PA, T**

MANUKA NATURAL AREA RESERVE
Hawai'i Dept. of Land and Natural Resources
Div. of Forestry and Wildlife
Hawai'i District Office, PO 4849
Hilo, HI 96720-0849
(808) 933-4221   **BW, H, MT**

**MAUNA KEA ICE AGE
NATURAL AREA RESERVE**
Hawai'i Dept. of Land
and Natural Resources
Div. of Forestry and Wildlife
Hawai'i District Office, PO 4849
Hilo, HI 96720-0849
(808) 933-4221
Four-wheel-drive necesary; area suscep-
tible to sudden weather changes; in-
cludes LakeWai'au   **H**

**MAUNA LANI BAY HOTEL AND
BUNGALOWS**
1 Mauna Lani Drive
Kohala Coast, HI 96743
(800) 327-8585 (from mainland)
(800) 992-7987 (interisland)
                        GS, H, I, L, T, TG

**OLD KONA AIRPORT
STATE RECREATION AREA**
Hawai'i Dept. of Land
and Natural Resources
Div. of State Parks
Hawai'i District Office
PO 936
Hilo, HI 96721-0936
(808) 933-4200   **F, PA, S, T**

BT Bike Trails	**CK**	Canoeing, Kayaking	**F**	Fishing	**HR**	Horseback Riding
BW Bird-watching	**DS**	Downhill Skiing	**GS**	Gift Shop	**I**	Information Center
C Camping			**H**	Hiking		

Parker Ranch
PO 458, Kamuela, HI 96741
(808) 885-7655   **GS, HR, I, T, TG**

Punalu'u Black Sand Beach
Hawai'i Dept. of Parks and Recreation
25 Aupuni St., Hilo, HI 96720
(808) 961-8311   **C, F, S, T**

Pu'ukohola Heiau
National Historic Site
National Park Service, PO 44340
Kawaihae, HI 96743
(808) 882-7218
  Bring own drinking water
                        H, I, RA, T, TG

Royal Waikoloan
HC02; PO 5300
Kohala Coast, HI 96743
(808) 885-6789
(800) 537-9800
  Offers tours of anchialine pools

Thomas Jaggar Museum
Hawai'i Natural History Association
PO 74, HI Volcanoes National Park, HI 96718
(808) 967-7643

Wailuku River State Park
Hawai'i Dept. of Land
and Natural Resources
Div. of State Parks
Hawai'i District Office
PO 936, Hilo, HI 96721-0936
(808) 933-4200
  Includes Rainbow Falls and Boiling Pots;
  Rainbow Falls best viewed in morning

Waimanu Valley
Hawai'i Div. of Forestry and Wildlife
Hawai'i District Office
PO 4849
Hilo, HI 96720-0849
(808) 933-4221
  Experienced hikers only; carry rain gear,
  shelter, and emergency rations   **C, H**

Waipi'o Valley Overlook
Hawai'i Dept. of Parks and Recreation
25 Aupuni St.
Hilo, HI 96720
(808) 961-8311
  Call for access information   **PA, T**

Maui

'Ahihi-Kina'u Natural Area Reserve
Hawai'i Dept. of Land
and Natural Resources
Div. of Forestry and Wildlife
Natural Area Reserves
54 South High St., Room 101
Wailuku, HI 96793
(808) 871-2620
  Call in advance for access information   **S**

Crater District—
Haleakala National Park
National Park Service
300 Ala Moana Blvd.
PO 50165, Room 6305
Honolulu, HI 96850
(808) 541-2693
          BW, C, H, HR, I, MT, PA, RA, T, TG

Honolua-Mokule'ia Bay
Marine Life Conservation District
Hawai'i Dept. of Land
and Natural Resources
Div. of Aquatic Resources
1151 Punchbowl St., Room 330
Honolulu, HI 96813
(808) 587-0100
  High surf conditions during winter   **S**

Hosmer Grove
National Park Service
PO 369, Makawao, HI 96788
(808) 572-9306
  Part of Haleakala National Park.
  Camping stays limited to three days   **C**

'Iao Valley State Park
Hawai'i Dept. of Land
and Natural Resources
Div. of State Parks, Maui District Office
54 South High St.
Wailuku, HI 96793
(808) 243-5354   **MT, T**

Kanaha Pond State Wildlife
Sanctuary
Hawai'i Dept. of Land
and Natural Resources
Div. of Forestry and Wildlife
54 South High St.
Wailuku, HI 96793
(808) 243-5352   **BW**

L	Lodging	**PA**	Picnic Areas	**RC**	Rock Climbing	**TG**	Tours, Guides
MT	Marked Trails	**RA**	Ranger-led Activities	**S**	Swimming	**XC**	Cross-country Skiing
				T	Toilets		

KANAIO NATURAL AREA RESERVE
Hawai'i Dept. of Land and Natural Resources
Div. of Forestry and Wildlife
Natural Area Reserves
54 South High St., Room 101
Wailuku, HI 96793
(808) 871-2620
    Call well in advance   **H**

KAPUNAKEA PRESERVE
The Nature Conservancy
1116 Smith St.
Honolulu, HI 96817
(808) 537-4508   **BW, H, TG**

**KEALIA POND NATIONAL
WILDLIFE REFUGE**
National Park Service, PO 340
Haleiwa, HI 96712
(808) 637-6330
    Special-use permit required; apply at
    least 6 weeks in advance   **BW, H**

KE'ANAE ARBORETUM
Hawai'i Div. of Forestry and Wildlife
54 South High St.
Wailuku, HI 96793
(808) 243-5352
    Prepare for extreme weather conditions
                                        H, S
**KIPAHULU DISTRICT–
HALEAKALA NATIONAL PARK**
National Park Service
300 Ala Moana Blvd.
PO 50165, Room 6305
Honolulu, HI 96850
(808) 541-2693   **H, I, MT, S**

KULA BOTANICAL GARDENS
RR2, PO 288, Kula, Maui, HI 96790
(808) 878-1715
    Call a week in advance to arrange guid-
    ed tour   **GS, MT, TG**

**MOLOKINI SHOAL MARINE LIFE
CONSERVATION DISTRICT**
Hawai'i Dept. of Land and Natural Resources
Div. of Aquatic Resources
1151 Punchbowl St., Room 330
Honolulu, HI 96813
(808) 587-0100
    Accessed by charter boats out of
    Lahaina, Ma'alaea, and Kihei   **BW, S**

**POLIPOLI SPRINGS STATE
RECREATION AREA**
Hawai'i Dept. of Land and Natural Resources
Div. of State Parks, Maui District Office
54 South High St.
Wailuku, HI 96793
(808) 243-5354
    Four-wheel drive recommended
                          BW, C, H, L, MT, PA

TROPICAL GARDENS OF MAUI
RR 1, PO 500, 'Iao Valley Road
Wailuku, HI 96793
(808) 244-3085   **GS, PA, T, TG**

WAIKAMOI PRESERVE
The Nature Conservancy, 1116 Smith St.
Honolulu, HI 96817
(808) 537-4508
    Reservations required; call at least one
    month in advance for monthly guided tour
                                    BW, H, TG

WAIKAMOI RIDGE NATURE TRAIL
Hawai'i Dept. of Land and Natural Resources
Div. of Forestry and Wildlife
54 South High St.
Wailuku, HI 96793
(808) 243-5352
    Bring drinking water   **BW, H, MT, PA**

WAI'ANAPANAPA STATE PARK
Hawai'i Dept. of Land and Natural Resources
Div. of State Parks
Maui District Office
54 South High St.
Wailuku, HI 96793
(808) 243-5354   **C, F, H, L, PA, S**

MOLOKA'I AND LANA'I

GARDEN OF THE GODS
Lanai Company
Lana'i City, HI 96783
(808) 565- 7233
    Four-wheel drive required

HALAWA VALLEY
Hawai'i Dept. of Parks and Recreation
Maui County, Moloka'i District Office
PO 1055, Kaunakakai, HI 96748
(808) 553-3204
    Four-wheel drive recommended
                                      H, PA, S

BT Bike Trails	**CK** Canoeing, Kayaking	**F** Fishing	**HR** Horseback Riding
BW Birdwatching	**DS** Downhill Skiing	**GS** Gift Shop	**I** Information Center
C Camping		**H** Hiking	

**HULOPO'E BAY MARINE LIFE
CONSERVATION DISTRICT**
Hawai'i Dept. of Land and Natural Resources
Div. of Aquatic Resources
1151 Punchbowl St., Room 330
Honolulu, HI 96813
(808) 587-01
Strong swells and currents   **C, F, S, T**

KAKAHAI'A NATIONAL WILDLIFE REFUGE
U.S. Fish and Wildlife Service
PO 340
Haleiwa, HI 96712
(808) 637-6330
Special-use permit required; apply at
least 6 weeks in advance   **BW, H**

**KALAUPAPA PENINSULA
NATIONAL HISTORICAL PARK**
National Park Service
Pacific Area Office
300 Ala Moana Blvd.
Box 50165, Rm. 6305
Honolulu, HI 96850
(808) 541-2693   **BW, H, PA, TG**

KAMAKOU PRESERVE (MOLOKA'I)
The Nature Conservancy
1116 Smith St.
Honolulu, HI 96817
(808) 537-4508
Call one month in advance to reserve
for guided tours   **BW, H, I, PA, TG**

KANEPU'U PRESERVE (LANA'I)
The Nature Conservancy
1116 Smith St.
Honolulu, HI 96817
(808) 537-4508
Call one month in advance for reservations on guided tours.   **H, TG**

KAPUAIWA COCONUT GROVE
Dept. of Hawaiian Home Lands
PO 1879
Honolulu, HI 96805
(808) 586-3820
Permission required

LOPA BLACK SAND BEACH
Lanai Company
Lana'i City, HI 96763
(808) 565-7233
Four-wheel drive required

MANELE BAY
Rock Resorts
Public Relations
680 Iwilei Road, #540
Honolulu, HI 96817
(808) 545-3913
       BT, F, GS, H, HR, L, MT, PA, S, T

MOLOKA'I FOREST RESERVE
Hawai'i Dept. of Land
and Natural Resources
Div. of Forestry and Wildlife
Natural Area Reserves
54 South St., Room 101
Wailuku, HI 96793
(808) 871-2620
Four-wheel drive necessary; strenuous
hiking. Includes Lua Moku Ilihai, Pu'u
Ali'i Reserve, Waikolu Lookout, and
Olokui Reserve.

**MOLOKA'I RANCH RECREATION
NETWORK**
Molokai Ranch Ltd.
PO 259
Maunaloa, HI 96770
(808) 552-2767   **BT, CK, F, GS, H, HR,
I, MT, PA, RA, S, T, TG**

MO'OMOMI DUNES PRESERVE (MOLOKA'I)
The Nature Conservancy
1116 Smith St.
Honolulu, HI 96817
(808) 537-4508
Call one month in advance for reservations for guided tours   **C, H, MT, S, TG**

MUNRO JEEP TRAIL
Lanai Company
Lana'i City, HI 96763
(808) 565-7233
Four-wheel drive required

PALA'AU STATE PARK
Hawai'i Dept. of Land
and Natural Resources
Div. of State Parks
Maui District Office
54 South High St.
Wailuku, HI 96793
(808) 243-5354 (person)
(808) 567-6435 (on-site)
Permit required for camping
       C, H, MT, PA, T

L	Lodging	**PA**	Picnic Areas	**RC**	Rock Climbing	**TG**	Tours, Guides
MT	Marked Trails	**RA**	Ranger-led Activities	**S**	Swimming	**XC**	Cross-country Skiing
				T	Toilets		

275

PELEKUNU PRESERVE (MOLOKA'I)
The Nature Conservancy
1116 Smith St.
Honolulu, HI 96817
(808) 537-4508
Please call to inquire about public access

SHIPWRECK BEACH
Lanai Company
Lana'i City, HI 96763
(808) 565-7233
Four-wheel drive required

OAHU

BISHOP MUSEUM
PO 19000-A
Honolulu, HI 96817
(808) 847-3511 **GS, PA, T, TG**

DIAMOND HEAD STATE MONUMENT
Hawai'i Dept. of Land and Natural Resources
Div. of State Parks
PO 621
Honolulu, HI 96809
(808) 587-0300
Bring flashlight; two tunnels on hike to
lookout **H, MT, PA, T**

FOSTER BOTANICAL GARDEN
Hawai'i Dept. of Parks and Recreation
Honolulu Botanical Gardens
50 North Vineyard Blvd.
Honolulu, HI 96817
(808) 522-7065 **GS, I, PA, T, TG**

**HANAUMA BAY STATE
UNDERWATER PARK**
Hawai'i Dept. of Land
and Natural Resources
Div. of State Parks
PO 621, Honolulu, HI 96809
(808) 587-0300
Limited parking; best to come before
9 A.M. **I, PA, S, T**

HAROLD L. LYON ARBORETUM
Univ. of Hawai'i at Manoa
3860 Manoa Rd.
Honolulu, HI 96822-1180
(808) 988-7378
Classes available; guided tours on first
Fri. and third Wed./Sat. of month
BW, GS, TG

IMAX THEATER WAIKIKI
325 Seaside Ave.
Honolulu, HI 96815
(808) 923-4629 **GS, T**

KA'ENA POINT NATURAL AREA RESERVE
Hawai'i Dept. of Land and Natural Resources
Div. of Forestry and Wildlife
Natural Area Reserves
Kawaiahao Plaza, 567 S. King St. #132
Honolulu, HI 96813
(808) 587-0051 **BT, BW, F, H**

KAHANA VALLEY STATE PARK
Hawai'i Dept. of Land
and Natural Resources
Div. of State Parks, PO 621
Honolulu, HI 96809
(808) 587-0300 (person)
(808) 237-8858 (on-site)
BW, C, F, H, PA, S,

KEAIWA HEIAU STATE RECREATION AREA
Hawai'i Dept. of Land and Natural Resources
Div. of State Parks, PO 621
Honolulu, HI 96809
(808) 587-0300 (person)
(808) 488-6626 (on-site)
Camping requires permit
BW, BT, C, H, MT, PA, RC, T

KOKO CRATER BOTANICAL GARDEN
Hawai'i Dept. of Parks and Recreation
Honolulu Botanical Gardens
50 North Vineyard Blvd.
Honolulu, HI 96817
(808) 522-7060 **BW, H,T**

MA'AKUA GULCH
Hawai'i Dept. of Land and Natural Resources
Div. of Forestry and Wildlife
Na Ala Hele
1151 Punchbowl St.
Honolulu, HI 96813
(808) 587-0166
Beware of flash floods, falling rocks,
and hunters **BT, C, H, MT**

MAKUA-KA'ENA STATE PARK
Hawai'i Dept. of Land and Natural Resources
Div. of State Parks, PO Box 621
Honolulu, HI 96809
(808) 587-0300
Bring own drinking water
BW, F, H, PA, S, T

BT Bike Trails	**CK**	Canoeing, Kayaking	**F**	Fishing
BW Bird-watching			**GS**	Gift Shop
C Camping	**DS**	Downhill Skiing	**H**	Hiking

HR Horseback Riding
I Information Center

MALAEKAHANA STATE RECREATION AREA
Hawai'i Dept. of Land and Natural Resources
Div. of State Parks
PO 621
Honolulu, HI 96809
(808) 587-0300
   C, F, H, L, MT, PA, RC, S, T

MAUNAWILI TRAIL
Hawai'i Dept. of Land and Natural Resources
Div. of Forestry and Wildlife, Na Ala Hele
1151 Punchbowl St.
Honolulu, HI 96813
(808) 587-0166   **H, MT**

MOKU 'AUIA (GOAT ISLAND)
Hawai'i Dept. of Land and Natural Resources
Div. of Forestry and Wildlife
1151 Punchbowl St.
Honolulu, HI 96813
(808) 587-0166
  Bring old pair of shoes; island accessible
  at low tide   **BW**

MOUNT KA'ALA NATURAL AREA RESERVE
Hawai'i Dept. of Land and Natural Resources
Div. of Forestry and Wildlife
Kawaiahao Plaza, 567 S. King St. #132
Honolulu, HI 96813
(808) 587-0051
  Access restricted   **BW, H**

NU'UANU PALI STATE WAYSIDE
Hawai'i Dept. of Land and Natural Resources
Div. of State Parks, PO 621
Honolulu, HI 96809
(808) 587-0300
  Light windbreaker recommended

PAHOLE NATURAL AREA RESERVE
Hawai'i Dept. of Land and Natural Resources
Div. of Forestry and Wildlife
Kawaiahao Plaza
567 S. King St., #132
Honolulu, HI 96813
(808) 587-0051
  Access restricted   **BW, C, H, MT, PA**

PARADISE PARK
3737 Manoa Rd.
Honolulu, HI 96822
(808) 988-0200
  Mosquito repellent recommended
         BW, GS, MT, T, TG

PEACOCK FLATS CAMPGROUND
Hawai'i Dept. of Land
and Natural Resources
Div. of Forestry and Wildlife
Na Ala Hele
1151 Punchbowl St.
Honolulu, HI 96813
(808) 587-0166
  Fires prohibited   **BT, C, H, MT**

**PEARL HARBOR NATIONAL
WILDLIFE REFUGE**
U.S. Fish and Wildlife Service
PO 340
Haleiwa, HI 96712
(808) 541-1201 (person)
(808) 637-6330 (on-site)
  Special-use permit required; apply at
  least 6 weeks in advance   **BW, H**

PU'U'UALAKA'A STATE WAYSIDE
Hawai'i Dept. of Land
and Natural Resources
Div. of State Parks, PO 621
Honolulu, HI 96809
(808) 587-0300   **BW, H, MT, PA, RC, T**

SACRED FALLS STATE PARK
Hawai'i Dept. of Land
and Natural Resources
Div. of State Parks, PO 621
Honolulu, HI 96809
(808) 587-0300
  Beware of flash floods
         BW, H, MT, PA, T

SEA LIFE PARK HAWAI'I
41-202 Kalanianuiaole Hwy., Suite 7
Waimanalo, HI 96795
(808) 259-7933
  Admission fee   **GS, I, T, TG**

**WA'AHILA RIDGE STATE
RECREATION AREA**
Hawai'i Dept. of Land
and Natural Resources
Div. of State Parks, PO 621
Honolulu, HI 96809
(808) 587-0300   **BW, H, MT, PA, RC, T**

WAHIAWA BOTANICAL GARDEN
Hawai'i Dept. of Parks and Recreation
1396 California Ave.
Wahiawa, HI 96786
(808) 621-7321   **MT, PA, T, TG**

L	Lodging	**PA**	Picnic Areas	**RC**	Rock Climbing	**TG**	Tours, Guides
MT	Marked Trails	**RA**	Ranger-led Activities	**S**	Swimming	**XC**	Cross-country Skiing
				T	Toilets		

277

WAIKIKI AQUARIUM
2777 Kalakana Ave.
Honolulu, HI 96815
(808) 923-9741 (day)
(808) 923-5335 (night)   **GS, I, T**

WAIMEA VALLEY
59-864 Kamehameha Hwy.
Hale‘iwa, HI 96712
(808) 638-8511
    Includes Waimea Falls Park
                        BT, BW, C, CK, GS, H,
                        I, MT, PA, S, T, TG

KAUA‘I

ALAKA‘I SWAMP
Hawai‘i Dept. of Land and Natural Resources
Div. of State Parks
Kaua‘i District Office
3060 Eiwa St., Room 306
Lihu‘e, HI 96766
(808) 241-3444
    Includes Pihea Trail, Alaka‘i Swamp
    Trail, Awa‘awapuhi Trail; bring drinking
    water and raincoat. Sign in at the Koke‘e
    Natural History Museum   **BW, H, I, MT**

BARKING SANDS BEACH
Access via permission of U.S. Navy
(808) 335-4229

HANALEI NATIONAL WILDLIFE REFUGE
National Park Service
PO 87
Kilauea, HI 96754
(808) 828-1413
(808) 828-1520 (hike information)
    Special-use permit required; apply at
    least 6 weeks in advance   **BW, H**

HULE‘IA NATIONAL WILDLIFE REFUGE
National Park Service
PO 87
Kilauea, HI 96754
(808) 828-1413
(808) 828-1520 (hike information)
    Special-use permit required; apply at
    least 6 weeks in advance   **BW, H**

Keahua Arboretum
Hawai‘i Div. of Forestry and Wildlife
Eiwa St.
Lihu‘e, HI 96766
(808) 241-3433
                        BW, H, PA, S, T

KILAUEA POINT NATIONAL WILDLIFE REFUGE
National Park Service, PO 87
Kilauea, HI 96754
(808) 828-1413
(808) 828-1520 (hike information)
    Special-use permit required; apply at
    least 6 weeks in advance   **BW, H**

KOKE‘E STATE PARK
Hawai‘i Dept. of Land and Natural Resources
Div. of State Parks
Kaua‘i District Office
3060 Eiwa St., Room 306
Lihu‘e, HI 96766-1875
(808) 241-3444
    Includes Koke‘e Natural History
    Museum, Koke‘e campground, and
    Kalalau Lookout; bring drinking water
                    BW, C, F, GS, H, I, L, MT, PA, T

NA PALI COAST STATE PARK
Hawai‘i Dept. of Land and Natural Resources
Div. of State Parks
Kaua‘i District Office
3060 Eiwa St., # 306
Lihu‘e, HI 96766
(808) 241-3444
    Includes Kalalau Trail, Hanakapiai
    Valley, Hanakoa Valley, Kalalau Valley;
    bring drinking water, mosquito repel-
    lent, camping gear for overnight stay
    when hiking Kalalau Trail; arrange for
    kayaking at Kapaa, Waihaa, or Po‘ipu
                    BW, C, CK, F, H, MT, PA, S, T

NATIONAL TROPICAL BOTANICAL GARDEN
PO 340, Lawa‘i, HI 96765
(808) 332-7361   **TG**

PO‘IPU BEACH
Hawai‘i Dept. of Parks and Recreation
4193 Hardy St.
Lihu‘e, HI 96766
(808) 241-6660   **S, T**

POLIHALE STATE PARK
Hawai‘i Dept. of Land and Natural Resources
Div. of State Parks
Kaua‘i District Office
3060 Eiwa St., # 306
Lihu‘e, HI 96766
(808) 241-3444
    Bring drinking water   **C, F, PA, S, T**

BT Bike Trails	**CK**	Canoeing, Kayaking	**F**	Fishing	**HR**	Horseback Riding
BW Bird-watching			**GS**	Gift Shop		
C Camping	**DS**	Downhill Skiing	**H**	Hiking	**I**	Information Center

SPOUTING HORN

Hawai'i Dept. of Parks and Recreation
4193 Hardy St.
Lihu'e, HI 96766
(808) 241-6660   **GS, T**

WAILUA RIVER STATE PARK

Hawai'i Dept. of Land
and Natural Resources
Div. of State Parks, Kaua'i District Office
3060 Eiwa St., # 306
Lihu'e, HI 96766
(808) 241-3444
    Includes Wailua Falls and Fern Grotto;
    kayak to Fern Grotto
                    CK, F, GS, H, I, PA, T, TG

WAIMEA CANYON STATE PARK

Hawai'i Dept. of Land
and Natural Resources
Div. of State Parks
Kaua'i District Office
3060 Eiwa St., Rm 306
Lihu'e, HI 96766
(808) 241-3444
    Bring drinking water
                    BW, F, H, MT, PA, T

ABOVE: *Visitors have long craved Hawai'i's vistas. On January 23, 1910, photographer Lawrence Edgeworth documented the motorized ascent of a well-dressed group who managed to make it to the top of the pali.*

L	Lodging	**PA**	Picnic Areas	**RC**	Rock Climbing	**TG**	Tours, Guides
MT	Marked Trails	**RA**	Ranger-led Activities	**S**	Swimming	**XC**	Cross-country Skiing
				T	Toilets		

INDEX

NOTE: **Bold** page numbers
refer to picture captions.

A *ali'i* shrubs, 97
balone, **168**
Admiralty Island and
  Admiralty Island
  National Monument, 162,
  169–71, **169**, 266
ae'o. See stilt birds
'Ahihi-Kina'u Natural
  Area Reserve, 60, **273**
ahole fish, 46
'Aiea Loop Trail, 112
'Aka'akai (bulrush), 46
'Akaka Falls State Park,
  45, 46, 271
'akala. See raspberries
alae ke'oke'o. See coot
  birds
Alaka'i Swamp and Trail,
  123, 132, 133–34, **133**,
  278
Alakoko Fishpond, 136
Alaska Maritime National
  Wildlife Refuge, 215–
  16, 266
Alaska Peninsula, 207,
  211–15
Alaska-Chilkat Bald
  Eagle Preserve, 174, 266
Alaska-Peninsula
  National Wildlife Refuge,
  212–13, 266
albatrosses, 90–91, 110,
  116, **136**, 139, 145
alder trees, 166, 178, 248
Aleutian Islands, 149, **153**,
  186, 188, 215–16
algaroba. See mesquite
alien species
  and the Hawaiian Islands, 8,
  11, 15, 31, 34, **44**, 124, 133,
  133
  *See also specific flora or
    fauna*
Alsek River, 179–80, 266
'ama'u. See ferns: *Sadleria*
  ferns
amica plants, 191, 253
Anchorage, Alaska, and
  the environs, 200–204
Anchorage Coastal
  Wildlife Refuge, **194**,

200–201, 266
Aniakchak National
  Monument and Preserve,
  214, 266
Annette Island, 162
apples, 117, 119
archaeological sites
  in Alaska, 204, 249,
    250–51, 252
  and early Polynesian
    colonizations, 11
  on Hawai'i (Big Island),
    32, **38–39**, 42, 50
  on Moloka'i, 84, 89, 90
  on O'ahu, 110, 112, 118
Arctic National Wildlife
  Refuge, 156, 242, 246,
  250, 253–57, 266
arnica plants, **251**
aspen trees, 219
auklets, 215
'auku'u. See herons
aven plants, 178, 191
avocado, 119
Awa'awapuhi Trail, 132

B amboo, 71, 76, **77**
anana trees, 14, 46,
  84, 98
banyan trees, 59, 76
Baranof Island, 171, 266
Barking Sands Beach, 134,
  278
barnacles, 160, 183
Bartlett Cove and
  Campground, **162**, 176
bats, 6, 46, 131, 211
bearberries, **247**
bears
  as an Alaskan natural
    resource, 153
  in Arctic Alaska, 245,
    248, 249, 253, **255**
  black, 160, 178, 179,
    183, 189, **191**, 200,
    224, 225, 236, 248, 249
  brown, 148–49, 160, 162,
    170, 178, 183, 189, 200,
    205, **206**, 207, 211, 212,
    215, 225, 249
  and the *Exxon Valdez*
    oil spill, 210
  food for, 189, **191**, 205,
  · **206**, 207, 212, 234, **235**,
    253, **255**
  glacier, 179
  grizzly, 153, 189, 211, 222,

224, 231, 234, **235**, 245,
  248, 249, 253
  and humans, 234–35
  in Interior Alaska, 222,
    224, 225, 231, 234, 236
  Kodiak, 211
  numbers of, 170
  polar, 253, **255**
  reserves for, 170
  size of, 189, 211
  in South-Central Alaska,
    183, 189, 200, 205,
    206, 207, 211, 212, 215
  in Southeastern Alaska,
    160, 162, 170, 178, 179
  Toklat, 234
  and wolves, 162
beavers, 162, 224, 225,
  236, 248
Becharof National
  Wildlife Refuge, 211–
  12, 266
Behm Canal, 166
Bering Land Bridge
  National Preserve, 222,
  237, **238**, 266
berries
  in Alaska, 149, 166,
    204, 234, **235**, **247**
  in the Hawaiian
    Islands, 45, 62–63
  *See also type of
    berries*
birch trees, 203, 219,
  225, **235**, 248, 249
birds
  in Arctic Alaska, 245
  arrival on Hawaiian
    Islands of, 6
  as extinct/endangered,
    11, 14, 15, 41, **47**,
    110, 132, **133**
  and the *Exxon Valdez*
    oil spill, 195, 210
  in Interior Alaska,
    223, 228, 229, 236
  in South-Central Alaska,
    192, 195,
    195, 198, 199, 200,
    201, 203, 207, 211,
    212, **213**, 214, 215, 216
  in Southeastern Alaska,
    162, 163, **163**, 167–68,
    170–71, **172–73**, 173–74,
    178
  See also specific bird
Bishop Museum, 104, 276

bison, 189
black sand, 35, 37, 43, 47, 50
Blue River, 166
blueberries, 166, 204, **235**
bogs, 113, 132, 133, 228
Boiling Pots, 47
boobie birds, 110, **113**,
116, 139, 145
Brady Icefield, 178
brant birds, 215, 238, 257
breadfruit (*ulu*), 14, 71,
76, 112
Bristol Bay, 211, **213**
Brooks Mountain Range,
241–42, 246–52, **250**, 253
bulrushes, 46
bunting birds, 163
butterfly fish, **58**, 60, 135

Cactus, 43, 76
Caesalpina Kauaiense
trees, 124
candlenut trees (*kukui*),
58, 71, 112, 119
Cape Krusenstern National
Monument, 246, 252-53,
267
caribou
in Arctic Alaska, **240**,
245-46, 249, 251,
252, 253-54, **256**
in Interior Alaska,
219, 222, 229, 231,
234, 236
prevalence in Alaska
of, 148-49, 152
in South-Central
Alaska, 212, 215
cattle, 11, 15, 43, **48–
49**, 54, 62, 92, 118, 216
cedar trees, 166, 167
cereus plants, 76
Chain of Craters Road, 32
Chichagof Island, 171, 267
chickens, 11, 14, 131-32
Chiswell Islands, 199
chitons, **168**
Christmas-berry, 89, 92-93
Chugach National Forest,
190, 193, 203, 267
Chugach State Park, 200,
267
cinder cones, **48–49**, 50,
52, 64, **65**, 68, **100**, 109
cinder deserts, **52**, 64
cinnamon, 112
cinquefoil plants, 252

clams, 106, 163, **168**,
183, 195-96
cloud forests, 9, 11
coconut palms, 14, **38–39**,
72, 85
coffee trees, 144
conservation
in Alaska, 155, **214**, 254-55
on the Hawaiian Islands, 15,
17, 110
of marine life, 40, 42, 106,
109
of seals, **214**
coot birds (*alae ke'oke'o*),
41, 56, 85, 135, 140
Copper River Delta, 189,
192, 267
coral, 6, **58**, 59, 60, 97,
106, 109
cormorants, 212, 215
cottonwood trees, 174, 225
crabs, **168**, 171, 195, 216
cranes, 224, **226–27**
curlew birds, 85, 238
currants, 204
cycad plants, 124
cypress trees, 69

Dall sheep. *See* sheep
damselfish, 59
deer, 15, 93, 96, 98. *See also*
caribou; moose
Denali National Park and
Preserve, **157**, 203, **218**,
222, **226–27**, 229-36, **230**,
234, **235**, 267
Denali State Park, 203, 267
Devastation Trail, **28**, 31
devilfish, 60
devil's club bushes, 166
Diamond Head, 101, 107, 109
Diamond Head State
Monument, 107, 109, 276
diapensia plants, 191
Dolly Varden fish, 162,
212, 214
dolphins, 40, 97, 110,
116, 162
donkeys, 41
doves, 93
dowitcher birds, **194**
dryas plants, 253
ducks
in Arctic Alaska, 240
eider, 238, 240, 257
on the Hawaiian
Islands, 46, 85, 135,

140, 145
Hawaiian *koloa*, 46, 85,
135, 140
in Interior Alaska,
224, 229, 236
Laysan, 145
in South-Central
Alaska, 203, 207, 215
in Southeastern Alaska,
173–74
dunes
in Alaska, 236, 249-50
in the Hawaiian
Islands, 80, 89-91,
90–91, 116, 135
dunlin birds, **195**

Eagle rays, 106, 110
eagles
in Arctic Alaska, 245
bald, 160, 162, 166,
168, 170-71, **172–73**,
174, 199, 200, 207, 211
food for, 171, 174
golden, 245
Hawaiian, 90
as Indian symbols, 163
in South-Central
Alaska, 199, 200,
207, 211
in Southeastern Alaska,
160, 162, 163, 166,
168, 170-71, **172–73**,
174
earthquakes, in Alaska,
179, 195-96
eelgrass, 215
eels, 60, 106, 110, 135
eider ducks, 238, 240, 257
ermine, **254**
eskers (glacial ridges),
204
eucalyptus trees, 11, 43,
62, 69, 71, 84, 92, 105
evergreens, 62. *See also* pine
trees; *specific evergreen*
'Ewa District, 102, 110-12
Exit Glacier, 198
Exxon Valdez oil spill,
193, 195, 196, 207,
210, 211

Falcons, 225, 227, 229,257
Fern Grotto, 136
ferns
on Hawai'i (Big
Island), 31, 34

on Kaua'i, 136
on Lana'i, 96–97
on Maui, 62, 63, 65–66,
68, **70**, **71**
on Moloka'i, 84, 88
on O'ahu, 106, 112, 118
in rain forests, 9
finches, 145
fireweed plants, 178,
181, **208–9**, **234**
fjords, 166–67, 169, **181**
floods, 16, 76, 117
flora and fauna
Alaskan endangered/
extinct, 149, 155–56, 171,
199, 216, 238
defense mechanisms of,
8, **9**, 31
Hawaiian alien/imported,
8, 11, 15, 31, 34, **44**,
124, 133, **133**
Hawaiian endemic, 8, 15,
44, 105–6, 109, 124, 132,
133, 139, **145**
Hawaiian endangered/
extinct, 15, 105–6,
116–17, 124, 131, 132,
133, **133**, **136**, 145
reintroduction of
Hawaiian extinct, 15–16
See also specific
arboretum, botanical
gardens, flora, or
fauna
forests
as an Alaskan natural re-
source, 153, 155, 156
as extinct/endangered, 9,
11, 14, 15
and hurricanes, 138
in Interior Alaska, 221, 222,
229
in South-Central Alaska, 196
in Southeastern Alaska, 159,
160, 166
taiga, 221, 222, 229
and tree decay, 9
See also cloud forests; rain
forests; *specific arboretum,*
preserve, or type of tree
forget-me-not plants, 253
Foster Botanical Garden,
104, 276
foxes, 153, 162, 200, 211,
216, 245, 248, 249, 252,
254
Frederick Sound, 168, 267

frigate birds, 110, **112**,
139

Gallinule birds, 135, 140
Garden of the Gods, 93,
94–95, 274
gardenias, **83**, 92
Gates of the Arctic National
Park and Preserve, 242,
246, 248, 267
geese
in Arctic Alaska, 240
Canada, **191**, 201, 215,
238
emperor, 212, 214, 215,
238
flightless, 90, **90–91**,
110
in the Hawaiian Islands,
31, 66, **68**, 90, **90–91**,
110
Hawaiian native, 31,
66, **68**
in Interior Alaska,
236, 238
in South-Central Alaska,
191, 201, 207, 212, 214,
215
in Southeastern Alaska,
173–74
Geranium arboreum, 63
ginger, 14, **14**, **45**, 46,
57, 71, 105, 106, **119**
Glacier Bay and Glacier
Bay National Park and
Preserve, **147**, **158**,
162, 169, 174–80, **175**,
176–80, 267
glaciers
age of ice in, 186
and the Alaskan
scenery, 148–49, 153,
160
and fjords, 166
and icefields, 167
in Interior Alaska,
222, 225–26, 235
and mountain peaks, 189
number of, 153, 160
size of, 160, 186
in South-Central Alaska,
183, 186, 189, 196, 203
in Southeastern Alaska,
160, 166
See also specific glacier
goats
in Alaska, 162, 178,

183, 189, 198
in the Hawaiian Islands,
15, 41, 65, 92, 144
goby fish, 46, 76
goldfish, 59
grasses/grasslands
in Alaska, 215
as endangered, 8–9
on Hawai'i (Big
Island), 41, 43, **48–49**
on Kaua'i, 144
on Lana'i, 97
on Maui, 62, 65–66
on Moloka'i, 91
grasshoppers, 8
grayling fish, 212
Great Kobuk Sand Dunes,
249–50
grebes, 191, 201
Green Sand Beach, **36**, 37
grouse, 189
guava groves, 15, 45, 76,
84, 119, 124, 144
gulls, 200
gum trees, 112–13
gyrfalcons, 229

Ha'alelepa'akai, 96
Hakalau Forest National
Wildlife Refuge, 46, 271
hala pepe (Dracaena), 69
hala. See pandanus trees
Halawa Valley, **83**, 84, 274
Haleakala National Park,
54, 62–68, 76, 273. *See also*
Kipahula District
Haleakala (volcano), 11
Halemau'i Trail, 66, 68
Halema'uma'u Crater, 28–
29, 31, **33**
Halema'uma'u Trail, **23**,
26, 29, 31
halibut, 162
Hamakua Coast, **45**, 46–50
Hana Coast, **12–13**, 54,
71–77, 135
Hanakapi'ai Beach, 141, 144
Hanakoa Valley, 144
Hanalei National Wildlife
Refuge, 135, **137**, 140–41,
278
Hanalilolilo Trail, 88
Hanauma Bay State
Underwater Park, 109, 276
hanging valleys, 77, 141, 144
Hapu'u. See ferns
Harding Icefield, 198

hares, 153, 224, 248
Harold L. Lyon Arboretum, 105-6, 276
hau. See hibiscus
Hauʻula, Oʻahu, 117
Hawaiʻi Tropical Botanical Gardens, **44**, 47
Hawaiʻi Volcanoes National Park, 22-35, 63, 271
Hawaiian Islands National Wildlife Refuge, 144-45
Hawaiian Volcano Observatory, 26, 28
hawks, 46
heliconia plants, **45**
heliotrope plants, 73, 76, 89, **90**
hemlock trees, **162**, 166, 167, 170, 171, 178, 193, 199
herons, 46, 56, 85, 118
herring, 195
hibiscus shrubs (*hau*), **14**, 71-72
hinahina. See heliotrope plants
honeycreepers
  ʻamakihi, 35, 59, 87
  ʻapapane, **26**, 35, 59, 87
  crested, **61**, 63
  evolution of, 7
  ʻiʻiwi, 35, 59, **72**
  nuku puʻu, 77
  ʻoʻo, **10**, 14, 132
  palila, **47**, 50
  See also parrotbill
Honolua, Maui, 59
Honolua–Mokuleʻia Bay Marine Life Conservation District, 59, 273
Honolulu District, 102, 104-10, **107**
Honouliuli Preserve, 276
Hosmer Grove, 62, 274
hot spots, 3, 6, **17**
Hualalai (volcano), 11, 19, 40
Hubbard Glacier, 180
huckleberry bushes, 166
Huleʻia National Wildlife Refuge, 135, 278
Hulopoʻe Bay Marine Life Conservation District, 97, 275
hunting, 149, 251
Hyatt Regency Waikoloa,

42, 271

ʻIao Needle, 57-58, **57**
  ʻIao Valley, 16, 56
ʻIao Valley State Park, 57-58, **57**, 273
ibis, 110
ice caves, **179**
icebergs, 203
icefields, 167, 178
iliau plants, 131
Iliau Trail, 131
ilima shrubs, 98
Imax Theater, 107, 276
inchworms, 7
Indian mulberry (*noni*), 84, 112
Innoko National Wildlife Refuge, 236, 267
International Biosphere Reserves, 22, 63
ʻio. See hawks
iris, **190**
ironwood trees, 11, 84, 138
Isodendrion plants, 106
Izembek National Wildlife Refuge, 214-15, 267

Jaggar (Thomas) Museum, 28, 273
jasmine plants, 252
jellyfish, 106
Juneau Icefield, 167, 173, 268

Ka Lae, **36**, 37, 271-72
Kachemak Bay State Park and Wilderness Park, 168, 199, 268
Kaʻena Point Natural Area Reserve, **113**, 116, **120–21**, 276
Kahana Valley State Park, 117-18, 276
Kahuna Falls, 46
Kailua, Hawaiʻi (Big Island), 40
Kaimu Beach, 47, 50
Kakahaiʻa National Wildlife Refuge, 85, 275
Kalalau Lookout, 132
Kalalau Trail, 141
Kalalau Valley, **130**, **142– 43**, 144
Kalaupapa Peninsula National Historic Park, 80, 86, **86–87**, 88-89, 275
Kaloko-Honokohau National

Historical Park, 41, 272
Kalopa State Recreation Area, 46, 272
Kamakou Preserve, 87, 275
kamaʻo birds, 132
kame terraces, 189
Kamoamoa area, **22**
Kanaha Pond State Wildlife Sanctuary, 56, 273
Kanaio Natural Area Reserve, 69, 274
Kanepuʻu Preserve, 92, 275
Kanuti National Wildlife Refuge, 236, 268
Kapuaiwa Coconut Grove, 85, 275
Kapunakea Preserve, 59, 274
Katmai Country, 204-10
Katmai National Park and Preserve, 155, 205-8, **206, 208–9**, 268
Kaʻu Desert, **33**, 35, 272
kaunaʻoa vines, 98
Kaupo Gap, 66, 69, 71
Kaupo Valley, 63-64, **64–65**
kava plants, 106
Kayak Island, 192-93, 268
Keahua Arboretum, 137, 278
Keaiwa Heiau State Recreation Area, 112, 276
Kealakekua Bay State Underwater Park, 37, 40, 272
Kealia Pond National Wildlife Refuge, 60, 274
Keʻanae Arboretum, 71, 274
kelp, 160
Kenai Fjords National Park, **196–97**, 198-99, 268
Kenai National Wildlife Refuge and Wilderness, 199-200, 268
Kenai Peninsula, 188, 193, 198-200
kettle ponds, 189, 204
kiawe. See mesquite
Kilauea Point National Wildlife Refuge, **136**, 138-39, 278
Kilauea (volcano), 3, **7**, 9, **18**, 20, 22-35, **23**, **28–29**
kingfisher birds, 163
kinglet birds, **162**, 178
kioea. See curlew birds
Kipahoehoe Natural Area Reserve, 37, 272

Kipahula District of
  Haleakala National Park
  66, 74–75, 76, 77, 274
kipuka islands, 50
Kipuka Puaulu, 35
kittiwake birds, 178,
  199, 212, 215
koa trees, 9, 35, 58, **61**,
  62, 77, 96, 118, 124
Kobuk Valley National
  Park, 236, **240**, 246,
  249–50, 268
Kodiak Island, 167, 210–
  11, 214
Kodiak National Wildlife
  Refuge, 210–11, 268
Kohala Coast, 41–46
Kohala (volcano), 19, 41, 43
Koke'e Lodge, 132
Koke'e Natural History
  Museum, 131, 133
Koke'e State Park, 130,
  130, 131, 278
kokia plants, 116–17
Koko Crater Botanical
  Garden, 109–10, 276
Koko Head, 101, 109–10
kolea trees, 35, 46
koloa. See ducks:
  Hawaiian *koloa*
Kona Coast, 35–41
Ko'olau Loa District,
  102, 117
Ko'olau Poko District,
  102, 117
Ko'olau Range, 101,
  104–5, 105, 110,
  117–19, **119**
kopiko trees, 46
Koyukuk National
  Wildlife Refuge, 236, 268
kukui. See candlenut trees
Kukui Trail, 131
Kula Botanical Gardens,
  68, 274

Lahaina, Maui, 59
Lahaina Pali Trail,
  58–59
Lake Clark National Park
  and Preserve, 200, 204,
  269
Lake Wai'au, 50
lantana plants, 15, 92–93
Lapakahi State
  Historical Park, 42, 272
LaPerouse Glacier, 178

larks, 245
lava
  'a'a, 32, 60, 132
  and the *ahu* lava
    cairns, 66
  in Alaska, 237
  and beach destruction, 50
  composition of, 3
  in Garden of the Gods,
    93, **94–95**
  and Lava Tree State
    Monument, 47
  pahoehoe, **18**, 32, 34,
    66, 132
  pali, 43, 56, 66, 68,
    102, **104–5**, 117, 118,
    134, 141
  Pele's hair on, 34, 62
  porous, 102
  tubes, **30**, 32, 42
  types of, 32, 34
Lava Tree State Monument,
  47, 272
leeward coasts of Hawaii, 6,
  8–9. *See also specific island*
leper colony, 80, **86–87**, 88
lichens, 62, 73, 166, 236
lilies, 84
lionfish, 135
liverworts, 85
lobelias, 57, 59
lobsters, 135
longspur birds, 228
loons, 191, 201, 203
Lopa Black Sand Beach,
  98, 275
lousewort plants, 191
lupine plants, **181**, **251**
Lynn Canal, 160, 174
lynx, 153, 200, 224, 225
Lyon (Harold L.)
  Arboretum, 105–6, 276

Ma'akua Gulch, 117, 276
Macadamia trees, 35, 68
MacKenzie State
  Recreation Area, 47, 272
McNeil River State Game
  Refuge and Sanctuary,
  205, 269
mahimahi fish, 107
mahogany trees, 112
Makaha Valley, 101, 119
Makapu'u Point, 110, **111**
Makua Valley, 101, 116, 120
Makua-Ka'ena State Park,
  120, 276

Malaekahana Bay State
  Recreation Area, 117, 277
mamane trees, 11, 35, **47**,
  50, 63, 65, 87
mamo birds, 14
Manele Bay, 97, 275
mango trees, 84, 124, 144
mangroves, 85
Manoa Falls, 105
Manoa Valley, 102, 105
manta rays, 60
Manuka Natural Area
  Reserve, 37, 272
marijuana, 17
marlin, 40
martens, 162, 236, 248
mauka forests, 124
Mauna Kea Ice Age
  Natural Area Reserve,
  50, 272
Mauna Kea Observatory, 51
Mauna Kea (volcano), 3,
  11, 19, 41, **47**, **48–49**,
  50–51, **51**
Mauna Lani Bay Hotel and
  Bungalows, 42, 272
Mauna Loa (volcano), 3,
  11, 20, 22–35, 50, 51
Mauna Ulu (volcano), 32
Maunawili Trail, 118, 277
Mendenhall Glacier, 173,
  269
Mendenhall Wetlands
  State Game Refuge, 173–
  74, 269
mesquite, 9, 41, 42–43,
  58, 85, 98
mikinalo plants, 133
miller birds, 145
mink, 162, 236, 248
mint plants, 8, 63, 84
Misty Fjords National
  Monument, 166–67, **169**,
  269
Mitchell Bay Bear
  Reserve, 170
moa. See chickens
moi fish, 46
Moku 'Auia (Goat Island),
  117, 277
Mokule'ia Bay, 59
mollusks, 46, 90
Moloa'a Bay, 138
Moloka'i Forest Reserve,
  85–88, 275
Moloka'i Ranch Recreation
  Network, 91, 275

Molokini Island, 60
Molokini Shoal Marine
    Life Conservation
    District, 60, 274
mongoose, 73, **76**, 131–32
monkeypod, 84, 85
monstera plants, **45**
Mo'omomi Dunes Preserve,
    80, 89–91, **90–91**, 275
moose
    in Arctic Alaska, 248,
        249
    in Interior Alaska,
        222, 224, 225, 231,
        234, 235
    in South-Central
        Alaska, 199, 200
    in Southeastern Alaska,
        176, 178
morning glories, 89–90,
    90, 92, 98, **99**, 134
mosquitoes, 16, 43, 63,
    199, 253
mosses, 34, 85, 87, 166,
    178, 219
Mount Ka'ala Natural
    Area Reserve, 113, 120,
    277
Mount McKinley National
    Park. *See* Denali
    National Park and
    Preserve
Muliwai Trail, 45
mullet, 46, 59
Munro Jeep Trail, 93, 96–97,
    96, 275
murre birds, 212, 215
musk oxen, 238, 245
mussels, 160, 163, **168**

Na Pali Coast, **122**, 123,
    128, 132, 134, **140**,
    141–45, **142–43**
Na Pali Coast State Park,
    141–45, **142–43**, 278
Naha, Maui, 98
Nancy Lake State
    Recreation Area, 203, 269
nanu. See gardenias
National Petroleum
    Reserve, 254, 269
National Tropical Botanical
    Gardens, 134-35, 278
native species of
    Hawai'i, 8, 15, **44**, 105–6,
    109, 124, 132, **133**, 139,
    145. *See also specific flora*

or fauna
naupaka plants, 73, 89,
    96, **134**
Nene. See geese:
    Hawaiian native
New Eddystone Rock, 166
Ni'ihau Island, 134
Noatak National Preserve,
    242, 246, 249, 269
noddie birds, 145
Nogahabara Dunes, 236
noni. See Indian mulberry
Northwest Coast (Arctic
    Alaska), 252-53
Nounou Ridge, 137
Novarupta (volcanic
    plug), 206, 207
Nowitna National
    Wildlife Refuge, 236, 269
nuku pu'u birds, 77, **133**
nunataks (mountain
    peaks), 198
Nunivak Island, 238
Nu'uanu Pali State
    Wayside, 105, 277

Octopus, 60, **168**
    helo bushes, 28, 35, 63
'Ohe'o Gulch, 76, **77**
'ohi'a trees
    on Hawai'i (Big Island), **23**,
        26, **27**, 31, 34, 35, 46, 47
    on Kaua'i, 133
    on Maui, 58, **61**, 63, 77
    on Moloka'i, 84, 87, 88
    in rain forests, 9
oil/oil industry
    as an Alaskan natural
        resource, 153, 156
    in Arctic Alaska, 254–55
    and the *Exxon Valdez*
        spill, 193, 195, 196,
        207, 210, 211
    in South-Central Alaska,
        193, 195, 196, 207, 210,
        211–12
'Ola'a Forest, 34
Old Kona Airport State
    Recreation Area, 40–41,
    272
olives, 92
olivine, **36**, 37
olopua. See olives
Onion Portage, **240**, 249,
    250–51
o'o birds, **10**, 14, 132
'opae'ula. See shrimp

'ope'ape'a. See bats
'opihi. See mollusks
orchids, **44**, **45**, 84, 104,
    105, 141
owls, 46, 90, 245, 257
oystercatcher birds, 163,
    163

Pack Creek Bear Reserve,
    170
Pahole Natural Area
    Reserve, 116, 277
paintbrush plants, **181**
pala'a. See ferns
Pala'au State Park, 89, 275
Pali 'Ele'ele, 57
palm trees, 14, **38–39**,
    72, 85, 104, 112–13,
    118–19
Palmer Hay Flats State
    Game Refuge, 203, 269
pandanus trees (*hala*),
    43, 73, 93, 96, 138, 141
Paradise Park, 105, 277
Parker Ranch, 43–44, 273
parrotbill, **61**, 63, 77
partridges, 93
Peacock Flats, 116, 277
Pearl Harbor, 101, 102, 110
Pearl Harbor National
    Wildlife Refuge, 110, 277
Pelekunu Preserve and
    Trail, 88, 276
penguins, 110
Pepe'opae bog, 80, 87–88
persimmons, 69, 92
petrel birds, 145
phalarope birds, 163
pheasants, 93
philodendron plants, **45**
phlox plants, 253
pigs, 9, 11, 14, 15, 16,
    34, 77
Pihea Trail, 132, 133
pike, 203, 212, 224, 236
pili grass, 8–9, 97
pine trees, 11, 62, 69,
    86, 93
pineapples, 62, 79, 80,
    83, 92, 97, 113
Pinnell Mountain National
    Recreation Trail, 228
plovers, 245, 252
plum trees, 84, 85, 138
plumerias, **14**, 46, 104
pohuehue. See morning
    glories

Poʻipu Beach, 135, 278
Polihale State Park, 134, 278
Polipoli Springs State Recreational Area, 64–65, 69, 274
pollock fish, 199
Pololu Valley Lookout, 43
poppies, 191
porcupines, 200, 248
porpoises, 139, 162, 166
Portage Lake and Portage Glacier, 203, 269
pothos plants, 42–43, 141
prawns, 46
Pribilof Islands, 186, **214**, 216, **217**
Prince of Wales Island, 162, 167
Prince William Sound, 183, 188, **191**, 193, 195–96, **195**, 269
protea plants, 53
ptarmigan, 189
puaiohi birds, 132
pueo. See owls
puffer fish, 60
puffins, 199, 212, **213**, 215
pukiawe shrubs, 35, 58, **60**, 62, 97
Punaluʻu Beach, 35, 37, 273
Puʻu Loa, 32
Puʻu o Kila Lookout, 132
Puʻu Oʻo (volcano), **18**, 23, **24–25**, 26, 31, 34
Puʻu ʻUlaʻula, 63
Puʻukohola Heiau National Historic Site, 37, 273
Puʻuʻualakaʻa State Wayside, 106, 277

Rail birds, 110
Rain forests
in Alaska, 148, **162**, 163, 166–67
on Hawaiʻi (Big Island), **28–29**, 34, 35, 46
Hawaiian, as safe and unique, 9, 16
on Kauaʻi, 131, 141
on Lanaʻi, 96
on Maui, 66, 77
on Molokaʻi, 87
Rainbow Falls, 47
raspberries (*ʻakala*), 7, 62
rat foot plant, 96
rats, 9, 14, 73, **76**, 216

ravens, 163
Red Hill, 63
reefs, 6, 106, 109
rhododendrons, 237, 252
river otters, 211
Royal Waikoloan, 42, 273
Russell Fjord Wilderness Area, 180, **181**
Russell Glacier, **182**

Sacred Falls State Park, 117, **118**, 277
Sadleria ferns (*ʻamaʻu*), 62, 63, 68, **70**, **71**, 96
salmon
chum (dog), 162, 174
as eagles' food, 171, 174
as food for bears, 189, 205, **206**, 207, 212
hatchery-reared, 156
humpback (pink), 162
and Indian beliefs, 163
in Interior Alaska, 224
king (chinook), 162
silver (coho), 162
sockeye (red), 148–49, 162, 205, **206**, 214
in South-Central Alaska, 183, 189, 193, 199, 205, **206**, 207, 211, 212, 214
in Southeastern Alaska, 162, 163, 171, 174
sand lances, 195
sandalwood, 11, 86, 92
sandpiper birds, 153, 167–68, 192, **195**, 228, 245, 252
Sandy Beach, 109
saxifrage plants, 191, 253
Scammon's spring beauty plants, 191
Sea Life Park Hawaiʻi, 110, 277
sea lions
in Hawaii, 110
in South-Central Alaska, 183, 193, 195, 198, 199, 210, 211, 212
in Southeastern Alaska, 162
sea otters, 149, 167, **168**, 171, 195
sea stars, **168**
sea urchins, 160, **168**
seals
in Arctic Alaska, 253, **255**
conservation of, **214**

as food, 253, **255**
fur, **196–97**, 216, **217**
harbor, 162, 178, 195, 212
and the Hawaiian Islands, 6, 90, 110, 116, **136**, 139, 145, **145**
monk, 6, 90, 110, 116, **136**, 139, 145
in South-Central Alaska, 195, **196–97**, 210, 212, 216, **217**
in Southeastern Alaska, 162, 178
Selawik National Wildlife Refuge, 236–37, 270
Seward Peninsula, 154, 237
sharks, 110
shearwater birds, **111**, 116, 139, 145
sheefishes, 236
sheep
in Arctic Alaska, 248, 249, 253
in the Hawaiian Islands, 92, 93
in Interior Alaska, **218**, 224, 225, 231, 234
introduction to Alaska of, 216
in South-Central Alaska, 189, 200, 216
shield cones, 3, 132
Shipwreck Beach, 98, **99**, 276
shrimp, 41–42, 46, **196–97**
Silversword Loop, 66, 68
silversword plants, 7, **9**, 53, 59, 65, **69**, **128**, **131**
sisal plants, 92
skunk cabbage, **191**
Skyline Trail, 64–65
Sliding Sands Trail, 64, 65–66
smelt fish, 168
snails, 17, 59, 116, **168**
snakes, 16
snapper fish, 59, 106
Solar Basin Refuges, 236–37
South Prince of Wales Wilderness Area, 167, 270
sparrows, 229
Spouting Horn, 135
spruce trees
in Arctic Alaska, 248, 249
in Interior Alaska, 219, 222, 225, 228

in South-Central Alaska,
191, 193, 199, 203
in Southeastern Alaska,
162, 166, 167, 170,
171, 178
squirrels, 215, 229, 234, 248
starfish, 160
steelhead fish, 162
Steese National
Conservation Area, 228,
270
Steller's jay birds, 186,
191, 193
Stephen's Passage, 168,
169
Stikine Icefield, 167, 270
Stikine River, 167-68, 270
stilt birds (ae'o), 41,
56, 85, 135, 137, 140
stinkbugs, 7
sugarcane, 14, 46, 54,
58, 62, 84, 113, 134, 136
Sunset Beach, 117
surgeonfish, 58, 59
Surinam cherries, 84
Surprise Lake, 214
swans, 224, 238
sweet potatoes, 14

Taiga, 219, 222, 229
Tangle Lakes
Archaeological Area,
204, 270
taro plants, 14, 44, 84,
137, 140
Tatshenshini River, 179-80,
266
teals, 174
terns, 111, 145
Tetlin National Wildlife
Refuge, 223, 270
Thomas Jaggar Museum,
28, 273
Three Forks Overlook, 207
thrushes, 87, 162, 163,
166, 178
Thurston Lava Tube, 30, 32
ti trees, 46
tidal waves, 42–43, 44, 84,
179
tides, in Alaska, 160, 200
Tongass National Forest,
159, 163, 169, 180,
181, 193, 270
Tracy Arm–Fords Terror
Wilderness Area, 169, 270
trade winds, 41

trapping, 149
Tree Molds, 34–35
trees. See forests; specific
arboretum, preserve, for-
est, or type of tree
triggerfish, 106–7
Tropical Gardens of Maui,
56–57, 274
tropicbirds, 40, 139, 144
trout, 162, 203
tuff cones, 102, 107,
109, 109–10, 111
tulip trees, 105, 124, 138
tundra
as an Alaskan natural
resource, 153
in Arctic Alaska, 240,
242, 245, 248, 249,
253, 257
in Interior Alaska,
219, 222, 225, 228,
229, 231, 235, 236,
237, 238
in South-Central Alaska,
189, 191, 204, 212, 215
types of, 219
turkeys, 93, 98
turtles, 37, 40-41, 90,
110, 116, 135, 139, 145

Uhaloa plants, 97
Ukak River Gorge, 207,
208–9
ulu. See breadfruit
uluhe. See ferns
United Nations. See
International Biosphere
Reserves

Valley of the Kings, 44
Valley of Ten Thousand
Smokes, 155, 206-7,
208–9, 268
violets, 59
volcanoes
active, 3, 7
as an Alaskan natural
resource, 148–49, 155
dormancy/extinction of,
3, 6
and erosion, 6
and fjords, 166
formation of, 17
height of, 3
in Interior Alaska, 238
and island formation,
3, 6, 17, 50

magma from, 3, 50
predictions about, 26, 28
shape of Hawaiian, 3
in South-Central Alaska,
183, 204, 205, 206–7,
208–9, 210, 212, 214,
215, 216
in Southeastern Alaska,
166
See also specific
volcano
vole, 211

Wa'ahila Ridge State
Recreation Area,
106, 277
Waha'ula Heiau, 34
Wahiawa Botanical
Gardens, 112-13, 277
Wahiawa District, 102,
112-13
Wai'ale'ale (volcano),
123, 128, 130
Waialua District, 102, 113
Wai'anae Coast, 119-20,
120–21
Wai'anae-Ka'ala Trail, 120
Wai'anapanapa State Park,
12–13, 72-73, 274
Waikamoi Gulch Nature
Trail, 63
Waikamoi Preserve, 61,
62, 274
Waikamoi Ridge Nature
Trail, 71, 274
Waikiki Aquarium, 106-7,
278
Waikolu Lookout, 86
Wailua Falls, 136
Wailua River area, 128, 136-37
Wailua River State Park,
136, 279
Wailuku River State Park,
47, 273
Waimanu Valley, 45-46, 273
Waimea Canyon, 123, 126–
27, 128, 129, 131, 132
Waimea Canyon State Park,
130, 131, 279
Waimea Falls Park, 116-17
Waimea Valley, 116, 278
Waipi'o Valley, 42–43,
43, 44-45
Waipi'o Valley Lookout, 44,
273
Walrus Islands State Game
Sanctuary, 211, 213, 270

The Pacific

walruses, 211
water pipit birds, 228
wawae'iole (rat foot
   plant), 96
weasels, 211, 215, **254**
whales
   as an Alaskan natural
   resource, **153**
   and the Hawaiian
   Islands, 54, 59, 139
   humpback, 54, 139, 168,
   178, 195, **196–97**, 199
   hunting of, **153**
   orca, 195, 199
   in South-Central Alaska,
   195, **196–97**, 198, 199
   in Southeastern Alaska,
   162, 168, 178
   and the whaling industry, 59
wheatear birds, 228
White Mountains National
   Recreation Area, 228, 270

whitefish, 224
wildflowers, in Alaska,
   219, 228, **250**, **251**, 253
wiliwili trees, 109
willow trees, 166, 199,
   219, 234, 248
winds, in Alaska, 205,
   207, 212
windward coasts of
   Hawai'i, 6, 9, 16. *See also
   specific island*
wolverines, 162, 200,
   215, 225, 248, 249, 253
wolves
   as an Alaskan natural
   resource, 153
   in Arctic Alaska, 245,
   248, 249, 252, 253
   in Interior Alaska,
   222, 225, 231, 235, **238**
   in South-Central Alaska,
   200, 215

in Southeastern Alaska,
   162, 167
Wood-Tikchik State Park,
   211, 271
Wrangell–Saint Elias
   National Park and
   Preserve, 155, **182**,
   187, 188–92, 271
wrasses, **58**, 59

Yakutat Bay region,
   180, **181**
yams, 14
Yukon–Charley Rivers
   National Preserve, 222,
   225–28, 271
Yukon Delta National
   Wildlife Refuge, 155,
   237–38, 271
Yukon Flats National
   Wildlife Refuge, 229, 271

PHOTOGRAPH CREDITS

*All photographs in the Hawai'i section are by
Richard A. Cooke III except the following; all
photographs in the Alaska section are by Kim
Heacox except the following.*

Front Cover: Richard A. Cooke III; i, iv: Kim Heacox;
viii: Richard A. Cooke III; ix: Tom Bean, Flagstaff,
AZ; x–xi: Richard A. Cooke III; xiv: Kim Heacox; 10:
California Academy of Sciences, San Francisco, CA;
14, top: Douglas Peebles, Kailua, HI; 14, bottom: J.R.
Mau/Photo Resource Hawaii; 14, right: Douglas
Peebles; 26: Jack Jeffrey/Photo Resource Hawaii; 30:
Tai Sing Loo/Bishop Museum, Honolulu, HI; 38–39:
Bronwyn Cooke, Eugene, OR; 47: Jack Jeffrey/Photo
Resource Hawaii; 58: Bill Curtsinger, Portsmouth,
ME; 68: Greg Vaughn, Eugene, OR; 69: Len Jenshel,
New York, NY; 70: G. Brad Lewis/Photo Resource
Hawaii; 71: Greg Vaughn; 72: David S. Boynton/
Photo Resource Hawaii; 76: Kevin and Cat Sweeney/
Photo Resource Hawaii; 83: Kenneth M. Nagata/
Photo Resource Hawaii; 107: Lithograph by G.H.
Burgess/Bishop Museum; 112: Franco Salmoiraghi/
Photo Resource Hawaii; 113: Erwin and Peggy
Bauer, Livingston, MT; 114–115: Gary Hofheimer/
Douglas Peebles Photography; 119: Douglas Peebles;
128: David S. Boynton/Photo Resource Hawaii; 133,
right: California Academy of Sciences; 136, top:
Greg Vaughn; 136, bottom: Erwin and Peggy Bauer;
145: Bill Curtsinger; 146–147: Bates Littlehales,
Arlington, VA; 152–153: RIPSA 2126, RIPSA 2115/via
Smithsonian Arctic Studies Center, Washington, DC,
courtesy Anchorage Museum of History and Art;
158: Tom Bean; 163: Rosamond Purcell, Medford,
MA; 164-165, 168: Tom Bean; 172-173: Thomas D.
Mangelsen/Images of Nature; 175: Bates Littlehales;
176: John Shaw, Colorado Springs, CO; 182, 187,
208-209: Fred Hirschmann, Wasilla, AK; 213: Tom
Bean; 214: Henry Elliot Collection, University of
Alaska Museum, Fairbanks, AK; 217: Tim Thompson,
Bainbridge Island, WA; 226-227: Thomas D.
Mangelsen/Images of Nature; 238: John Shaw; 239:
Tim Thompson; 244-245: Tony Dawson,
Anchorage, AK; 254, top: Erwin and Peggy Bauer;
254, bottom: Thomas D. Mangelsen/Images of
Nature; 255: John Shaw; 279: L. E. Edgeworth/
Bishop Museum; Back Cover: Tom Bean (puffins),
Kim Heacox (bear).

ACKNOWLEDGMENTS

The author of Hawai'i is grateful to Papillon
Helicopters, Captain Zodiac, the Oshiro family,
Snuba, Trilogy, and Bill Heacox. Above all, much love
and aloha to Ron and Linda Nagata.

Richard A. Cooke III, the photographer for Hawai'i,
would like to thank Keoni Wagner/Hawaian Airlines;
K. C. Cronin; Jeffrey B. Judd/Volcanoes National Park;
G. Brad Lewis; Jim Watt; William Waterfall; Robert
Sabuan; Diana Reuter/Shiela Donnelly & Associates;
Mark White/Nature Conservancy of Maui; Susan
Conway; Jennifer Mack Urquhart/Island of Lanai
Company; Lynn Johnson; Randy Moore.

The editors gratefully acknowledge the assistance
of Tim Allan, Marni Davis, Judith Ann Hancock,
Jane Hoffman, and Bob Mon. The following consul-
tants also helped in the preparation of this volume:
Bob Dittrick, Wilderness Birding Adventures; Glenn
Elison, U.S. Fish and Wildlife Service; Lorin Gill,
Education Director, Moanalua Gardens Foundation;
Robert Pyle, Bishop Museum; John E. Grassy; Dallas
Rhodes, Professor and Chair of Geology, Whittier
College; Bud Rice; and Keith P. Tomlinson,
Education Specialist, Bishop Museum.